W9-CZB-462

PASTORAL THEOLOGY

Rev. Michael Pfliegler

PASTORAL THEOLOGY

Translated by John Drury

THE NEWMAN PRESS
WESTMINSTER, MARYLAND
1966

PASTORAL THEOLOGY is a translation of the German *Pastoral Theologie* by Michael Pfliegler, first published by Herder & Co., Wien.

Nihil Obstat: Very Rev. Msgr. Carroll E. Satterfield
Censor Librorum

Imprimatur: His Eminence, Lawrence Cardinal Shehan
Archbishop of Baltimore

July 27, 1965

The *Nihil Obstat* and the *Imprimatur* are official declarations that a book or pamphlet is free of doctrinal and moral error. No implication is contained therein that those who have granted the *Nihil Obstat* and the *Imprimatur* agree with the contents or with the opinions expressed. *Library of Congress Catalog Card Number:* 65–25981. Printed in the United States of America.

FOREWORD

Pastoral theology appeared as a distinct discipline in the latter half of the nineteenth century. At first theologians were occupied trying to define its scope and delimit its subject matter. Not much attention was paid to practical problems.

Even today the situation is much the same. Two world wars have produced great changes in the world. The earlier manuals have become outdated. Their authors never dreamed of the problems which would face their successors. The present-day reader can still learn something from these books, but he will not find what he is looking for. The theological principles remain constant, but the subject matter is quite different. Anthropological, psychological, sociological, and historical conditions have changed radically. The theological doctrine on man is ever true: man is a creature of God, tainted by original sin and redeemed by Christ. But fallen man lives his life in a given historical epoch with its own conditions and problems. He can be approached and saved only if these realities are taken into account. The earlier manuals cannot satisfy because they dealt with a different world and a different generation of men.

We need pastoral manuals which deal with today's world. We already have many valuable commentaries on specific problems, and these are noted in the bibliography. But there is no up-to-date work on pastoral theology which considers modern man and his problems. It is a large project; but it must be undertaken because the need is critical. This writer is keenly aware of the risks involved.

The fundamental theological substrate is clearly delineated in the first part of the book. But even behind the countenance of modern man, which we must come to know as well as possible (Book II), hovers the face of the crucified Redeemer. He is still the eternal Redeemer calling out to His flock.

In Rome, the center of Christendom, a central agency has been established to direct and coordinate pastoral activity (Centrum orientationis et coordinationis pastoralis, Secretaria generalis, Roma, Piazza Pio XII, n. 3). This, more than anything else, indicates the critical urgency of the pastoral question. The present volume is meant to contribute to this work.

One final word of clarification: pastoral theology, as it is usually taught, embraces three (or even four) separate activities corresponding to the priest's threefold office:

1. *Hodegetics* (pastoral direction)—pastoral theology in the strict sense.

2. *Homiletics* (or Kerygmatics)—the art of preaching. *Catechetics*, the art of religious instruction, also belongs here. It has received great attention in recent years, and there is an extensive bibliography on the subject. The task is often delegated to professional catechists. But this division between homiletics and catechetics is not always a good thing.

3. *Liturgy*—its subject matter is clearly defined, and much has been written about it.

The present volume is concerned with *Hodegetics*.

Biblical passages are quoted from:

Old Testament

1. New Confraternity of Christian Doctrine translation:
   Vol. I—Genesis to Ruth
   Vol. III—Job to Sirach
   Vol. IV—Prophetical Books

2. Otherwise, the Douay version

New Testament

New Confraternity of Christian Doctrine translation

CONTENTS

CONTENTS

PART FOUR: *The Parochial Ministry Today*

BOOK TWO

THE PASTORAL CLIENT

PART ONE: *Human Development*

PART TWO: *Pastoral Direction in the Various Stages of Life*

PART THREE: *Man, Woman, and the Family*

BOOK ONE

The Pastoral Office

PART ONE: THE PASTORAL MISSION

I. CHRIST, THE PASTOR OF SOULS

The pastoral care of souls is nothing else but the fulfillment of the mandate which Christ left to His disciples upon His return to the Father: "All power in heaven and on earth has been given to me. Go, therefore, and make disciples of all nations, baptizing them in the name of the Father, and of the Son, and of the Holy Spirit, teaching them to observe all that I have commanded you; and behold, I am with you all days, even unto the consummation of the world" (Mt. 28: 18–20). Christ transmits to them His own power, His own authority, and His three offices: His *teaching* office—"Go and make disciples"; His *priestly* office—"Baptizing"; and His *pastoral* office—"teaching them to observe all that I have commanded you."

In the economy of salvation there is no real pastoral ministry unless it is rooted in and patterned after Christ's mandate. But more is involved than the mere transmission of Christ's ministry to His disciples.

Christ is not just a transmitter: He is the *one and only pastor* of souls. No one else can bear that title unless he is truly united to Christ. "I am the way, and the truth, and the life" (John 14: 6).

There is no other Way (Shepherd), no other Truth (Teaching), no other Life (Source of Grace). With these words Christ outlines the threefold function of the pastor for all times and all places.

§ *1. The Way: Christ the Shepherd*

Christ is "the Way," the Shepherd who leads His flock along the right path, as the shepherds of Palestine do to this very day. Thus He is pictured in *Isaia* (40: 10–11): "Here comes with power the Lord God . . . Like a shepherd he feeds his flock; in his arms he gathers the lambs, carrying them in his bosom, and leading the ewes with care." In *Ezechiel* (34: 2) He complains about the shepherds of Israel who have neglected the sheep and looked out for themselves. "I swear I am coming against these shepherds. I will claim my sheep from them and put a stop to their shepherding . . ." (34: 10). "The lost I will seek out, the strayed I will bring back, the injured I will bind up, the sick I will heal, but the sleek and the strong I will destroy shepherding them rightly" (34: 16). You, my sheep, you are the sheep of my pasture, and I am your God . . ." (34: 3).

Christ calls Himself "the good shepherd" (John 10: 11). And in John's gospel the good shepherd refers to Himself not just as *agathós* but as *poimèn ho kalós*. There is a hint of heaven itself in the use of this image. Christ lays down His life for His sheep. A good shepherd is willing to sacrifice everything for His sheep, even His own life. He is no hireling who tends the sheep solely for money and runs off when a wolf appears. Christ is always the *summus pastor,* the over-lord of creation (Eph. 1: 32; Col. 1: 18), the *archipoimen,* the arch-shepherd.

He is the eternal mediator between God and men, and He has an everlasting priesthood (Heb. 7: 24); there is no other legitimate priesthood, only the one which is truly united to His (Heb. 9: 15).

§ 2. *The Truth: Christ the Teacher*

Christ has not only brought us the truth: He is *Truth.* He is the truth underlying all reality. The Father's eternal Word was made flesh, and entered our world. "The word was made flesh, and dwelt among us" (John 1: 14). But Christ's message is not just a philosophical teaching; it is a gospel of salvation. When it is taught as the life-giving message of Jesus and becomes a vital force in the lives of men, in short, when it transforms a man into an "alter Christus," it saves men's souls. The Holy Spirit, the Spirit of Truth, "will not speak on his own authority . . . He will glorify me; because he will receive of what is mine and declare it to you" (John 16: 13–14). Those who serve this truth, even if only by being hospitable to their brethren, are "fellow-workers for the truth" (3 John 8).

Faith depends upon the preaching of the word—"fides ex auditu" (Rom. 10: 17); therefore it is entrusted to messengers. Christian faith involves more than the acceptance of a body of doctrines; for Christ is the "author and finisher of faith" (Heb. 12: 1).

§ 3. *The Life: Christ the Eternal High Priest*

Christ is *Life,* the new life of holiness. "In him was life, and the life was the light of men" (John 1: 4). Faith is everlasting life (John 3: 36), a participation in God's eternal life granted by the Father (John 5: 26; 6: 33). Under the form of bread, the food which nourishes our human body, He has given us the bread of eternal life—Himself (John 6: 35). This life comes to us through His death. As the eternal High Priest, He offered Himself up for us. And His self-sacrifice sets the example for every priesthood which bears His name. For us His life is embodied in His Eucharistic Presence (S. Th. 3, q. 50, 4, ad 4). When a priest pronounces the words of consecration, he makes Christ's priesthood present for himself and his flock.

II. CHRIST, THE SENDER

Christ Himself sends all those who are sacramentally and juridically empowered to preach, rule, and sanctify in His name.

§ 1. *His Choice*

Christ chooses His messenger and priest. What was true for the Apostles is true for all their successors. The words of Jesus at the Last Supper apply to each one: "You have not chosen me, but I have chosen you, and have appointed you that you should go and bear fruit, and that your fruit should remain; that whatever you ask the Father in my name he will give you" (John 15: 16).

A man does not choose the priesthood; rather Christ calls him. In the eyes of the Church the genuineness of this call rests in the faith of the one called, his qualifications and his ability. It is not that we have any right to confirm Christ's call. But being men, we can only base our decisions on human criteria. The Church, the bishop, and the candidate pray that their decision may be in accord with God's will.

§ 2. *His Authorization*

The Lord authorizes the priest's mission and confers His own powers on him: "All power . . . has been given to me. Go, therefore . . ." (Mt. 28: 18). This conferral of power is a mission to the whole world. Individual parishes will be established, and ought to be. But the pastor of souls will remain true to Christ's universal mission only if he continues to look beyond his parish to the surrounding world. The pastoral ministry must be mission-orientated, not only in the large European cities where the workers have fallen away and in un-Christianized territories, but everywhere. It is essentially a world-wide mission, a "going forth" (*poreia, poreuthentes*). Every flock has its strays, its lost sheep. Christ's mandate involves missionary work both inside and outside the fold. The water-level must be the same in both compartments.

§ 3. *His Message*

This mission is essentially a preaching one. The message of John the Baptist, Christ's forerunner, was: "Repent, for the kingdom of heaven is at hand" (Mt. 3: 2). In His first appearance Christ carried out this advice literally (Mt. 3: 17) and then passed on the message to His disciples (Mk. 6: 12; Mt. 10: 8). Every subsequent follower of Christ until the end of time echoes this introductory refrain: repentance alone leads us to the door of God's kingdom. The Lord and His word alone is the door: "I am the door. If anyone enter by me, he shall be safe, and he shall go in and out and shall find pastures" (John 10: 9). The kingdom of heaven suffers violent assaults. And constant effort must be the hallmark of those called to salvation. Christ's message is a call to baptism as well, but it does not end there. The baptismal robe symbolizes man's rebirth, his new life. And life by its very nature struggles to maintain itself in existence.

§ 4. *His Abiding Presence*

The mission is a heavy responsibility which goes beyond man's natural strength. "But take courage, I have overcome the world" (John 16: 33). The apostle of Christ follows in the footsteps of his victorious master. And what is more, "I am with you all days, even unto the consummation of the world" (Mt. 28: 20). He is always beside His apostle. Knowing that Christ is always nearby, the apostle can carry out and complete the mission entrusted to him. On the night before He died the Lord assures His disciples: "Amen, amen I say to you, he who believes in me, the works that I do he also shall do, and greater than these he shall do, because I am going to the Father. And whatever you ask in my name, that I will do . . ." (John 14: 12–13). In His priestly prayer (John 17) He implores the Father on their behalf: "I am no longer in the world, but these are in the world, and I am coming to thee. Holy Father, keep in Thy name those whom thou hast given me, that they may be one even as we are . . . Sanctify them in the truth. Thy word is truth" (17: 11–17).

The mission is really a direct (vertical) commission from the Father to His Son and to every apostle until the end of time. "Even as thou has sent me into the world, so I also have sent them into the world. And for them I sanctify myself that they also may be sanctified in truth" (John 17: 18–19). And after the resurrection, Christ tells them: "Peace be to you! As the Father has sent me, I also send you" (John 20: 21).

III. THE CHURCH

§ *1. The Visible Manifestation of Christ's Presence*

The Lord has returned to the kingdom which He shares with the Father and the Holy Spirit from all eternity; but He is "semper vivens ad interpellandum pro nobis" (Heb. 7: 25). He remains with us through His Word, His sacraments, and His indwelling in the souls of men. But He has put His Church in charge of the Word, the sacraments, and the channels of grace. In short, Christ has put the Church in charge of His mission. "I am with you" (Mt. 28: 20) as a group, not just as individuals. Christ is referring to the community of the faithful, the Church, as well as to its individual members.

1. *Christ is the invisible head.* Christ is "the head of his body, the Church" (Col. 1: 18). But men require some concrete, visible manifestation of this body. And the community of the faithful is called the visible body of the Lord, the mystery of His salvific presence, the "corpus mysticum." The unity of this body is not the unity of a mob in which the individual

loses his identity. The Lord's mystical body, like the human body, has different members; and each member has its own function. "For as the body is one and has many members, and all the members of the body, many as they are, form one body, so also is it with Christ" (1 Cor. 12: 12).

2. *Christ continues His work of salvation in the Church.* The Scriptures indicate that Christ's threefold office persists in the Church. The *priestly office:* "And the bread that we break, is it not the partaking of the body of the Lord" (1 Cor. 10: 16). The *teaching office:* "He who hears you, hears me; and he who rejects you, rejects me; and he who rejects me, rejects him who sent me" (Lk. 10: 16). Here again we find a direct (vertical) commission—from the Father to the Son to the Church. The *pastoral office:* "Thou art Peter, and upon this rock I will build my Church . . . And I will give thee the keys of the kingdom of heaven; and whatever thou shalt bind on earth shall be bound in heaven, and whatever thou shalt loose on earth shall be loosed in heaven" (Mt. 16: 18–19). "Feed my lambs . . . feed my sheep" (John 21: 15–17).

3. *The Church distributes Christ's powers.* "Now you are the body of Christ, member for member. And God indeed has placed some in the Church, first apostles, secondly prophets, thirdly teachers; after that miracles, then gifts of healing, services of help, power of administration, and the speaking of various tongues" (1 Cor. 12: 27–28).

§ 2. *The Body of Christ*

The Church, the body of Christ, contains the mystery of our salvation. In the course of her history she has built up an organized structure to meet the demands of her mission.

1. The *Hierarchy:* The Pope, the Patriarchs, the archbishops

(Metropolitans), the bishops; in mission lands—the Vicar Apostolic, the Prefect Apostolic, and the "praelati nullius" who have juridiction over a territory not yet set up as a diocese (Canons 271–328). The College of Cardinals is traditionally the Pope's top advising body, and the Pope himself freely appoints them.

2. At the center of the Church there is also the Roman Curia. It settles canonical, administrative, and juridical questions in the name of the Pope and is composed of twelve congregations, three tribunals, six offices, and seven papal commissions (canons 242–264).

3. The Code of Canon Law outlines the requirements for clerics and their appointments. In short, it outlines the things required of a pastor of souls,

for the *pastoral office:* c. 218–275; c. 1407–1551;
for the *priestly office:* c. 731–1321;
for the *teaching office:* c. 1322–1408.

§ 4. *Canon Law and Christian Love*

The need for Church Law became apparent as the Church developed from a small community into a universal body. But no matter to what extent the Church's work of salvation is inscribed in cold matter-of-fact canons, the pastor of souls should never forget that the Holy *Father* heads the universal community of the faithful, and that it is always *Mother* Church who rules us.

His love for his own country and people must not obscure his love for the universal community of the faithful. In fact, his love for all men will expand and deepen his love for those around him. "Sentire cum ecclesia" is more than a meaningless phrase. It is meant to express the love between the members of the Church, and it should be the goal of every pastor of souls. Rooted in this love is the power to convert souls, the missionary spirit, and the apostolate of every baptized Christian to those around him—in his family, his place of work, and his social life.

IV. THE IMMEDIATE MISSION (MISSIO)

1. *The Bishops*

The bishops are the true successors of the Apostles and inherit their powers by divine appointment (c. 329, 1). They possess the full powers of the priesthood, and by virtue of their appointment possess *potestas ordinaria* in their own diocese (*diokesis*—sphere of administration). They possess the full powers of their office, but not the extraordinary powers granted to the first Apostles: they do not enjoy personal infallibility nor can they found churches.

§ 2. *His Powers of Ordination*

As a rule, the bishop—through the imposition of hands—ordains the pastoral ministers of his diocese.

1. In the ordination of deacons: "Accipe Spiritum sanctum ad robur et resistendum diabolo et tentationibus eius, in nomine Domini," in accordance with the example and the mandate of their master (John 20: 22). "Accipe potestatem legendi Evangelium in ecclesia Dei."

2. In the ordination of priests: We beseech Almighty God "ut super hos famulos suos, quos ad Presbyterii munus elegit coelestia dona multiplicet . . . benedictionem sancti Spiritus et gratiae sacerdotalis infunde virtutem."

He anoints their hands and gives them the power to celebrate the Eucharist: "Accipe potestatem offerre sacrificium Deo, Missasque celebrare pro vivis quam pro defunctis in nomine Domini." Then he gives them the power to forgive sins, using the same words the Master used to confer this power on His Apostles (John 20: 23).

3. The newly ordained minister pledges obedience to his bishop. The latter takes the hands of the ordained and places them in his (the symbolic act, based on Feudal custom, represents a personal pledge of service): "Promittis mihi et successoribus meis reverentiam et oboedientiam?" The ordinand responds, "Promitto." Then the bishop gives him the kiss of peace.

According to present-day law (c. 111, 1), every priest has to belong to some diocese. This is necessary for good order in the activities of the universal Church. The priest is also subordinate to his Ordinary in his personal conduct.

4. The bishop gives his priests the "*missio canonica*" which represents their jurisdictional powers. He appoints them and fills the pastoral offices in his diocese. And in accordance with canonical procedure he has the right of recall.

PART TWO: THE PASTORAL MINISTER

I. THE PRIEST

When one refers to a "pastor of souls," one thinks first of the priest.

A. HIS CALL

§ *1. Our Lord Himself called His Apostles to be the first priests and the pastors of souls*

1. Christ did not confer His threefold office on all those who came to Him, but only on His Apostles and disciples. Scripture consistently distinguishes between "the multitude" which followed Him and the select group of "disciples" which He Himself picked out—72 in all (Lk. 10). The twelve Apostles are often referred to simply as "disciples" (Mt. 10: 1; 20: 17); but Saint Luke reports (6: 12–16) that Jesus chose twelve of these disciples and called them "apostles" ("those sent forth"). To be sure, our Lord often mentions a call sent out to everyone, but in these instances He is referring to their cooperation in the work of the kingdom. He always distinguishes between being called and being chosen. Many are *called,* and are therefore qualified; but few are *chosen.* The call is always directed toward men with free will; whether or not they are "chosen" depends on their free decision.

2. Christ clearly indicates that the call comes through Him (John 15: 16). He makes clear His role as middleman in the transferral of the heavenly mission–Father, Christ, Apostle (John 20: 21). And this process continues today in a different form–Christ, bishop, priest. The Lord confers His priestly powers on them—the power to offer sacrifice (Lk. 22: 19;

1 Cor. 11: 24 ff.), to preach and to baptize (Mt. 28: 18), to forgive sins (John 20: 22; Mt. 18: 18).

§ 2. *The priestly call is the same today*

1. *God Himself initiates the call.* No one can presume to enter this state without this divine summons. This was true under the old covenant, and it is still true (Heb. 5: 4). God confers the dignity of this office on men; even Christ, the high priest of the new covenant, did not glorify Himself in this office (Heb. 5: 5).

Great saints, like Gregory of Nazianzen and John Chrysostom, regarded themselves as unworthy and tried to flee this call; but God found them. In his rule, Pachomius forbade his hermits to take on this *honor,* used here in a sacramental context, not a sociological one. Thus there can be no mistake about the call and the candidate's acceptance. God makes the decision and sends out the call; man's decision is an act of obedience to God. "Dei judicio relinquendum est, quem velit et si velit, assumere sibi ministerium vel sacerdotium" (Rufinus, *Historia monachorum,* vol. 1). Nor is the priesthood of the New Law based on blood descent (Heb. 7: 16).

2. The call to the priesthood is often regarded as a burden, not as an *honor* and a *gift of grace.* But this does not change its true nature. God has stretched out His hands and touched a human life; that is all that matters. Even in the Old Testament one prophet (Jonas) tried to shun this call, and others argued against it (e.g., Jer. 1: 4–10); but God did not retract. And with this call God also grants the appropriate grace. His words to Jeremia are ever true: "Have no fear before them, because I am with you to deliver you" (Jer. 1: 8). Trusting in these words, the candidate accepts God's call. "Whatever unworthiness we may see in ourselves, we can still do every thing God asks of us with the help of Jesus

Christ. All things are possible with the help of Him who strengthens me. We are never so weak that Jesus Christ cannot help us to fulfill the demands of our call."[1]

3. Around the turn of the century this question was being discussed in France: who can consider himself called to the priesthood? Some[2] regarded the God-given call as the decisive factor, while others[3] maintained a different position. They said that any man could accept the priestly call, if he possessed the necessary spiritual, moral, and intellectual qualifications. A commission appointed by Saint Pius X reached a similar conclusion (A.A.S., IV, 485). It emphasized these points: a) "personal inspiration," understood as a sensible call from God, is not necessary; b) a personal inclination toward the priestly office is not a necessary pre-requisite; c) all that is required of the candidate is the proper intention, the necessary spiritual and moral qualifications, and freedom from canonical impediments; d) the bishop decides whether a given candidate is to be admitted to the priesthood; e) the bishop's decision cannot be challenged by an appeal to God's call; f) if a candidate were to reject a valid call from God, it would be a sin against charity, but not against justice.

§ 3. *Indications of a divine call*

1. A *personal inclination* or attraction to the priestly state, which may take one form or another: negatively, a person may feel a spiritual uneasiness about his refusal to follow an inner call; positively, he may be convinced that God is calling him and that he can reach self-fulfillment only by accepting this call. The motives may be supernatural or natural, e.g., the needs of the people. "The harvest indeed is great, but the

[1] Charles de Condren, *Geistliche Briefe* (Freiburg, 1939), pp. 38 f.
[2] L. Brancherau, *De la vocation sacerdotale* (Paris, 1896).
[3] J. Lahitton, *La vocation sacerdotale* (Paris: 1922²).

laborers are few" (Mt. 9: 37). The example of a zealous priest never ceases to attract young men to this calling.

2. Rarely are these indications of a true call unmistakably convincing, but that is not surprising. The most vital decisions in human life are necessarily based on man's liberty and represent ventures freely *chosen*.

3. A person who feels that he has a call to the priesthood, has the duty and the moral obligation to follow it. John Climachus warns: "Let us beware lest we be found guilty before the judgment seat of God of having lightly rejected His divine call or having been slow in answering it." Family ties do not determine our decision one way or the other. As Saint Jerome says: "Honora patrem tuum, sed si te a vero Patre non separat. Tamdiu scito sanguinis copulam, quamdiu noverit Creatorem" (Ep. 54: 3).

Will a man be "blessed" in accepting this call? Every man will find his full measure of happiness in carrying out his God-given task.

B. THE PRIESTLY STATE

§ 1. *Its Dignity*

Through his ordination the priest is marked with an indelible character and enters a new state (i.e., acquires a new status).

The Latin word for the sociological concept *status* is *ordo,* and it connotes the dignity attached to it. Like any other state the priestly order involves a select community of members, its own way of life, its own code of honor, its own peculiar duties and rights, and even its own manner of dress. In a society which no longer recognizes "estates," it stands as a witness to an ancient societal setup. And this may be a cause of antipathy in a "classless" society.

The dignity of the priesthood stems from the nature of the state itself. Even in pagan societies the priest, who mediates between men and the deity, was regarded as the representative of a higher power and a spiritual world, bringing divine gifts to men. "At the start of every cultural group two distinct ranks are already formed—the nobles and the priests. They are the first societal groups in the farming communities."[4] In later ages the priesthood has been replaced by theories such as "Rationalism, Liberalism, and Socialism."[5]

With the coming of Christ the Old Testament priesthood lost its significance and its rights; and with the destruction of the temple, it ceased to exist. The New Testament priesthood, as "the ministration of the spirit," stands in contrast to the Old Testament priesthood, "the ministration of death." The latter is founded on a code of law, engraved in letters, which kills. "Now if the ministration of death, which was engraved in letters upon stones, was inaugurated in such glory that the children of Israel could not look steadfastly upon the face of Moses on account of the transient glory that shone upon it, shall not the ministration of the spirit be still more glorious?" (2 Cor. 3: 7–8)

§ 2. *The Basis of This Dignity*

1. The priest participates in the imperishable priesthood of Christ (Heb. 7: 23 ff.): "We have such a high priest, who has taken his seat at the right hand of the throne of Majesty in the heavens . . ." (Heb. 8: 1). Thus every priest can echo the words of the Apostle Paul: "Let a man so account us, as servants of Christ and stewards of the mysteries of God" (1 Cor. 4: 1).

2. The priest has power over the physical and mystical Body

[4] Oswald Spengler, *Der Mensch und die Technik* (1931), 64. Trans. *Man and Technics* (Knopf, 1963).

[5] *Ibid.*, p. 65.

of Christ—to change bread and wine into Christ's body and blood, and to forgive sins. Not even the greatest saint can appropriate these powers to himself (S. Th., Suppl., q. 19, a. 4).

3. The priest has the power to bless. This is most fully appreciated by the people when they seek the blessing of the newly ordained priest. But the power remains forever the same.

4. The priest is the preacher of the divinely revealed truth—John 1: 7; Phil. 2: 17—and of Christ's love—John 21: 15 f.; 1 Pet. 5: 2; 1 Tim. 5: 12 ff.; 2 Tim. 2: 3 ff.; 1 Cor. 4: 3; 2 Cor. 5: 20 ff.

§ 3. *Privileges Protecting This Dignity*

The priestly claim to special attention and esteem (c. 119, c. 1209, 2) involves the following privileges:

1. *privilegium canonis:* c. 119, c. 2334, 3. Injury inflicted on the person of a cleric is regarded as a sacrilege and involves a corresponding sanction.

2. *privilegium fori:* c. 121, c. 2341. The right to be tried exclusively by a clerical tribunal.

3. *privilegium immunitatis:* exemption from military service, public service, and other offices which are not in keeping with the priestly state: c. 121; c. 139, 2, 3; c. 141.

4. *beneficium competentiae:* c. 122. The right to financial aid in economic distress.

Whether these privileges are respected or not depends, of

course, on the state with which the Church makes agreements or concordats.

§ 4. *Other Protective Measures*

According to canon 138, there are certain functions, offices, and professions which *do not fit in with the dignity of the priesthood:* "clerici ab iis omnibus, quae statum suum dedecent, prorsus abstineant." Traditionally the commentators list the following: the acting profession, the post of executioner, and innkeeping. The priest should not participate in gambling games, carry weapons, or join in hunting parties (Decision of the Conc. Congregation—June 11, 1962). A bishop can forbid his priests to attend any and all hunts (A.A.S., XIII, 498). Visiting taverns without grave necessity is forbidden.

Canon 139, 1, forbids the priest to visit places, good in themselves, where he, as a cleric, would be conspicuous: public bathing spots and theaters, and well known health resorts. Canon 139, 2, forbids him to practice medicine or surgery. To be sure, our Lord gave His disciples this commission: "Cure the sick, raise the dead, cleanse the lepers, cast out devils" (Mt. 10: 8; Lk. 9: 2). But He was speaking of the charismatic healing which He Himself worked. The canonical interdict may also be a result of the way surgery was practiced in older days. It was once the avocation of hangmen and executioners; and it was not regarded as a respectable profession. Today, in order to enter the medical profession a priest must get a papal indult (c. 139, 2). In special cases a priest may accept a public office (president, minister, mayor, parliamentary delegate) with permission from the Church (c. 139, 3, 4). Clerics must also keep away from such things as plays, dances, and public gatherings, when their presence might cause scandal (c. 140). Clerics may not volunteer for military service (c. 141) or run a business enterprise—even through a middleman (c. 142).

§ 5. *Clerical Decorum*

The priest must live among men in a manner befitting his dignity. His residence should be simple, dignified, and in good taste; it should not be gaudy or luxurious. As the representative of an ancient class, the priest wears a distinctive garb which varies in different places and countries; but it should always be clean and neat. The priest must take proper care of his body, as good etiquette demands. The priest who appears in public unkempt and unshaven lowers himself in the eyes of others. A priest may work in his garden, and the people will be quite pleased. But certain jobs should be left to others, and his people feel the same way.

C. CLERICAL TRAINING AND DEVELOPMENT

In the course of history the training of priests has taken many different forms. In the earliest days of the Church the candidate received a charismatic appointment and thus was admitted to the sanctuary. In the Patristic Age much depended on the efforts of the individual to mold his own character and deepen his learning. Later, in the Middle Ages we find a rudimentary training system in effect. The would-be priest was taught the rudiments of Christian doctrine and the nature of priestly work by a parish priest; then he took a final examination in some cathedral school or cloister. The theological and ascetical training required today was set up by the Council of Trent, which established the seminary system (Trid. S. XXIII. c. 18 *De ref.*). Though slight differences in detail may exist from place to place, the basic system is the same for the universal Church. The "vagans clericus" is no more.

Clerical training is under the supervision of the diocesan bishop. Minor seminaries begin this formation. Afterward the candidate enters a major seminary for his theological and ascetical training. The general rule is that the candidates live and study in a certain area set aside for this purpose. These "seed-grounds" (*seminarium, semen*), cloistered from the passing world, are able to give the candidates a more comprehensive training for their future ministry and a more thorough spiritual formation. But this communal training should not hinder the full development of individual personality. In *The Diary of a Country Priest* George Bernanos puts these words into the mouth of a priest: "I am an old priest and know full well how seminary training can level spirits to a common denominator of mediocrity." This must be avoided at all costs, because the Church needs mature and manly laborers.

§ 1. *Theological Training in the Seminary*

The Church demands (c. 1365 ff.) that the seminarians have two full years of philosophy and four years (*saltem integro quadriennio*) of theology. Canon 976, 3 stipulates that the theology course may not be private; it must be taken in a seminary.

By its very nature theological study can never be a purely speculative pursuit. The great theologians of the past meditated on sacred theology on their knees. A purely intellectual approach is not just insufficient; it is a profanation, often deplored more by the uninitiate than by theologians. "I have heard students speaking about God's nature in such a way that I found myself blushing. They knew everything about God except the fact that He was listening to them; yet they did not blush. And they were theology students."[6] Theology

[6] R. Huessy in M. Mueller, O.F.M., *Die Begegnung im Ewigen* (Freiburg, 1954).

must work toward conceptual clarity and try to provide answers to the seminary student; but it must also trace back his calling to its roots in revelation. It must help to lead him to wisdom and holiness.

Theological study cannot restrict itself to a "pat" presentation of the theological material. It must concern itself with contemporary religious questions and problems. In response to a letter sent out by German seminary rectors after World War I various lay people made this comment: "The great pity is that we find it so hard to initiate a discussion on religious questions with the average priest." A set of textbook questions and answers does not equip the priest for the problems he will encounter outside the seminary. Even a thorough grounding in the humanities provides only a partial preparation. Very often priests are reluctant to teach religion in secondary schools and trade schools because they encounter problems for which they are not prepared.

The mark of a sincere theology student is his unceasing quest for knowledge. He may devote his special attention to a particular theological work (*timeo virum unius libri*) or to a particular Church Father. And every priest should develop a special interest in some particular branch of the sacred sciences—mindful, of course, of the danger inherent in overspecialization.

§ 2. *And after Ordination*

1. The priest has a duty to broaden his theological background after his ordination. Canon 129 warns him not to discontinue his study (of theology especially) after leaving the seminary. He should hold to the solid traditional teaching and not be taken in by novelties or pseudo-intellectual aberrations.

2. For the first three years after his ordination, the priest must take the annual clergy examinations (established in 1918).

They will test his knowledge of theology, remind him of his duty to continue studying, and show him how he can integrate his study into the work of the ministry. Only the Ordinary can exempt a priest from these examinations. According to a decision of the Consistorial Congregation (April 30, 1918—A.A.S., X, 237) priests attending secular universities are not to be exempted, because they especially need a good theological background. However, special arrangements can be made for them. The results of these examinations are to be considered in filling vacant ecclesiastical posts (c. 130).

3. Clergy conferences are another means of broadening the priest's knowledge. In larger dioceses they are to be held in the various deaneries, several times a year if possible (A.A.S., XIV, 526). Canon 131 lists questions of moral theology and liturgy as the preferred subject-matter. Pious devotions should be an integral part of these meetings. Besides these diocesan conferences it is recommended that the clergy of a particular area hold conferences among themselves to discuss pressing problems. Should it be impossible to hold such conferences, then the clergy are to submit their answers or opinions in writing and forward them to the Ordinary (c. 131, X, 2). Those obliged to attend the clergy conferences are: all secular and all religious priests who are engaged in pastoral work; all religious who have been given faculties to hear confession in the diocese and do not have similar conferences in their cloister. The bishop can take canonical action to make attendance compulsory (c. 2377).

4. Special tests must also be taken by those seeking a pastorate or a teaching position in schools of higher education.

§ 3. *Cultural Formation*

1. Any priest who is involved in pastoral work, or in teaching, needs a solid training in the subjects and the problems con-

nected with his work for the kingdom of God. This means specialized training in some fields and formal training in such areas as speech and homiletics. These subjects are not studied for their own sake, but for their contribution to the intellectual formation of the cleric. The natural foundation must be laid well, if the priest is to make full use of God's grace in His quest for perfection—*gratia supponit naturam.* Maturation is the development of the basic nature which God bestows on all men. Just as the *lex naturalis* is the foundation of the *lex humana* and *lex divina,* so a well-developed human nature is the best foundation for growth in holiness and individual self-fulfillment. The ultimate objective is the formation of a human personality which has reached its full natural and supernatural potential. This objective has not been reached if cultivated non-Christians can say of a Christian or even a priest: he lacks the rudiments of culture.

2. Only a priest who has been so trained will be able to judge discriminately and sift the views he encounters in the world. Only such a priest will be able to maintain his independence amid the world's changing opinions, fashions, and ideologies. He alone will be able to uphold his convictions and defend them confidently when challenged by others.

The world is a mission land; and only a priest well formed naturally and supernaturally can be a successful propagandist.

3. What this clerical training will involve in the concrete is determined by several factors, e.g., the hierarchy of values to be instilled, the needs of the time and place in which the priest works, and his own personal preferences. The priest cannot read and digest everything which he encounters. He must study those things which will prepare him for his calling. He must make good use of his time because he will have to render an account to God.

The cleric should read with pencil in hand and correlate

the knowledge he acquires, always remembering that it is primarily intended to serve him in his pastoral work.

§ 4. *Spiritual Formation*

This is the heart and soul of priestly training and crowns the other aspects of his formation.

1. Canon 124: "*Clerici debent sanctiorem prae laicis vitam interiorem et exteriorem ducere, eisque virtute et recte factis in exemplum excellere.*"

The priest is more than a cultured man: he is a spiritual man. He has a greater obligation than the ordinary Christian to live a holy life. Indeed, it is his duty to set an example for the laity. In this context "spiritual" is opposed to "worldly," insofar as the latter implies an inordinate preoccupation with purely temporal realities. The "spiritual man" is the "*pneumatikòs anér*" whose life is rooted in Christ (1 Cor. 2: 15), whose thoughts and actions radiate from the supernatural life he has received. He is a "man of God" (1 Tim. 6: 11). It is a heavy duty to be an exemplar, and a dangerous burden to assume. But the priest has been given an order by his Lord and Master: "You are the light of the world. A city set on a mountain cannot be hidden. Neither do men light a lamp and put it under the measure, but upon the lamp-stand, so as to give light to all in the house. Even so let your light shine before men, in order that they may see your good works and give glory to your Father in heaven" (Mt. 5: 14–16).

2. Holiness of life is not enjoined on the priest simply as a moral law; for him it is a God-given vocation, a guiding motto for life. It is enjoined on every redeemed human being, but especially on the priest.

The same command is implicit in the striking words of St.

Paul: "For God, who commanded light to shine out of darkness, has shone in our hearts to give enlightenment concerning the knowledge of the glory of God, shining on the face of Jesus Christ" (2 Cor. 4: 6). The revelation of God's glory radiating from the face of His Incarnate Son is the light of our hearts. And it should be reflected in our faces too. Human beings who come in contact with the priest should be able to glimpse this reflection.

3. Imitation of Christ is the guiding principle of priestly existence. And it cannot be feigned because it springs from the inmost depths of our being. "*Agere sequitur esse.*" It is not rooted in an act of the will, but rather in our very mode of existence. The effectiveness of our pastoral labors depends essentially on the divine light radiating within us.

4. In short, the priestly vocation involves a moral obligation to lead a holy life (*vita spiritualis*). The "man of God" must lead "a life hidden with Christ in God" (Pius XII).

The full significance of this obligation becomes clear when we consider the case of a priest who fails to live up to it. If a layman fails to live up to his moral obligations, his calling (farmer, businessman, doctor) is not radically affected. But if a priest fails to live up to his obligations, his life becomes one enormous contradiction. His infidelity strikes at the heart of his existence and his sacred functions: Mass, sermons, administration of the sacraments, recitation of the breviary. In such circumstances he should have a chance to regain his senses and rectify his conduct.

§ 5. *The Church's Solicitude*

1. Canon 124 obliges all clerics to lead a holier life than the laity. In his *Adhortatio ad clerum universum de sacerdotalis vitae sanctitate* (September 23, 1950), Pope Pius XII singled

out the following aids to growth in holiness: a) the Mass, b) the breviary, c) meditation, d) Marian devotion (the Rosary), e) visits to the Blessed Sacrament.

2. The Pope was referring to daily Mass in his exhortation. And the laity takes this for granted. Canon 805 obliges the priest to celebrate Mass "*pluries per annum.*" Bishops and religious superiors are to make every effort to say Mass on Sundays and Holydays of Obligation at least. Those who are involved in pastoral work must, of course, make sure that all the traditional divine services are available to the people.

3. The Mass is celebrated properly when the priest's external decorum expresses his internal devotion. He should pay particular attention to the rubrics as they are commonly interpreted. Undue haste, half-hearted attention, or a perfunctory air can scandalize the worshipers, whereas a devoutly celebrated Mass is the best possible sermon.

4. All clerics in Major Orders are obliged to "say" the Divine Office (c. 135). But this common expression is rather misleading. It is not just a question of reciting words or getting through the hours. The cleric must *pray* the Divine Office. It is the second great means of sanctification for the priest. Every day he has an opportunity to immerse himself in the Church's universal prayer—or to misuse it. Throughout the Church year it plunges him daily into the mystery of God's salvation-history. Canon Law prescribes that it be "*oratio vocalis,*" but this does not mean that it has to be "*oratio labialis.*"

5. Canon 125, 1, obliges the bishop to see to it that his priests receive the sacrament of penance "frequenter." Many interpret this to mean once a week, or at least once a month. Obviously one should be in the state of grace to receive and dispense the sacraments.

6. Canon 126 insists upon daily meditation, daily recitation of the Rosary, daily examination of conscience, and a daily visit to the Blessed Sacrament.

7. According to canon 126 priests ought (*debent*) to make a retreat at least once every three years.

II. THE PASTORAL MINISTER

At the very outset we are confronted with a basic question. Does priestly ordination itself oblige the priest to exercise the powers he receives at that time? Or, to rephrase the question: must every priest be a pastoral minister, to some extent at least?

There are theologians who answer "no" to this question. It cannot be shown on theological grounds that ordination imposes a pastoral obligation on the ordinatus. But in certain situations there may be such an obligation: 1) in an emergency, it could become an obligation in charity; 2) if a priest is assigned to a pastoral office, he has a pastoral obligation; 3) canon 128 requires that a priest accept the task assigned by his bishop. The obligation remains as long as a need exists. And the bishop decides whether the need does or does not exist. The obvious shortage of priests in the world today makes the question purely theoretical.

Does every priest have at least the desire to be a pastor of souls? I think so.

1. The priest was not ordained for self-glorification. As the ordination ritual reiterates again and again, he is ordained "*tam pro vivis quam pro defunctis.*"

2. The priest would be abusing his sacred anointing if he did not regard it as a "talent" for which he must render an account before the Lord (Mt. 25: 19).

3. In his *Regula pastoralis* (1, 5) Gregory the Great points out that no motive, however lofty it may be, excuses the priest from showing a pastoral concern for souls: "Some very talented priests zealously pursue the quiet path of contemplation, but refuse to give others the benefit of their preaching. They long for silent corners and undisturbed meditations. Undoubtedly they are guilty of wrongdoing to the extent that their preaching could have benefited the souls of other men."[7] In the light of these words every priest who undertakes a non-pastoral assignment (librarian, procurator)—even with the consent of his Ordinary, or at his bidding—must scrutinize his priestly life continually.

A. HIS PERSONALITY

The priest who is to do God's work in the world must have a supernatural call and the spiritual and theological formation provided by the seminary. All this was pointed out in a previous section and is presupposed in what follows.

§ 1. *The Basic Requirement*

The pastoral minister must possess a well integrated personality rooted in a living faith. Why?

1. The priesthood is not a job or a profession. In many jobs a man need only perform his duties uncomplainingly. His basic character make-up does not affect his work to any significant degree (e.g., ticket agent, postman).

Some occupations deal with various aspects of human

[7] "Sunt itaque nonnulli, qui magnis muneribus diati, dum solius contemplationis studiis inardescunt, parere utilitati proximorum in praedicatione refugiunt, secretum quietis diligunt, secessum speculationis appetunt. De quo, si distincte judicentur, ex tantis proculdubio rei sunt, quantis venientes ad publicum prodesse potuissent."

existence, e.g., lawyer, doctor, scientist. Here again competence in one's specialized field is the main requirement, although we have come to realize the value of a well-rounded outlook. Many teachers still think they can do without it, but no professional educator does.

The pastoral minister must reach the spiritual core of man, the unique center which sets each person off as an individual and determines his course for time and for eternity. If the pastoral minister himself does not have a well formed personality, he will not be able to appreciate individuality in others; he will not reach them. In his eyes Christ's call to the individual and God's eternal law are immediately reduced to a set of formulas in a moral textbook. He sees sins rather than sinners, cases rather than frail human beings. He does not see human nature in the concrete, the individual and personal characteristics of human behavior. To put it bluntly, he sees nothing but a two-legged animal who either keeps or breaks the Commandments. He does not consider the human factors involved in human conduct; he misses the over-all picture because he sees only bits and pieces of information. He has no understanding of the individual as such, and he does not realize this—how could he? This failure on the part of the pastoral minister is one of the main reasons why men reject his "guidance." For social encounters between human beings are dependent on interpersonal rapport.

2. What do we mean by "personality" in this context? A man has a mature personality (i.e., is a "person") when he has developed or is trying to develop his full natural and supernatural potential as an individual human being, when he has integrated or is trying to integrate all this into a well balanced unity. Such a man is an "adult" human being, one who can make mature decisions in God's sight and exhibit that "*perfectio potentiae ad actum*" of which Saint Thomas spoke (S. Th. 2, 2, q. 55, a. 1). In particular the true adult dis-

plays a certain spiritual and intellectual maturity which suffuses all his actions.

There are certain rational virtues proper to the pastoral ministry. Traditionally they are divided into speculative and practical virtues. The speculative virtues are: *intellectus*—the sure-footed ability to judge correctly on matters of principle, acquired by study and experience; *scientia*—keen insight into the workings of men's souls, acquired by study and by listening with the "third ear"; *sapientia*—the ability to correlate abstract principles and concrete actions in the light of eternal truths (S. Th. 1, 2, q. 57, a. 3).

Possessing a certain moral maturity, the true adult knows quite well that he is still far from his ultimate goal. Directly opposed to him is the self-righteous hypocrite who spends his time passing judgment on others. Moral maturity reveals itself in these characteristics: a frank and open character, a mode of life guided by conscience, an inner consistency between thought and action, a selfless idealism striving for true nobility of soul.

In the religious sphere maturity is revealed in our ceaseless efforts to fashion ourselves naturally and supernaturally in God's image. As we have already noted, the New Testament characterizes the Good Shepherd as *kalos,* not just *agathos,* thus hinting at the supernatural qualities he should possess.

Even when the pastoral minister has done his best to mold a mature personality, he feels a trace of sadness for his inability to complete the job and for the tragic elements which are an integral part of earthly existence. He is patient with himself and with others; and thus he avoids falling into pharisaism.

Personality always implies individuality. Even the priestly call from God is a unique call directed to a specific individual. When we speak of "originality," we are expressing our admiration for a person's individual uniqueness in some respect; when we speak of "eccentricity," we are referring to a distorted expression of individuality. It is important to realize that the solitary priest assigned to some lonely post can easily succumb to this distorted behavior pattern. One of the most important tasks of the seminary is to inculcate in the young cleric a true appreciation of personality and its pastoral significance. This point needs stressing because many ascetical guides seem to be rooted in the assumption that the mature priest is one whose spirit has been "broken." This is a mistaken view which has no legitimate connection with the ascetical ideal of the "*natura cruciata.*"

§ 2. *Agere sequitur esse*

The competent pastoral minister must be a mature human being, a mature Christian, and a mature priest. "*Gratia supponit naturam.*" A person whose natural growth has been stunted cannot grow into a mature disciple of Christ. "*Agere sequitur esse.*" Christian morality and pastoral activity are not summed up in a set of normative rules. They are embodied in the natural and supernatural activities of a mature human being living in the state of grace. The great canonized saints who founded religious orders and did outstanding missionary work, possessed strong individual personalities.

B. PASTORAL VIRTUES

Canon 543, 2, requires two particular virtues of a pastor (besides theological training and his exemplary life, of course) —zeal for souls and prudence.

§ 1. *Zeal for Souls*

The Apostles saw the words of the psalmist (68: 10) fulfilled in their Master: "*Zelus domus tuae comedit me*" (John 2: 17). Every pastoral minister must be consumed with this same zeal for the kingdom of God. Zeal for souls is a burning desire, enkindled by the grace of priestly ordination, to save souls and lead them to God—no matter what the personal cost.

1. Pastoral zeal for souls has its theological roots in love for one's neighbor, love for the souls entrusted to one's care. This sacred Eros, which is enkindled in the days of youth, must grow into an all-consuming flame in the heart of the pastoral minister. Without this love he will not be able to discern the crying needs of the world around him and of the individual soul. "We cannot fathom the secret depths of the human heart; they are revealed only to those who love."[8] If a man has great love, he will gain a deeper knowledge of all things than reason alone could ever give him" (Louis Thomassin, 1695).

This love strengthens and solidifies our faith (*fides caritate formata*). It is the love of the Good Shepherd who goes looking for the one lost sheep.

Christian love is the "new commandment" (John 12:34) which stands in radical contrast to every previous conception of love. It must be displayed by every true Christian. And when it is a living force in a pastor of souls, it can change the world. Why? Because it is something which this world has never seen or experienced before. "That unique and wondrous supernatural force was injected into the heart of human existence. . . . The world of antiquity had been a breeding ground for hate (even as neo-paganism is today), a hate which corroded the hardest material and poisoned the most intimate human relations. It was a fearsome and sinister beam piercing every corner of human existence."[9]

This new love must be a living force in every pastor of souls. It should be apparent to all who come in contact with

[8] Nicholas Berdyaev, *Von der Bestimmung des Menschen* (1935). Trans. *The Destiny of Man* (C. Scribner's Sons, 1937), p. 150.

[9] Frank Thiess, *Das Reich der Daemonen* (Vienna, 1941), p. 159.

him. Human reasoning and theological principles deal only with universal notions and abstract concepts. Only love sees concrete realities and frail human beings calling for help. And the pastoral minister must deal with frail human beings.

2. Brotherly love causes that holy uneasiness which every pastoral minister feels. He re-echoes the words of Saint Paul: "the love of Christ impels us" (2 Cor. 5: 14) and "Do bear with me! For I am jealous for you with a divine jealousy" (2 Cor. 11: 1).

The pastoral minister who is not aglow with his love will preach and labor in vain. "*Qui non ardet, non incendit*" (Gregory the Great). What did Our Lord Himself say? "I have come to cast fire upon the earth, and what will I but that it be kindled?" (Lk. 12: 49) The pastoral minister shows himself to be his Master's disciple by spreading this flame.

3. Out of this love grows that great compassion which is the mark of the "omnipotens et misericors Deus." Christ's disciple must echo His feelings: "I have compassion on the crowd" (Mk. 8: 2). This compassion for others will preserve him from a pharisaical hardness. "Every high priest taken from among men . . . is able to have compassion on the ignorant and erring, because he himself also is beset with weakness . . ." (Heb. 5: 1–3).

4. The zealous pastor of souls is ever solicitous for the welfare of his flock. The concept itself—care of souls—is a Christian one, and the basic word is *care*. The pastoral minister is dedicated to a life of service. Unselfishness and a willingness to serve others are his watchwords for life. His Master gave His life for His sheep. The pastor's needs are provided for by the people. But his relationship to the goods of this world is a spiritual one. His pastoral vocation is not a call to "make a living." Like his Master, he is a shepherd, not a hireling who tends the sheep only for a salary (John 10: 12).

5. Opposed to pastoral zeal are despairing pessimism and over-zealousness. The pessimist shakes his head and says: "It's hopeless, nothing can be done." So he does nothing or performs his duties mechanically. Such a pastor would do well to remember the words of Saint Augustine: "*De nullius hominis correctione desperet, quem patientia Dei videt vivere, non ob aliud, nisi adducatur ad poenitentiam*" (*De catechizandis rudibus*, c. 26). If God allows an unrepentant sinner to remain alive, He does so only that the sinner may be brought to repentance. We have no right to give up hope. And this is doubly true for young men.

Overzealousness, zeal not tempered with patience and love, is also out of order. Impatience and pressure tactics accomplish no lasting results—"*nil violentum durabile.*"

§ 2. *Pastoral Prudence*

Saint Gregory the Great calls this the "*ars artium.*" It is one variety of the cardinal virtue of prudence (*phronesis*) which the Scholastics defined as "*rectitudo rationis.*"

Prudence has two facets. It involves a) making the right decision and b) choosing the right means to carry it out. A man can spoil a good endeavor by using the wrong means to carry it out. The pastor of souls must work prudently. In Saint Thomas' treatment of the virtues, prudence heads the list of practical virtues and is described as the ability, born of experience, to carry out the right decision in the right way.

1. Prudence involves, first of all, judicious insight.

a) The prudent man has a keen appreciation of the strong points and the weaknesses in his character and his fund of knowledge. No human being can blindly pattern himself after another or ape him—in preaching or dealing with others—even when the would-be prototype is appealing and original.

People have a way of seeing through poses and postures. A trait which seems genuine in one person may seem phony in another. Even some of the traits and practices of the saints are not to be imitated. The confessional practices of Saint Klement Hofbauer show that he was original and inventive (Johannes Hofer, *Der heilige Klemens Maria Hofbauer*, Freiburg, 1923). But moral theologians could well regard some practices as indirect betrayals of the confessional seal (pp. 368 ff.). And on one occasion he presumes to change the baptismal ritual (p. 352).

b) In certain instances the prudent man can borrow the insights of other men. He can profit from books on psychology, psychiatry, ethnology. But he will learn more from his own contacts with men.

c) The prudent man learns from experience. He knows how to adapt his ministry to the concrete situations in which he must work. Dr. Karl Sonnenschein once said: "In the slums I cannot start out by preaching the gospel. Living in these hard circumstances, they are not yet ready for it." We must regard his words as a prudent judgment based on the realities of the situation.

2. Prudence is also the judicious choice of the proper means. In deciding whether a boys' club should be established in a given area the pastoral minister must consider, not only the value of such a club, but also the needs of the area. The club might restrict the pastor's attention to a select group of young people and cause him to neglect the rest. All this must be taken into account.

In its early days some proponents of the liturgical revival sometimes advocated reforms which were good in themselves, but premature. And they introduced these reforms without the approval of ecclesiastical authorities. Their imprudence hurt the movement itself. They were not justified by the fact that many of their measures are now being supported by the authorities themselves. This is the tragic story of many avant-garde reformers. But, on the other hand, this does not exonerate those who mistook their own laziness and inertia for prudence.

Prudence is never calculating. The prudent pastor of souls is not looking for personal advancement or a higher office. He does not try to get around someone by showing favoritism, or backing down on matters of principle, or demeaning his office.

Finally, prudence is trust in God. With love and patience he puts all his undertakings into God's hands (2 Tim. 3: 10). And when he is perplexed about something, he follows the advice of St. James: "But if any of you is wanting in wisdom, let him ask it of God . . ." (Jas. 1: 5).

§ 3. *Exemplary Conduct*

Conduct, too, is a social entity.

1. Everyone's conduct sets a good or a bad example for society as a whole. The higher up a man stands on the social scale, the greater is his influence on his contemporaries. But everyone contributes something to his environment—for good or for ill. The first adulterer or rake in a country district still shocks the sensibilities of his neighbors. But gradually the people grow accustomed to the situation, and register no surprise when others follow suit. Sinful acts which are public knowledge cause scandal and invite imitation: "If so and so can do it . . ." People think that another's behavior excuses or even justifies their own sinful acts.

It is very important that people be made to realize the effect of their behavior on others. We all can unwittingly contribute to the bad behavior of another; we must, therefore, examine our conscience and echo the prayer of the psalmist:

"Cleanse me from my unknown faults! From wanton sin especially, restrain your servant . . ." (Ps. 18: 13–14).

2. The pastoral minister is a model for others in a very special sense. He is not called just to champion good conduct and holiness of life in his sermons. He must be a living exemplar of what he preaches. His way of life speaks louder than his words. And men believe their eyes more readily than their ears. When a person has a lofty vocation and is expected to set a good example, the discrepancy between his preaching and his behavior is more glaring.

The pastoral minister can give scandal in ways which the press would never label "scandal." The way he celebrates Mass, the way he acts in the sacristy or in the church, affects the behavior of his parishioners. It is a sad state of affairs if people get the impression that he is at best "lukewarm" in his ministry, if they detect semblances of avarice, hard-heartedness, unruliness, and anger.

To be sure, in these days there is not as much cause for complaint as there was in the days of Savonarola. The latter complained that Florence could be transformed into the new Jerusalem, if it were not for the bad example set by priests and monks.[10] And more than once Saint Clement Mary Hofbauer complained about the bad example of a priest which put the fruits of his labor in doubt.[11]

3. The pastor's duty to be a model for others involves a certain amount of danger, and a paradox.

a) The minister's desire to serve as a model for others, even though it is rooted in his sacred calling, involves certain moral dangers. A priest suffers from doubts and uncertainties too. Yet he is supposed to conduct himself as a model of steadfastness and confidence. Who but our Lord has a right to say:

[10] Jos. Schnitzer, *Savonarola*, I, 236.
[11] Joh. Hofer, *Der Heilige Klemens Maria Hofbauer*, pp. 215 f., 325.

"Learn from me"? (Mt. 11: 29) Who can honestly echo the words of St. Paul: "be imitators of me, as I am of Christ (1 Cor. 4: 16) or "be imitators of me, and mark those who walk after the pattern you have in us"? (Phil. 3: 17)

What minister can offer his people an example untainted by self-delusion, spiritual pride, and personal sins? What minister does not feel the weight of inner contradictions and personal insincerities? Strangely enough, much insincerity and hypocrisy find their roots here.

b) Pharisaism is one term used to describe this insincerity. The pharisaical person gloats over his own goodness and looks down on others, sometimes going so far as to pass judgment on them.

c) The Christian ideal is a lofty one; the priestly ideal is even loftier. It is very difficult to live a life which measures up to that ideal. Yet a priest is expected to be a model for others! How easy it is for him to adopt pious poses, overbearing mannerisms, and unctious ways.

d) The pastoral minister can avoid these pitfalls if he approaches his task with the proper attitude. He should try to be an example rather than to give example. *Agere sequitur esse.* He should always strive to live up to his sacred calling in his daily life.

He cannot allow himself to become a Pharisee. He will always feel some sadness over the fact that he has not fully satisfied His Master's command—to be the light of the world, the city set on a mountain. His life cannot be a source of self-satisfaction. He should live in such a way that men will see his good works and praise the Father in heaven (Mt. 5: 14).

Nevertheless, the divine command is there. St. Paul admonishes Titus (1: 7): "A bishop must be blameless as being the steward of God." And he tells Timothy (1 Tim. 3) that the bishop must set an example for others. The minister's life must be a pattern for those entrusted to him (1 Pet. 5: 3).

The words of Isidor are still true: "The king who follows the law is its living embodiment; so too the priest who follows the commandments is a living exemplar."[12] The bad example of a priest is always more powerful than his fine words.[13]

4. The social activity of the pastoral minister and his helpers varies greatly from place to place. The Church is a worldwide organization planted in countries with different cultures, languages, and histories. So we can only make some general observations.

a) As a priest, the pastoral minister is "*segregatus a populo.*" Of necessity he leads a somewhat lonely life and must, therefore, sustain himself with prayer and meditation. But he is also sent to help his people. So he must try to reach them by using every means compatible with the dignity of the priesthood.

b) He is concerned about the souls of men. So he does not question their background or their affiliations. He is equally responsible for all the faithful under his care. And he has a mission to all the unbaptized in his jurisdiction.

c) He must show equal courtesy to everyone he meets—beggar and prince, farmer and factory worker. Good manners are one form of brotherly love, and they stem from an appreciation of man's natural and supernatural worth. Gentlemanliness finds its roots in the depths of our faith: "*Modestia vestra nota sit omnibus hominibus*" (Phil. 4: 5).

d) Neatness in dress and personal appearance is more than a question of social etiquette, for a sloppy appearance may repel those who need his help. In recent years several novels about

[12] Isidore of Pelusium, *Letters* (M. G. 78, 976 B).

[13] "Nemo quippe amplius in Ecclesia nocet, quam, qui perverse agens, nomen vel ordinem sanctitatis habet. Delinquentem namque hunc nullus praesumit et in exemplum culpa vehementer extenditur, quando pro reverentia ordinis peccator honoratur" (Gregory the Great, *Regula pastoralis,* 1.2 M. L. 77, 16 A).

a holy priest and his adventures have presented a different opinion. But in the ordinary course of events social decorum attracts people more frequently than interior holiness.

e) By virtue of his sacred office the priest is exempted from certain social customs and courtesies. And the people fully realize this. They do not expect him to kiss the bride, for example. The slightest trace of vanity in his dress or manner lowers him in their eyes. He must be sociable, but he is not expected to be the life of the party.

f) Canon 138 permits him to go to taverns if there is some need, or if the Ordinary sees a good reason for it. There he may meet people whom he does not encounter elsewhere. The pastoral minister has every right to enjoy legitimate forms of recreation. The rules of Canon Law and the norms laid down by diocesan synods are good guide-posts in this area.

III. THE PASTORAL OFFICES

This section deals with the three canonical offices which carry on the pastoral work of the Church. They are often called the "little hierarchy," but a better word would be the Greek term *diakonia*. The Ordinary appoints priests to these offices. Our treatment is based on the stipulations of Canon Law.

A. THE DEAN

§ 1. *The Name and Its Meaning*

1. The word *decanus* (*dekadasches*) was a military term, the title of an officer in charge of ten men. In the course of the Church's history the term has had several meanings.

a) In the large monastic communities the *decanus* was appointed by the Abbot to take charge of ten monks. He in turn was responsible to the Abbot (*Rule of St. Benedict*, c. 21).

b) The *decanus capituli* was the chairman of the bishop's advisory council, the cathedral chapter whose members led a *vita communis.*

c) When the people living in country areas were converted to the Faith, parishes were established. The *decanus* was a pastor "*primus inter pares*" among the pastors of a given province. He had to conduct the monthly pastoral conference.

The reforms of Gregory VII prompted the rise of *capitula ruralia* among the rural clergy. These were priestly associations which anyone could join. One member was put in charge of the association and given the title of *Decanus.* He was not only an arm of the bishop, but also an elected chief. He had the same position as the head of a Religious Order.

2. Canon 445 describes the dean (*vicarius foraneus*) thus: "*Decanus est sacerdos, qui vicariatui foraneo ab Episcopo praeficitur.*" He is appointed (and deposed, c. 446, 2) by the bishop. In regions where it is an immemorial custom, the dean is chosen from among the pastors of a region (c. 57). This custom goes back to those associations which arose in the eleventh century.

§ 2. *His pastoral functions*

1. He has some measure of supervision over the conduct and the ministry of priests in his deanery (c. 447, 1). In particular he is to see to it that they fulfill the residence requirements (c. 465, 494), that preaching (c. 1325, 1344) and catechetical instruction (c. 1330–1333) take place, and that the sick are provided with pastoral care (c. 468).

2. He must see to it that the bishop's instructions, especially those given at the time of his visitation, are carried out (c. 447, 1, n. 2).

3. He will take special pains to see to it that the Holy Eucharist is properly housed and renewed at regular intervals in accordance with canonical regulations (c. 447, 1, n. 3, 4).

4. To some extent he has supervision over the proper maintenance of churches, church ornaments, sacred vessels. He must make sure that the liturgical regulations (especially regarding the celebration of Mass) are followed.

5. He oversees the administration of the different churches and makes sure that the parish records are being kept correctly.

6. Thus he has a right to visit the parishes in his deanery. How often this is to occur is decided by the bishop (c. 447, 2).

7. If a pastor is seriously ill, he must see to it that he has spiritual and physical assistance. When a pastor in his deanery dies, he must provide for his decent burial. When a pastor is seriously ill or has just died, he must make sure that the parish books, records, and assets are not misplaced or lost.

8. He is to convoke and chair the pastoral conferences ordered by the bishop (c. 131, 448).

9. At least once a year he must report the pastoral condition of his deanery to the bishop (c. 449).

10. He must take care that there is no traffic in relics in cases of death (c. 1289, 1). He also has some supervising power over the care and disposition of the goods of a benefice (c. 1478).

§ 3. *His Rights*

1. The dean has no *de jure* jurisdiction over the other pastors

in his deanery. He is simply "*primus inter pares.*" Usually he is chosen from their ranks (c. 446, 1). His general powers are determined by canon 446, 1, and are specified more clearly by diocesan law.

2. Some of his *de jure communi* rights:
He must be invited to a diocesan synod (c. 358, 4). Usually the bishop delegates to him the power to absolve certain sins reserved to himself (c. 899, 2). He can give permission for the initiation of a lawsuit over a question of property rights or church administration, when the matter is urgent and the bishop cannot be easily reached (c. 1526).

§ 4. *The Ideal Dean*

1. He is the shepherd of his confreres. This does not mean that he is to be their father confessor, since this might cause difficulties. But it means that he is to show concern for the priestly souls in his deanery.

2. He should be the guiding force coordinating the spiritual, pastoral, and cultural activities of his area and promoting cooperation among his fellow-workers in the ministry.

3. He should also promote camaraderie among his fellow-workers. Hospitality has always been a characteristic trait of deans.

§ 5. *A Pastor Too*

Since the dean is usually a pastor himself, an arch-dean visits his parish as the bishop's representative.

B. THE PASTOR

§ 1. *The Name and Its Meaning*

1. The word *pastor* is usually traced back to the Greek word *paroikos,* the master of a local postoffice in the Roman empire. The word was also used to designate an inhabitant in that particular postal zone. The area itself was called a *paroikia.* And perhaps the religious leader of the area was given the same title.

Other terms were also used: in the primitive Church—*presbyter;* in the Middle Ages—*pastor, rector, ecclesiasticus, parochianus.* To distinguish the parish priest from the monk, the word *plebanus* was used. And this is the root-word behind the terms used in many modern languages. The now official designation *parochus* was established by the Council of Trent.

2. Canon 451 defines the meaning of the term. "*Parochus est sacerdos vel persona moralis, cui paroecia collata est in titulum, cum cura animarum, sub ordinarii auctoritate exercenda.*"

a) The pastor is either a physical person (an ordained priest) or a moral person (a Cathedral Chapter, an Order, or a Cloister). In the latter case the pastoral work is put under the supervision of one priest who is designated vicar (c. 452, 2).

b) A pastor is given a parish *in titulum.* It thus becomes his parish and is placed under his pastoral care. He acquires jurisdiction in it (c. 873, 1).

c) He is entrusted with the *cura animarum* of all those in his parish.

d) His pastoral ministry is under the supervision of his bishop, who is the pastoral minister of the whole diocese (c. 334) (1326, 1327). But he is not just an arm of the bishop. He enjoys *potestas ordinaria* and his office, securely established by Canon Law, is respected by the bishop.

3. Canon Law makes a distinction (c. 454, 1), between movable (*amovibiles*) and irremovable (*inamovibiles*) pastors. In Europe irremovable pastors are the rule; but in the United States, for example, irremovability is only granted as a mark of distinction. Canon 454, 2, makes an important stipulation: a bishop can change a removable pastorate into an irremovable one after consulting his chapter; but papal permission is needed to change an irremovable pastorate into a removable one. And this is intended to further his ministry. A pastor should be able to make plans from one year to the next. But he could not do this if the threat of removability was hanging over his head.

§ 2. *His Qualifications and Appointment*

1. Only an ordained priest can validly receive a pastorate (c. 453, 1). Thus we no longer have the annoying problem whereby a benefice was entrusted to a non-priest who then appointed a vicar to handle the pastoral ministry. This practice is expressly forbidden in canon 154.

For the licit reception of a pastorate, Canon Law (c. 453, 2) requires that the pastor possess certain qualities: good morals, proper training, and two specific virtues—zeal for souls and prudence. (We have discussed these virtues above.) But the point is made that the nominee should also possess those virtues (*virtutes*) and qualities (*qualitates*) which this particular pastorate calls for: "*Quae ad hanc vacantem paroeciam cum laude gubernandum requiruntur.*"

Not every priest is qualified to fill a particular vacancy. A particular type of man may be best suited for a rural parish, an urban parish, a spiritually decadent parish, and so forth. The pastor should not be chosen simply on the basis of age, or education, or even holiness. Canon 459, 1, lays a heavy responsibility on the bishop in the matter of choosing a pastor: "The ordinary has a grave duty in conscience to choose the man he regards as best qualified to run the vacant parish, without allowing personal likes and dislikes to influence his decision."

2. The bishop makes the pastoral appointment (c. 455, 1). In cases where nomination is reserved to the Holy See, the parish is handed over by it (c. 1435). The sanctioned privileges of some areas (parts of Italy and Switzerland) to nominate or elect their own pastors remain in force (c. 455, 1, c. 1542); so also do the historical rights of the patron (c. 1462). Canon 1452 and custom determine when and how such rights become legitimate.

Priests who seek a vacant pastorate on their own initiative must prove their qualifications. In churches run by a Religious Order, the head of the Order proposes candidates to the bishop.

The parish is entrusted to the new pastor through the bishop or his representative in the Ceremony of *Investiture:* the pastor is "invested" (c. 461). Canons 1443–1445 describe the ceremony. Through this ceremony the pastor receives title and right to the parish entrusted to him.

The "installation" of the new pastor through the dean has no legal significance. This ceremony can be omitted, but it does have pastoral value. The new shepherd is presented to his flock in a solemn ceremony and thus he introduces himself.

§ 3. *The Office of Pastor*

1. As yet, there is no well developed "theology of the pastor." According to traditional teaching his office is *not juris divini.* The opposite view was condemned by Pius VI (Denz., 1509 ff.). According to Karl Rahner,[14] however, the pastor is "in a very real sense the living and tangible representative of the Church." "The Church, as an historical entity, is necessarily

[14] In the anthology, *Die Pfarre*, edited by Hugo Rahner (Freiburg, 1956).

localized in time and place"; and "the pastor is her prime representative."

2. The pastor has *potestas ordinaria* which is conferred with the office itself. In the *forum internum* he possesses *jurisdictio ordinaria* which cannot be delegated *in se* (c. 873, 1). But in many dioceses special regulations permit a pastor to give confessional and preaching faculties to a priest from another diocese for two weeks (e.g., the diocesan synod of Vienna, 1937, c. 165).

3. A pastor can only hold one parish *in titulum;* and a given parish can only have one pastor (c. 460, 1; c. 156). But due to the ever increasing shortage of priests many pastors supervise more than one parish.

4. There is a certain parallel between the bishop's relationship to his diocese and the pastor's relationship to his parish:

a) The parish is his spouse, the object of his love and care.

b) It is his life's work and should occupy all his attention and energy.

c) In assuming a given pastorate, he should be consumed with a special love for it and its people.

d) He should only relinquish his pastorate for pastoral reasons —e.g., because he has "preached himself out" or has nothing more to contribute. The make-up of the parish may have changed greatly, for example, and he may no longer feel qualified to handle it. Industrialization, urbanization, and immigrations can cause radical changes and create a need for new pastoral techniques. The pastor who honestly feels he cannot handle these new developments is to be commended if he requests a change.

"The pastoral life is a nomadic existence. And it is a time-honored rule that the flock must be moved to new grazing ground every other night" (Konstantin Noppel, *Aedificatio Corporis Christi*).

e) Some pastorates are harder; some are easier. But none can be regarded as sinecures.

§ 4. *His Canonical Obligations*

1. *Basic Obligations*

a) Wherever possible, the pastor should reside in the parish rectory located in the vicinity of the parish church (c. 465). For a just reason the bishop can exempt a pastor from this obligation, if the dwelling in question is not too far from the church and does not interfere with his pastoral ministry.

Canon 465, 2, allows the pastor a maximum of two months vacation a year. The bishop can extend this period if a just reason exists (e.g., sickness). The retreat period is not included in this two-month vacation (§ 3); but only one week per year can be allowed for it.

A pastor can only leave his parish for more than a week when the following conditions are fulfilled (c. 465, 4): he must get the written permission of his bishop; he must leave an acting pastor (*vicarius substitutus*) in his place, who is acceptable to the Ordinary of the place; a vicar belonging to a Religious Order must also have the permission of his superior. A sudden, unforeseen absence (e.g., in a case of death) must be reported to the bishop subsequently with an explanatory note (§ 5). Anytime the pastor is going to be absent, he must designate a substitute (§ 6). The penalties for failing to observe the residence requirements are mentioned in canons 2168–2175.

b) On all Sundays and Holydays the pastor must offer Mass on behalf of his parishioners—*Missa pro populo* (c. 466, c. 339). The Holydays are those thirty-five established by

Urban VIII in his constitution *Universa* (September 13, 1641). The pastor cannot be dispensed from this obligation, even when the income of the parish is scanty (c. 339, 1).

On days other than Holydays of Obligation the pastor can accept Mass stipends in most dioceses. But those stipends must be set aside for the use of the diocese. If the pastor administers more than one parish, he need only say one Mass for all the parishioners. This *Missa pro populo* should, if possible, be celebrated in the parish church with the parishioners present (§ 4).

c) As a priest the pastor is obliged to say the breviary. According to canon 1475 he should say it for his parishioners. The many problems of the parish ministry should induce the pastor to devout prayer. He will soon learn the living value of the Psalms.

2. *Pastoral Obligations*

a) Canon 464, 1, delimits their scope. All those who belong to a parish are under the pastor's care, unless they are exempt Religious. The bishop can also exclude non-exempt Religious Orders and pious societies from his care (c. 2382).

b) The basic guiding principle is this: the pastor should show greatest concern for those souls which are in spiritual danger. His model is always the good shepherd who leaves the ninety-nine and goes after the one lost sheep.

A pastor has no legitimate right (or excuse) to separate himself from his flock (c. 467, 1). His fatherly love should be directed especially toward the wayward, the poor, the needy, and the young people. Many parishes, especially in large cities, call for a real missionary pastor.

c) At least every ten years the pastor must provide a mission for the people (c. 1349). But even more important is a regular program of parochial mission work which will stem from Missions and other spiritual programs.

d) Special attention should be paid to the danger of mixed marriages (c. 1064). The pastor should try his best to discourage them (n. 1). If a mixed marriage does take place, he must see to it that the parties do not violate the commands of God and the Church. He must make sure that the pledges made are kept (n. 3).

e) Since there is only one Church and one baptism, the pastor should realize that (c. 1350, 1) baptized non-Catholics are also under his care ("*sibi commendatos habeat*"). In dealing with them, however, he must use tact and show respect for their personal convictions. According to an Instruction of the Holy Office (March 1, 1950) concern for non-Catholic Christians "is one of the foremost pastoral duties." But a person can only be received into the Church when he enters freely out of a personal conviction (c. 1351).

f) Communism is discussed by a decree of the Holy Office dated July 1, 1939. Those who hold its doctrines, or defend them, or spread them are excommunicated. Those who freely and knowingly join the party are not to be admitted to the sacraments. But naive people, or anyone who has been forced to join the party, should be left alone. The growth of Communism in a country is rooted in the social inequities which exist; so the elimination of these inequities should be a pastoral concern.

3. *His Central Duties*

a) First and foremost: to offer the Holy Sacrifice as often as possible (c. 467, 1; cc. 802–844). Attendance at Mass should not be regarded simply as the fulfillment of a Church law (c. 1248 f.). It should represent God's "chosen race" (1 Pet. 2: 9) gathered around the altar to worship Him. The people must be brought to participate in the sacrifice in accordance with the Church's directives and the fruits of the liturgical revival. Where this participation is not yet a reality, the people should be thoroughly trained in the principles of liturgical worship. The new practices cannot be introduced simply with an announcement from the pulpit. No lasting results are produced by this method.

The people must come to realize once again that they participate in the Mass as the community of God's faithful. Once they realize this, countless difficulties fade away.

Worship of the Blessed Eucharist should be a prime concern of the pastor. To that end he should hold such services as Benediction, Holy Hours, and Forty Hours'. The church should remain open so that people can visit the Blessed Sacrament during the day. Pious local customs connected with Eucharistic devotion should be maintained if possible. In some places administration of Communion to the sick is a public ceremony. The people accompany the priest prayerfully, and he blesses all who pass. In other areas the bell tolls at the moment of Consecration, and the people living and working in the surrounding area kneel down to join in the prayer of those at Mass.

b) All the sacraments should be administered with the greatest possible solemnity. This is especially true of *baptism* (cc. 755–761). When a dead parishioner is being carried to the cemetery, the church bells toll his departure. But it often happens that a child is reborn into the Church in an atmosphere of hushed silence. Sometimes only the god-parents know what has taken place. So some pastors announce every baptism, invite people to attend, and have the church bells ring during the ceremony itself. For the early Christians this was the crowning experience which prepared them for martyrdom. Adults thus should be continually reminded of this fact. All those who may have to administer emergency baptism on some occasion—midwives, nurses—should receive appropriate instruction (c. 743). Children should be given a Christian name (c. 761). If the child is given several names, at least one should be a Christian name. The common Christian names and their local variations are pretty well known throughout the world: there is no restriction in choice among them. Nicknames are out of the question.

The sacrament of confirmation (cc. 755–761) is unique in that the ordinary minister is the bishop. In many places the essential ritual is surrounded with additional ceremonies. The pastor should discreetly eliminate any ornamentation which does not contribute to the significance of the ritual itself.

A decree of the Sacred Congregation of the Sacraments dated September 14, 1946 (A.A.S., XXXVIII, pag. 349–58) granted pastors of the Roman Rite an extraordinary privilege. They can administer confirmation validly and licitly with the following conditions stipulated: 1) the pastor must be in his own territory; 2) the pastor must make sure the candidate is seriously ill and in danger of death; 3) only the pastor has this power; 4) the power cannot be delegated; 5) the power can be used only if the bishop is not available; 6) the pastor must use the rite found in the *Rituale Romanum* (Editio Pii XI, 1925). The confirmation is to be recorded on the baptismal record.

Every pastoral minister must be prepared at all times to administer the sacrament of penance. A schedule for confessions should be set up and published in every church. Usually it is found on the permanent announcement-schedule at the entrance of the church, where everyone can find it. At least several times during the year (e.g., Eastertide, the octave of Corpus Christi), the pastor should bring in priests from outside the parish so that his parishioners may confess to them if they wish.

c) Preaching the Word of God (cc. 1344–1348) is one of the pastor's personal duties (c. 1344, 1). If possible, he should preach at the service with highest attendance. It is only by way of exception that the pastor can fulfill this obligation through another priest. He must get his bishop's permission if he wishes to delegate the duty permanently (c. 1344, 2).

It is the Church's wish that at least a short homily be preached at every Mass (if possible) on Sundays and Holydays of Obligation (c. 1349). Even pastors belonging to Religious Orders must follow the special directives of the local Ordinary. The faithful should be urged constantly to attend services where sermons are preached (c. 1348). Pastors who are negligent in this matter will have much to answer for.

d) Catechetical instruction is primarily the duty of the pastor and his assistants (cc. 1329–1336). This canonical position must be kept in mind, even when the catechetical program is organized on a wider scale through a centralized organization. Pastoral ministers should show special concern in preparing children (and others) for confirmation, First Communion, and first confession (c. 1330, n. 1, 2). And catechetical doctrine should be reviewed and explained to adults again and again, especially on Sundays and Holydays (c. 1332). Where such things as "Sunday school" programs already exist, they are to be kept up. Often the pastor can fulfill this obligation only by preaching an ordered series of doctrinal sermons.

If the pastor cannot handle this task alone, he can bring in other clerics and also good skilled laymen, especially those who belong to the Confraternity of Christian Doctrine (c. 711, 2).

Priests and clerics belonging to the parish have a duty to assist the pastor in this work, as long as they are not canonically forbidden to do so (c. 1333, 2). Members of Religious Orders also (c. 1334) have this obligation. But they are to devote their special attention to the instruction of adults in their own churches.

e) The pastor also has an obligation to preserve intact the faith and morals of his territory. He himself takes the *professio fidei* upon assuming his office (c. 461 and c. 1406, 1, n. 7). He must keep an eye out for erroneous teachings and strange sects within the parish. He must adopt prudent measures to arrest and reform corrosive elements. He must work tactfully to stop the spread of harmful books (c. 1405, 2) and help to provide good books, papers, and magazines for his people. In places where it seems necessary, every parish should, if possible, establish a lending library.

f) Every pastor must show concern for the growth of priestly vocations within the diocese (c. 1353). He, before anyone else, can spot the seeds of a vocation: and he has the duty to test and nurture them. Much depends on the pastor and his ministry. For is it not true that there have always been certain parishes and certain pastors who know how to foster potential vocations?

g) Repeatedly and insistently the Church urges the pastoral minister to care for the sick and the needy. The second great commandment is now an official duty for him (c. 468). He is constantly reminded of his duty to administer the sacraments to the sick (cc. 847; 858, 2; 882; 900, n. 1; 937–949; cc. 864 ff.). And since the earliest days of the Church, care for the needy has been not only a pastoral concern, but the very touchstone of Christianity (c. 463, 4; c. 1235, 2).

§ 5. *His Administrative Duties*

It is conceivable that these duties may seem to be quite unimportant to a zealous pastoral minister. They can occupy so much of his time that the pastoral needs of his flock may be seriously neglected. On the other hand, a pastor with some predilection for accounting may devote so much time and energy to these duties that he turns into an office clerk. While a pastor may be able to delegate many duties to his subordinates in a small parish, he will have to handle them himself in a large one. But the duty remains, and the responsibility is his alone.

1. In assuming the office of pastor he has taken on the obligation to keep the parish books conscientiously—"*accurate conficere*" (c. 470, 1, 3; c. 2283).

a) The parish registers: the baptismal (and confirmation) record, the marriage book, and the record of deaths. A copy of these records is to be sent to the Chancery each year.

b) In many places the parish must also keep a record of the *status animarum*. It provides accurate, up-to-date information on the spiritual condition of the parish, listing new converts, those who have fallen away from the Church, and those who have been brought back.

c) The pastor must also keep the parish archives (c. 470, 4; c. 383 f.; cc. 2383, 2406).

d) In places where it is required or customary, he must also keep the parish chronicle or history. Only significant events should be recorded. It is not the place for the pastor to make comments on his parishioners, judge his predecessors, or criticize his assistants. Such remarks would leave him open to the criticism of those who come after him.

2. The pastor has other administrative duties:

a) He must manage the property and the goods belonging to the parish church. He must keep an inventory of the property's value, and this inventory is open to examination. He must do his best to prevent these goods from being destroyed or damaged. All this means that he must also use the parish assets wisely, and keep accurate account books. The parish trustees can assist him in these affairs (cc. 1182–1184; 1518–1528).

b) He must also manage the parish benefice (cc. 1473–1482) and its revenues, all the money used to support the pastor himself and his assistants. The benefice may be real estate or hard currency, but it must be estimated in accordance with canonical regulations and local norms.

§ 6. *His Rights as Pastor*

1. The following functions are reserved to the pastor according to canon 462.

a) The solemn (i.e., according to the ceremony in the Roman Ritual) baptism of his own parishioners.

b) Administering confirmation in accordance with the decree of 1946.

c) The public administration of Communion to the sick and the administration of Viaticum, the Last Anointing, and Solemn First Communion.

d) Publishing the banns of marriage and giving premarital instructions (cc. 1094–1097).

e) Receiving converts into the church and taking back fallen-away Catholics.

f) In general, he has charge of all those extra-sacramental services which involve some degree of public solemnity (processions, house blessing). He can bless the sacred vessels belonging to the parish church and any chapels in his territory (c. 1304, n. 3).

g) Administering the Last Rites to his parishioners and celebrating their obsequies.

h) He has the right to obtain Holy Communion for the sick from any church in his parish (c. 483).

i) In Eastertide he has the power to absolve all sins reserved to the bishop himself (cc. 873, 1; 880, 2; 899, 2; 2253, 1).

j) He can dispense from certain marriage impediments if it is no longer possible to have recourse to the bishop, or if a special need exists on the part of the couple (cc. 1044 ff.).

k) In individual cases he can dispense from the laws of fast and from the obligation to attend Mass on Sundays and Holydays.

2. *Restrictions*

a) Today the pastor's rights are somewhat more limited *de jure* because of the exemptions enjoyed by Religious Orders and other pious foundations.

b) Parishioners are no longer bound to fulfill their Mass obligation or their Easter duty in their parish church.

c) Certain things are not his business:

a) He has no right to introduce new processions or drop existing ones (c. 1294).

b) He has no right to introduce changes in the liturgy. Since the Council of Trent, liturgical matters in the Roman rite are the province of the Apostolic See (c. 2, c. 1267): "*Unius Apostolicae Sedis est tum sacram ordinare liturgiam, tum liturgicos approbare libros.*"

γ) He has no right to interfere with pious institutions within his territory as far as the administration of their temporal goods is concerned (c. 691, 1).

δ) He cannot impose canonical penalties (c. 2220, 1), nor can he pass a judicial sentence; if he does either, he incurs a "latae sententiae" censure. However, as a pastoral minister or a theologian he can give his opinion on a case. He can also insist upon the observance of a canonical penalty within the boundaries of a parish, if the crime is notorious (c. 2232, 1). He can, of course, deny Christian burial; but in such a case it would be wise for him to get in touch with the bishop.

C. THE PASTOR'S ASSISTANTS

§ 1. *The Vicarius*

1. The priests who come under this heading are given different titles. Here we shall mention the three which are most common.

a) *Chaplain.* This word is derived from the Latin word *capella,* a diminutive of *capa* or *casa,* meaning little house. In the Middle Ages it also meant "mantle," referring to the mantle of Saint Martin, the patron of France. It was preserved in a room which soon was called *capellanus.* He had to accompany the Frankish king on all his royal expeditions, carrying the mantle of Saint Martin. The room in which the mantle was kept at the royal palace became known as the *capella.* Already round the year 800 the word referred to any small room where prayers were said. After 850 *capellanus* referred to any clerical assistant.

b) *Cooperator.* This is a Biblical term (*Sunergós*) meaning "co-worker." Saint Paul designated his disciple Epaphroditus as the first cooperator. He was serving his first prison term in Rome. The community at Philippi, which was deeply attached to St. Paul, sent Epaphroditus to Rome with a sum of money for him. Epaphroditus fell sick and almost died. Upon his recovery St. Paul sent him home with an accompanying letter. In this letter we find the theological roots of the concept. "But I have thought it necessary to send to you Epaphroditus, my brother and *fellow-worker* and fellow-soldier, but for you a messenger and the minister to my need. For he was longing for all of you and was grieved because you had heard that he was sick" (Phil. 2: 25–26). In a previous passage, St. Paul describes his beloved disciple Timothy as *unanimis* (*isópsuchos*): "For I have no one so *like-minded* who is so genuinely solicitous for you. For they all seek their own interests, not those of Jesus Christ. But know his worth: as a child serves a father, so he has served with me in spreading the gospel" (2: 20–23).

c) *Vicar.* This term has been adopted by Protestant sects and is no longer in general use among Catholics. In ecclesiastical usage it is the general designation for the chief representative of a certain group (vicar-general, vicar-capitular). *Vicarius cooperator* is the canonical term for the priests who assist the pastor.

2. We must distinguish this concept from other offices which have similar designations:

a) The *vicarius actualis* (or *vicarius curatus*) is the acting minister in a parish whose official director is a moral person—a Chapter, Religious Order, or Cloister (c. 471, 1). In practice, he has the same duties and responsibilities as a physical pastor. Usually his official title is administrator.

b) Canon 475, 1, stipulates that a *vicarius adjutor* can be appointed to a parish if a pastor can no longer perform his duties because of old age, feebleness, forgetfulness, incipient blindness, or some other chronic infirmity. The appointment is made by the bishop. In a cloister church, the superior has a right to nominate the candidate.

Canon Law does not recognize age-limits or compulsory retirement. If a pastor refuses to resign, he can only be removed for very serious failures. And the process is long and drawn out. For an old and failing pastor, withdrawal from the parish could very well be a death-blow. So he is allowed to remain in the parish, and the pastoral duties are entrusted to a *vicarius adjutor*. When the pastor is completely incapacitated, the latter assumes all his rights and duties. But in his letter of appointment his rights and duties can be restricted or spelled out in detail.

c) According to canon 472, 1, 2, the *vicarius oeconomus* is one who acts as the administrator of a vacant parish and performs the pastoral duties until a new pastor is appointed. In rural areas a neighboring pastor is usually entrusted with this temporary assignment. In city parishes the first assistant usually assumes the task at the bishop's order. His new status is only temporary. He may not introduce measures which would encroach upon the decisions of the new pastor.

d) The *vicarius substitutus* is the priest who takes a pastor's place during his absence, with the bishop's approval (c. 465, 4; also c. 474 and c. 1923, 2).

e) Here we are discussing the *vicarius cooperator* only. His function is described in canon 476, 1.

According to paragraph 2 of canon 476, the assistants can be called upon to perform all the parish functions which are not reserved to the pastor himself by Canon Law. The work assigned to the assistants can be pinpointed spatially. Thus, in a mountain area, he might be assigned to a sister church; or, in a city parish, a certain block might be his assignment. It can also be pinpointed to specific persons or groups of persons, e.g., a minority group or the working class in the parish. Usually the duties are assigned on the basis of purely practical considerations. Besides conducting divine services and preaching sermons the assistant is the moderator of a particular parish organization, or youth groups, or school activities. His sphere of duty can be spelled out in his appointment notice.

3. The appointment of an assistant is no longer the same as it was before the Council of Trent. In those days the pastor made the appointment, and the local Ordinary then approved it. Today the appointment is made by the Ordinary, "*audito parocho.*" Most likely this last stipulation will never gain the force of custom. Religious superiors have the right to nominate candidates for their parishes.

4. The conditions necessary for fruitful collaboration in the ministry are binding on the assistant as well.

a) Residence in the parish. Usually he lives in the parish rectory. In some country areas, he has his own house and household staff (Ireland, Switzerland). How this duty is to be fulfilled in a given place depends on the diocesan statutes and praiseworthy local customs (*secundum laudabiles consuetudines*); such customs are very rare.

b) The Ordinary will take pains to see that the cooperative endeavors of the parish ministry are founded on a common way of life shared by the parish ministers. As canon 134 states: "*Consuetudo vitae communis inter clericos laudanda ac servanda.*" The emphatic wording of this canon underlines the importance and the seriousness of the request. Primarily it is the bishop's responsibility to see that the Church's wish is fulfilled. But in actual practice much depends on the pastor and his assistants. "*Vita communis*" means more than living under the same roof, eating at the same table, or even reciting the breviary in common. First and foremost it means a deep common concern and love for souls which must underlie the efforts on their behalf.

5. An assistant can be recalled *ad nutum* by the bishop or the vicar-capitular. But the seriousness of the action is emphasized by the fact that the vicar general needs the *mandatum speciale* of the Ordinary (c. 477, 1).

An assistant can be transferred to another post. Apart from this he can also be removed if he is seriously remiss in his duties or acts against the commands of his pastor. This holds true, even if he proves to be right. It is the pastor who is responsible for the pastoral work in his parish. He remains secure and irremovable.

§ 2. *His Office*

We have a well developed theology of the papacy and the episcopacy. A theology of the pastor may be on its way. But we cannot find any clear biblical foundation for a theology of the vicarius, because the position—as we know it—did not exist in those days.

1. But the Apostles (especially St. Paul) did have anointed co-workers who were called *cooperatores,* and Scripture tells us how the Apostles regarded this office. So perhaps we can speak of a theology of the vicarius in an analogous sense.

The word *sunergós* occurs twice with this meaning. But the first instance has no relevance here. In his third Epistle (v. 8) St. John bids his beloved Gaius and his flock to show hospitality toward the messengers of the Gospel. He calls all those who receive them *sunergoí tē alētheía* (*cooperatores veritatis*—in the Vulgate). Thus he is clearly referring to all the faithful and their duty to one another.

The word occurs again in Philippians 2: 25. St. Paul is speaking of his *sunergós Epaphróditos* and characterizes him in this fashion. He is 1) a brother—*adelphós;* 2) a fellow-worker—*sunergós;* 3) a fellow-soldier—*sustratiōtēs;* 4) a minister to my need—*leitourgòs tēs chreias mou.* If we add to these epithets the one he used to describe Timothy—*isopsuchos* (*unanimis*), we would have a good foundation for the development of a full-fledged theology of the vicarius.

2. These fundamental notions pervade the description of the vicarius and his work as outlined in Canon Law: c. 476, 6.

a) The assistant must supplement (*supplere*) the work of his pastor, helping him when he has reached the limits of his capacity for one reason or another. He must assist him in his need as a "brother" and a "helper."

b) The assistant has a duty to assist the pastor "*in universo paroeciali ministerio.*" As the pastor's co-worker, he must step in to handle any parochial work which the pastor cannot take charge of personally.

c) It is with good reason that all priests are called "confreres." But the assistant must remember the phrase "*subest parocho.*" Priests today must realize this just as Epaphroditus and Timothy did. The pastor is more than a confrere. He is something of a father to his young assistant—"*qui eum paterne instruat.*" He introduces the young apprentice to pastoral work and watches over his progress. At least once a year he is to send a report about his assistants to the Ordinary, because the latter must know about their abilities and their competence as pastoral ministers.

Timothy died as Bishop of Ephesus, Epaphroditus as Bishop of Terracina. The latter, who was the first to be called a *cooperator,* is the patron of parochial assistants; his feast-day is celebrated on March 22.

§ 3. *His Relations with the Pastor*

1. Theological principles and canonical regulations do not completely settle the relationship between the pastor and his assistant. In actual practice tensions may develop between them and lead to open quarrels. Their hostility to one another may scandalize the parishioners and have tragic consequences for the young curate. Experience shows that the first assignment of a newly ordained priest plays a great role in his future as a priest. The fact that there may be moral guilt on one side or the other, or on both, is not the point at issue here.

The ideal relationship between them is proposed by the Psalmist: "*Ecce quam bonum et quam jucundum habitare fratres in unum*" (Ps. 132: 1). Their harmonious life together will teach their parishioners more than any sermon. It will serve as an example and an inducement to all the families in the parish. History provides us with another example of this ideal—the oratories of the early Middle Ages where the parish priests lived a common life.

Here we shall discuss only the common causes of tension, the ones which lie outside the moral sphere and are, therefore, easily overlooked. Once these factors are present, parochial work can become a torture for both parties, even if they are well intentioned.

a) Some causes of tension are rooted in the age difference between the old pastor and his young assistant. They are pinpointed by developmental psychology and described in terms of a binary opposition.

α) the young man is still at the beginning of life; the old man has reached the end of his life. Thus they have quite a different outlook on life. One feels that his life is still ahead of him; the other sees life slipping away from him. So their attitude toward earthly life and its problems is radically different, if not diametrically opposed.

β) The young man is still involved in a process of growth and becoming; the old man has already gone through this process. So the former boldly abandons himself to this process, while the latter is now pretty well set in his living habits, convictions, feelings, and plans.

γ) This can lead to tension between the young man's daring and the older man's attitude of resignation. What young man does not love to take some risks and face some dangers! All this is a thing of the past for the older man. Yet both are harnessed to the same wagon. The young man plunges forward; the older man holds back, considering the matter calmly in the light of his own convictions and experiences.

δ) Tension can develop between the inexperienced young man and the experienced older man. The former thinks he knows what is involved; the latter has gained insight from his long experience. But the young man does not appreciate this, and his critical comments hurt the pastor's feelings.

ε) Frequently it is the age-old conflict between the idealist and the realist; or between the optimist and the pessimist. Age may not enter into the picture at all. It may be a question of temperament.

ζ) The young man may want to do something; and he may look for the opportunity. Then the pastor may step in and put a damper on the project because he prefers quiet. Don't rock the boat!

η) Strangely enough, these opposing attitudes can find suitable mottos to justify themselves. The older man says: "*Quieta non movere*"; the younger man says: "*Ecce nova facio omnia*" (Apoc. 21: 5). There is a hint of tragedy in all this because neither side can fully sympathize with the other. Psychological factors, of which the older man is not even conscious, make him reluctant to undertake new endeavors. The younger man cannot really appreciate their influence on his pastor's outlook.

All these factors can lead to ill feelings or harsh words which make cooperation impossible between them.

b) Other causes of tension are rooted in personal temperament and the contrast between psychological types. They crop up in every life and give considerable impetus to the tensions provoked by age difference. Some temperaments, such as the sanguine and the phlegmatic, do not get along well with each other. And watch out if two people of choleric temperament are co-workers, each one wanting to have the last say! It is an oft-told tale that the assistant who complains the loudest about a domineering pastor, later proves to be an overbearing pastor himself. Or it may happen that the extrovert and the introvert are forced to work together. The former is understanding, trusting, and open to his environment; the latter is withdrawn, distrustful, and critical. Yet they must somehow cooperate with each other.

c) Some tensions between young and old arise from the fact that they grew up at different points in history. The old priest is still inclined to regard liberalism or socialism as diabolic evils. The young priest knows that much has changed in the past fifty years and that the attitude of the pastoral minister must change accordingly. Fifty years ago, young assistants had to face the opposition of their pastors when they tried to carry out the decree of Pius X regarding Communion for children. Yet today many of them are violently opposed to the liturgical reforms which must come.

d) Different individuals approach their work with different attitudes. And these differences can easily create conflicts. One man likes a good fight; the other only wants results. One brings politics into his sermons; the other sticks to pastoral problems only. One is content to stay with the faithful, the "*pusillus grex*"; the other has a missionary outlook. One enlists the active help of the laity; the other regards them as clients only.

e) These tensions can have tragic consequences for the newly ordained curate. The young priest comes to his first parish with high ideals and lofty objectives. But he finds a pastor who does not correspond to these ideals. The pastor has many years behind him. The young curate must suddenly adapt himself to this pastor. It is a slow and painful process. Or else he drops his ideals in a very short time and becomes a caricature of all they stand for.

f) Should an open quarrel develop from these tensions, the assistant may find himself in a tight spot. In the eyes of Canon Law, he is not on an equal footing with the pastor. The latter is firmly entrenched in his office and protected by Canon

Law; the former can be removed *ad nutum*. So the curate's sense of justice is hurt because he must go even if he is in the right; and he often is. In such a situation one is justified in appealing to the pastor's gallantry. But a contrary decision should not embitter the young cleric and squelch his optimism.

2. What is the solution to these problems? It may be pointed out that the differences and even the oppositions between individuals are meant to complement and enrich the parties involved. Old age has its own particular functions and assets; so does youth. There is much truth in the words of the old pastor who said: "I learn something from each new curate. Each one brings new enthusiasm and new ideas along with him." If—and only if—the assistant adopts this same attitude will he learn much from his pastor.

Guide-Lines in Dealing with Disputes:

a) After examining individual cases, one might venture to say that in most cases the assistant is right in theory, but wrong in the way he goes about handling it.

b) It is better to leave a pastoral project alone if it will create dissension in the rectory.

c) The situation is worse, in fact, inexcusable, if the dispute spreads to the parishioners themselves.

d) No new project should be initiated against the pastor's wishes. He remains, while assistants come and go.

e) The pastor should not disregard the importance of youthful initiative, nor should the assistant overlook the necessity for careful planning.

f) The assistant must not lose his respect for his immediate superiors. The pastor, on his part, will have much to answer for, if he squelches his assistant's initiative, independence, and idealism.

Novels which deal with parochial life and its problems:
P. A. Sheehan, *My New Curate* (1899)
G. Powers, *The Encounter* (1950)
H. M. Robinson, *The Cardinal* (1950)
Father X, *Everybody Calls Me Father* (1951)
Edwin O'Connor, *The Edge of Sadness* (1961)
J. F. Powers, *Morte d'Urban* (1963)

§ 4. *Other Helpers*

Three main groups come under this heading.

1. The religious teachers appointed by the bishop to give instruction in the parish schools. Canon Law (cc. 1329–1336) imposes a duty on the pastor to provide religious instruction in his parish. If he and his assistants cannot handle this task by themselves, the diocesan office assigns religious teachers who must have a *missio canonica* from the bishop. Because they assume a duty primarily incumbent on the pastor, it is obvious that they will work in close cooperation with him. They should present themselves to him and regard their work as a pastoral undertaking, even if they are lay people appointed and paid by the state or the community. They should stay in close contact with the pastor and lend a hand at services conducted for the young people. Religion teachers cannot be mere teachers.

These principles hold true for all catechists, whether they teach in elementary schools, trade schools, or other high schools. But the pastor must remember that the high school pupils come from many parishes: the catechists are not his exclusive property.

2. The rectors of other churches and benefices within the parish. They should cooperate with the pastor insofar as they are able. In accordance with canon 609, 3, and the orientation

of all priestly work toward the good of souls, it is only right that the schedule of divine services in the churches within a parish should not clash with one another.

3. Religious Orders for Men within the Parish.

a) The Problem:

Religious Orders are pastorally orientated to a large extent. They must stay on good terms with the pastor in carrying out their public activities. Their churches usually have a larger number of priests and preachers: and their services can be conducted more solemnly and splendidly.

Since they are not burdened with the duties incumbent on diocesan clerics, they have more free time for pastoral work itself.

The result is that often the best parishioners prefer to go to a church staffed by a Religious Order. Strained relations can arise as a result.

b) The Solution:

Canon 608, 1, makes the wise provision that, at the pastor's request, Order-priests may lend assistance in pastoral work both in their own churches and elsewhere. Canon 1334 further insists that if the local Ordinary needs their help in providing catechetical instruction to the faithful, their superior is obliged to answer this request—provided, of course, that it does not disrupt the discipline of his community. If communal life would be disrupted, then they should be restricted to giving instruction in their own churches. This stipulation applies even to exempt Religious Orders. For canon 608, 1, indicates that Order-priests have a definite link with the diocese in which their establishment is located.

The pastoral ministry of the diocesan priest has different roots than that of the Order-priest. But these roots are not mutually exclusive. Konstantin Noppel, S.J., formulates it thus: "Religious orders represent extra-territorial communities freely entered by individuals, while the hierarchy is built upon communities in which the church is linked to local territories" (*Aedificatio Corporis Christi*, 24). But the diocesan priest also ministers to individuals, even as the Order-priest does. Besides his other parochial duties, he gives spiritual direction to individuals and takes charge of various societies.

In any case, there must be no "*invidia spiritualis.*" The motto guiding all pastoral endeavors is: *dummodo praedicetur Christus.*

The parochial ministry of the Order-priest is closely tied up with that of the diocesan priest. And throughout the centuries they have worked together in the greatest harmony.

PART THREE:
THE PAROCHIAL MINISTRY—YESTERDAY

I. TO THE END OF THE MIDDLE AGES

§ *1. In Apostolic Times*

Parishes, as we understand them, did not exist in the days of the Apostles or their immediate successors. As far as we can judge from the available data, there were three types of parochial communities.

a) An Apostle resided and presided over (*proestótēs*) the community. St. James the Younger lived and died as the bishop of Jerusalem. He worked in that city and presumably in the surrounding area.

b) St. Paul provides us with the best example of the second type, the missionary apostle. We know a great deal about his manner of living. He journeyed all over, establishing new communities and setting someone over them. But he did not stay in one place.

c) St. John the Evangelist shows us a third type. He established communities and put "angels" (*ángelos*) over them. But he exerted personal influence on these "angels" or "servants" from some central point, realizing full well that he was their "brother and partner in the tribulation and kingdom and patience that are in Jesus" (Apoc. 1: 9). We may assume that the first type of parochial community was the dominant one by the second century.

§ 2. *In Post-Apostolic Times*

The *prototype* of the present-day parish may be pinpointed (Konstantin Noppel) in those primitive Christian communities headed by one man who was not a bishop. The Church (community—*ekklesía*) had been established by the Lord and founded on the rock of Peter. But Christians perceived and experienced this church as a localized community of the faithful. According to Alfred Wickenhauser (*Die kirche als mystischer Leib Christi*), St. Paul used the term *ekklesía* in three senses:

a) referring to the Christian community gathered to celebrate the Eucharistic banquet;

b) referring to a local Christian community as such;

c) referring to a local community as a particular embodiment of the Church as a whole ("*Ecclesiae Dei, quae est Corinthi*"—2 Cor. 1: 1). The local community shared the characteristics of the Church as a whole.

Only later was the term applied to the house in which the salvation-mystery was celebrated. In those days there was no distinction between *ekklesía* and *dioikesis*.

2. The titles of the one who headed the local communities were varied and interchangeable: elder—*Presbuteros;* overseer—*epískopos;* leader—*hegoúmenos.* In the Latin areas of the West there was also a number of titles used interchangeably: *Dominus, Pastor, Episcopus,* even *Papa.* Even Gregory of Tour (d. 594) uses *sacerdos* and *episcopus* as synonyms (*De gloria confessorum,* c. 79).

When we read a report from the fourth century which says that five hundred bishops are living in North Africa, we may assume that they were consecrated bishops with the powers of an Ordinary and "pastors," in our sense of the term, in the range of their activities. It is hardly likely that the concept of a clearly delimited area (parish) under the pastoral care of one bishop existed. Even the "*tituli*" in Rome were not parishes as we understand them. The bishops of Rome, surrounded by their priests, celebrated Mass, preached, and baptized in them. Later, the head of the titular churches (consecrated bishops) celebrated Mass in these churches. But every Sunday they brought along a piece of the host consecrated by the Pope (*fermentum*) to emphasize the Pope's prerogatives and the unity of their sacrifice with his. Sidonius Apollinaris (433–479) was the first to distinguish between bishops and "second-class bishops," i.e., priests who did not preside over any diocese (parish).

What functions did priests have in those days?

a) They constituted the bishop's "council of elders" (*Presbyterium*).

b) Usually they did not celebrate Mass alone, but rather con-celebrated with the bishop; to be sure, one of them had to celebrate Mass when the bishop could not.

c) Even preaching, confessional absolution, and baptism were the bishop's concern. The priests instructed the catechumens, prepared penitents for confession, visited the sick, and performed other similar functions at the behest of the bishops.

d) Only priests con-celebrated with the bishop. But very often they were not esteemed as highly as the deacons by the community, because the latter had charge of administrative and charitable activities. So it is easy to understand why the new Pope was often chosen from the ranks of the latter.

§ 3. *The Church in the City*

For centuries Christianity was essentially an urban religion. The surrounding farmlands remained pagan for the most part. The clearest proof of this is the fact that the Latin word for *rustic—paganus*—has come down to us as the word for "pagan."

1. In the days of the Church Fathers the Church gradually spread from the city into country areas, converting the rural population. The missionary program varied greatly from place to place. First priests (or even deacons) were sent to the country to prepare the groundwork. In the early days even bishops themselves went to the missions and established churches. Many of them left their sees later on and went to found new missions (e.g., St. Martin). The missionary priests were to sow the seeds and do the preparatory work. They recruited the catechumens and instructed them in the Faith. But it was the bishop who had to preach, baptize, celebrate Mass, and hear confessions. The concept of suffragan bishops (*chōrepískopos, epískopos tōn chōrōn*—"country bishops") appeared in the fourth century and, in the East, endured into the high Middle Ages. They were consecrated bishops who had no see of their own, hence, no ordinary jurisdiction, as we would say. They were sent into the mission areas by the Ordinary of their city.

From the sixth century on, the urban bishops allotted permanent parochial territories to the missionary priests. They in turn promised him *obedientia* and *stabilitas loci.* The prototype for this practice may well have been the system of titular churches in Rome.

2. With the appearance of these independent parochial areas under the jurisdiction of the city Ordinary, the modern parish was born. Up to that time the bishop, surrounded by his priests, had been the sole pastor. But now the missionary pastors received the power to preach, to celebrate Mass, and to administer the sacraments (confirmation and ordination being excluded, of course). A large parochial territory was soon split up into smaller sections. Each section had its own small

church closely linked to the "*ecclesia matrix*" of the territory. And thus the modern "deanery" came into being.

3. All these innovations altered the older concept of the episcopacy. Up to then the bishop had been the sole pastoral minister. Now he was a bishop, as we understand the term today. Under him stood the territorial deaneries and their parishes. Now he was really an *epískopos* who ruled and watched over an organized diocese; and the latter term became a genuine administrative concept. But as late as the Synod of Frankfurt (747) *parrochia* and *dioceses* were used interchangeably.[15]

4. The priests who exercised a relatively independent ministry under the bishop's jurisdiction formed clerical communities which later became known as Oratories. Like the monastic Orders they had certain spiritual activities in common—prayer, meditation, and pastoral work. Up until the ninth century these communities handled the work of the pastoral ministry. Those who felt they had a priestly vocation entered the oratory; there they received theological and ascetical training, and were made acquainted with the duties of the priesthood.

Even after a deanery had been divided into smaller parochial communities, certain pastoral functions were frequently the prerogative of the *ecclesia matrix* (as they once had been the prerogative of the bishop's home church). On the vigils of Easter and Pentecost all the catechumens of the area had to assemble in this church for baptism. Often on great feast-days all the faithful of the deanery had to journey there for Mass.

Paralleling the developments of deaneries and local parishes was the establishment of manor churches for lords and their fiefs. Here again smaller churches were erected around

[15] Hefele, *Konziliengeschichte*, III, 54 ff. Trans. *A History of the Councils* (Edinburgh, 1871).

a focal point. Thus more and more "parishes" sprouted up in the countryside. And since they were dependent on the lord of the manor, they were somewhat beyond the bishop's influence.

Up to the fourth century (St. Augustine) we have no information on the training of parish priests. From the fifth century up into the Middle Ages the city clergy were trained in the cathedral schools. One member of the cathedral chapter was put in charge of this task. In rural areas candidates were trained by the local pastor, unless an oratory existed. After his training the prospective candidate had to take a test in a cathedral school or monastery. Only in the thirteenth century did secular priests begin studying in universities.

§ 4. *The Carolingian Period*

Henceforth parishes are the pastoral posts assigned by the diocesan bishop. Most of them are geographically delimited. In the Roman Empire they may have existed in the fifth century; but they appear in the territory of the Franks only a hundred years later. With the advent of Charlemagne the parochial system is fully established everywhere. But the constitutive elements were in existence before this: 1) a pastoral sphere localized within certain geographical limits; 2) an obligation on the part of the parishioners to fulfill their sacramental and liturgical obligations in the parish church under pain of imprisonment or other corporal punishment; 3) the establishment of a full-fledged parish "plant" supported by stole-fees, tithes, and other assets accruing from donations and legacies.

§ 5. *The High Middle Ages*

1. In the eleventh century Italian cities were the first to establish more parishes in the city itself. But baptism was still the legal prerogative of the bishop's own church. This new

development soon spread to other countries. It introduced another change, a decisive one, in the episcopal office and its actual function. No longer is the bishop a shepherd exercising his threefold office directly on his flock, as his pastors do; now he is an arch-shepherd overseeing the pastoral work of others. He is now removed even from the faithful in his city. The pastor now exercises a quasi autonomy (*jurisdictio ordinaria*). His irremovability is taken for granted.

2. The establishment of manor churches gradually gave rise to the right of *patronage* (Lateran III, 1179). The bishop appoints pastors, but the lord nominates them. Oratories no longer flourish. The typical pastoral minister is now the isolated priest with one or more helpers. The ranks of the priesthood were still swelling, and new offices appeared. Some priests resided in manor churches; some lived on the endowment of a benefice; some lived on Mass stipends, saying several Masses daily. The Synod of Seligenstadt on the Main (1022) forbade priests to say more than three Masses daily! *Vagantes clerici* included not only priestly candidates, but also ordained priests looking for a post. This *clerical proletariat* did great harm to the reputation of the priesthood. Even pastors were frequently poor and had to find additional means of support (e.g., by running a spa). Often they were compelled by the lord of the community (who had the right to choose their pastor) to perform some service quite unconnected with the ministry. This was especially true in Slavic lands where they had to tend to cattle. A. Veit (*Volksfrommes Brauchtum*) cites a case which had to be corrected by the Synod of Eichstadt (1453).

3. In the thirteenth century we find an important distinction —between Church property (*fabrica ecclesiae*) and benefice (*mensa parochialis*).

The system of large parishes lasted even beyond the High Middle Ages. In country places a parish might stretch over more than ten villages. And in the cities the rule was one parish per city, even though there were obvious problems involved. "The establishment of new parishes met the opposition of the bishops in the cities and of the pastors in the country areas. They realized that it would mean a loss of revenue for them."[16]

In cities where the bishop was also the pastor, he carried out his pastoral activities through the "Archipresbyter" and his administrative duties through the "Archidiakon."

In country areas the pastor had to supervise the training of diocesan priests. Often he had to take on this work personally. Recommended works, besides the Bible, included the pastoral writings of Gregory the Great and Hrabanus Maurus, and the many *manualia sacerdotum* which appeared during the High Middle Ages. A test in the cathedral school concluded the training period. The pastor vouched for the candidate's moral and spiritual formation before the ordaining bishop. City clerics were able to get better training.

§ 6. *The Mendicant Orders*

No problems arose between the pastor and the Religious Orders as long as pastoral activity lay outside the province of the latter.

The situation changed radically when the mendicant Orders arose in the thirteenth century. In a few decades they had spread over Western Europe, founding communities and preaching zealously. The diocesan clergy objected strenuously when the friars mounted the pulpit with a papal *missio* and captivated many of their parishioners. The traditional law demanded that the faithful fulfill their religious obligations in the parish church, and the pastors stressed this obligation, often motivated by economic considerations.

[16] Alois Schrott, *Seelsorge im Wandel der Zeiten* (Graz: Vienna, 1949) p. 25.

The dispute was ameliorated by Pope Boniface VIII and definitely settled by the Council of Vienna (1311): 1) the mendicants have a right to preach in their own churches: they can preach in parish churches only with the pastor's permission; 2) confessional faculties must be obtained from the local Ordinary. Once granted these faculties, the mendicants are "delegated priests" in accordance with Lateran IV (1215); 3) their churches are also allowed to conduct burial services. But they must give the stole fee to the parish church.

This discussion highlighted a weighty problem in pastoral theology which is just as important today—the conflict between the rights of the parish as a local representation of the universal Church and the prerogatives of an individualized charismatic ministry. St. Paul, the great charismatic minister, established communities wherever he went. And he too had to contend with this problem (Cor. 3–4).

§ 7. *Civil Law and Christian Obligations*

The following remarks apply only to the Church in the western Roman Empire. But elsewhere the situation was much the same.

1. The national rulers (emperors, kings, princes) were the protectors of the Church. They felt themselves responsible for the temporal well-being of their subjects and even for their spiritual well-being. Religion was not a private matter by any means. It was the central concern of the government. An emperor such as Charlemagne regarded himself as a kind of archbishop. This is clearly indicated in the *Capitularia francorum: "Rex admonitor fidelium domnus imperator sit et omnes fideles adjutores ipsius."* Only after this fundamental principle is laid down, does he present his decisions on the episcopal office. "We have decided that in accordance with canonical prescriptions we shall not allow any bishop or priest

from anywhere to celebrate divine services before he has been tested by the synod" (1 *Capitularia* 2, 4). "We have decided that every bishop should tour his diocese once a year" (*Ibid.*, 8).

2. The Christian life was a civic obligation everywhere. The pastor did not have to take great pains to see to it that people attended Mass and received the sacraments. He just had to preach, say Mass, administer the sacraments, and bury the dead. The people were obliged to attend Mass by civil law.

3. Religious instruction, as we know it, did not exist. Parents and god-parents were responsible for this. The Capitulary dated 813 prescribes: "*Unusquisque compater vel parentes vel proximi filios suos spiritualis catholice instruat, ita ut coram Deo ratiocinare debeant.*" Thus the emperor emphasized their God-given obligation by making it a civil law as well.

To a certain extent Sunday sermons provided instruction to all the parishioners. During the Mass the community recited the more important prayers, the Pater Noster, the Apostles' Creed, and the Ten Commandments. Since sermons were the sole means of acquiring the necessary religious knowledge, failure to attend them was often regarded as a mortal sin (Schrott, p. 35). In monastery and cathedral schools adequate knowledge of the Faith was regarded as the most important item.

4. Attendance at Sunday Mass and fulfillment of the Easter duty were civic duties backed up by legal sanctions. (In many moral manuals it is still asserted that a person makes an integral confession even if he goes against his will.) In short, this was the Catholic Middle Ages, when religious ideals pervaded the public conduct of life—superficially, at least. It was a period of great naïveté as well, in which the people worshiped the saints avidly and reveled in miracles.

5. Besides the numerous cloisters, the many Third Orders and pious brotherhoods enabled the laity to deepen their spiritual life. Just before the Reformation, Hamburg had over one hundred brotherhoods. Other large cities had similar numbers. But the historical events of the sixteenth century do not testify to their effectiveness. Every guild had its own particular devotions; many were organized by the Church along the lines of a pious association. Each one had its own patron and its own insignia. Care of the sick and the needy was a prime concern. The *devotio moderna,* which arose in Deventer (Holland), was to a large extent a pious lay movement.

6. All in all, we can say that the pastoral care of souls, as we understand it, did not exist in this period. The whole spirit of the age was orientated toward religious ideals and practices. It moulded the character of the individual or at least kept his wayward tendencies in check. This Christian atmosphere lightened the burden of the pastoral minister. His ministry was a functional one: he celebrated the sacred rites for the people. In certain areas this is still true. But in general the pastoral ministry has changed radically in the past few centuries. The individual grows up in a secularized world where religion exerts little pressure. The pastoral minister must go out to the individual and try to convert him. He must try to transform his whole outlook on life. This becomes clearer every day.

II. COLLAPSE AND REFORM

§ 1. *Collapse*

The seemingly impregnable ministry of the Middle Ages collapsed under the storm of events which ravaged the Church in the sixteenth century.

1. *The Causes*

a) Catholic morality, as a state duty backed up by civil law, had forgotten how to stand on its own resources. Its collapse was inevitable when the moment for individual decision and personal choice arrived.

b) Once the functional ministry failed to touch and influence the hearts of individuals, it led to false security and delusions about the Christian life. The religious life of a parish often degenerated into pious customs, and this augured ill for pastor and flock.

c) Thus it often happened that those who were searching for a deeper inner life were the first to succumb to the "reformers."

d) The moral decadence of the times had tinged the clergy too. Schrott (p. 58) cites a medieval Italian proverb: "If you would come to hell, become a priest." Savonarola maintained that he could make Florence a city of saints if it were not for the bad example of priests and monks. The vice of simony was widespread, especially in the administration of the sacraments and the granting of indulgences. A considerable number of pastoral ministers had concubines and often went through a public marriage ceremony.

The formal training of priests was scanty. In the late Middle Ages preaching reached its nadir. The essentials of the Faith—grace, the sacraments—receded into the background. The people's outlook was superstitious and primitive. They reveled in miracle stories and were berated with fire-and-brimstone sermons. In general the clergy were not prepared to face the new crisis and to handle the theological problems it raised.

2. *Underlying Problems*

These cannot be overlooked if one wishes to gain a full appreciation of the contemporary situation. The Renaissance

Popes and their Curias were guilty of many abuses. Bishops, almost without exception, came from the ranks of the aristocracy. Often they were princes without any priestly vocation. Having no concern for their flock, they would live with their noble relatives in some palace and rule their diocese through a vicar or coadjutor. Very often they did not have the necessary theological or even juridical training. To cite one example of the contemporary state of affairs, canons, who were usually the sons of lesser noblemen, had to prove their jousting ability before assuming their post.[17] They were frequently called "God's cavaliers."

Although the monasteries were full of monks and nuns, the religious life was at its nadir. The large number of apostate Religious is enough to prove this. Many cloistered communities adopted the Reformation doctrines en masse. Lacking any deep religious and ascetical training, they could not cope with the Protestant challenge. The older Religious Orders did not do pastoral work. Personal sanctification and divine adoration were their primary objectives. But those who had taken the vow of poverty found it hard to live up to this ideal. Their monasteries had grown wealthy from the donations of pious lay people, and abuses arose. No visitation could settle these disputes because the inspector was no better. The common folk trusted their eyes more than their ears, and had forgotten the high ideals of piety.

§ 2. *Tridentine Reform*

The reforms introduced by the Council of Trent represented a victory of the pastoral viewpoint over the state-church concept, in theory at least.

1. *Basic Principles*

a) Every parishioner should know his pastor personally. b)

[17] J. Lortz, *Geschichte der Reformation*, II, 84.

The pastor should know all his parishioners personally. He is responsible before God for every soul. c) The faithful should receive the sacraments from their own pastor (Trid., XXIV, de ref., c. 13). d) The pastor's conduct should exemplify what he preaches to those entrusted to him (*forma gregis*).

2. *Eliminating Abuses*

a) For the most part, parishes are geographically set off from one another. b) Benefices may not be entrusted to lay people (but they can be entrusted to ordained curates). c) The priest must avoid even the appearance of avarice, commercialism, simony (S. XXIV, c. 1). d) Before anything else, the bishop is the pastor of his diocese and the messenger of God's word, as the pastor is the minister of his parish and its parishioners. e) The exemptions enjoyed by Religious Orders are to be curtailed in some ways. In pastoral work, Religious priests are subject to the bishop's jurisdiction.

3. *Training Pastoral Ministers*

In contrast to the minimal requisites for ordination which had prevailed, we find the following reasonable prerequisites laid down by Trent. 1. For the reception of tonsure: confirmation, knowledge of the rudiments of faith, the ability to read and write, and a "*probabilis conjectura*" about the life of the candidate. Tonsure should not be given to someone who is merely seeking to escape temporal jurisdiction (S. XXIII, c. 4). 2. For the reception of Minor Orders (*Ibid.*, c. 5): the testimony of a pastor or a *magister scholae* concerning the candidate's academic training. 3. For the reception of Major Orders candidates must petition their bishop at least one month before Ordination. He in turn puts their pastor or some other priest in charge of their examination. The pastor presents the candidate's name to the community and announces his desire to be ordained a priest. He makes inquiries about his parentage, his age, his morals, and his life as a Christian. Then he forwards this information to the bishop in the *litterae testimoniales.* Four days before the Ordination they are to appear before experts in theology and Canon Law for testing. The minimum age for the reception of subdiaconate and diaconate is twenty-three (c. 5 and c. 6). 4. Bishops are to erect major and minor seminaries in their dioceses for the theological and ascetical training of priestly candidates (S. XXII, c. 18, de ref.). 5. The livelihood of every *ordinatus* must be guaranteed (S. XXI, de ref., c. 2). This provision was not motivated by economic considerations. It was meant to eliminate the clerical proletariat which caused so much scandal in the Middle Ages. 6. Like the bishop, the pastor has the duty to reside in his parochial territory. His curates have the same duty.

§ 3. *The Reforms in Practice*

St. Charles Borromeo (1538–1584) carried out the Tridentine reforms in an exemplary way in the diocese of Milan. He was the first to build major and minor seminaries for the training of pastoral ministers. He convoked many synods and held many pastoral conferences. His *Pastorum instructiones* may be regarded as the first modern treatise on pastoral theology. St. Peter Canisius strove to implement the Tridentine reforms in Germany. The prototype for the establishment of major seminaries was the Collegium Germanicum (1552) established in Rome by St. Ignatius. Next came the English Seminary founded by Cardinal Reginald Pole. This Tridentine directive was implemented very slowly and was often disregarded. Many dioceses were content to place their clerics in cloisters. The founding of minor seminaries took even longer.

§ 4. *Obstacles to Reform*

The old State-Church concept was stronger than the spirit of reform. 1. Manor lords still had the right to nominate episcopal candidates. And their nomination was binding for all practical purposes. 2. The Pope needed the support of these lords in carrying out these reforms. His prime concern was to keep Catholic within the fold and regain the lost territories. 3. The Augsburg treaty (1555) gave Protestant rulers added powers in the form of a supreme episcopate. So the rights of the Catholic leaders could not be curtailed, because the Church needed their cooperation. 4. In spite of the Tridentine decrees, certain practices continued. For example, a cleric could still become a valid canon after receiving tonsure. And time and again bishops were chosen by the cathedral chapter. 5. As was true of old, there was a surplus of priests acting as acolytes and chaplains in manor churches, and a corresponding lack of competent pastoral ministers. 6. The newly orientated parochial ministry, involving man-to-man contacts, was too novel; many refused to take a chance at it. 7. The Reformation revealed the sorrowful state of the traditional Religious Orders. These were not able to rehabilitate themselves quickly enough. New Orders, burning with zeal, jumped in to fill the gap. The Jesuits and the Theatines appeared in the cities and towns; the Capuchins and later the Lazarists, in country areas. Their work involved preaching, catechetical instruction, parish missions, and retreats. The Capuchins reintroduced the old practice of pilgrimages.

§ 5. *How Big Should a Parish Be?*

If a pastor is to fulfill his duties adequately, this question must be answered. Two factors are involved: the spatial dimensions of the parish territory and the number of parishioners. Both must be considered if the pastor is to know his people and care for them as Trent demanded. So we must ask whether the Church has made any official statements on these questions.

1. *The Territorial Extent of a Parish.*

The Council of Trent (S. XXI, c. 4) provides us with an official statement on this question in the chapter entitled "*Coadjutores curae animarum quando sint assumendi*"; it is dealing specifically with the question "*ratio novas paroecias erigendi.*" It bases its judgment on the principle of "*magnum incommodum,*" so basic in moral theology. A parish should be split if attendance at Sunday Mass involves great inconvenience to or possible harm for a large number of parishioners, thus excusing them from this obligation. The risks may be due to the distance involved or even to the difficulties of the travel-route itself. It is quite possible, especially in our day, that these difficulties would be circumvented by new means of transportation. But no one is obliged to use extraordinary means. In some areas these modern means of transportation cannot be used. So unless branch chapels (daughter churches) can be erected, the parish must be divided.

2. *The Number of Parishioners.*

Heinrich Swoboda (1861–1923), the noted pastoral theologian, approached this question from the ideal of the good shepherd (in his *Groszstadtseelsorge* [1911] and elsewhere). Our Lord Himself said: "[The shepherd] calls his own sheep by name and leads them forth. And when he has led out his own sheep, he goes before them; and the sheep follow him because they know his voice" (John 10: 3–4). *Oídasin* (*know*) signifies the immediate contact involved in human dialogue. This must be present. "I know mine and mine know me, even as the Father knows me and I know the Father" (John 10: 14). "And other sheep I have that are not of this fold. Them also I must bring, and they shall hear my voice, and there shall be one fold and one shepherd."

The good shepherd is the model for every pastor of souls. Even though the scriptural image cannot be pushed too far, it at least implies that the shepherd and his parishioners should know each other personally. And the pastor must work to bring the "other sheep" into his fold, because Christ's commission remains a permanent duty. On his departure from Miletus, Paul reminds the people (Acts 20: 31) that for three years "night and day I did not cease with tears to admonish every one of you." He is referring, of course, to the small community of the diaspora.

The Council of Trent (S. XXIV, de ref., c. 13) pays official recognition to the "good-shepherd" ideal. But it should be noted that it approached the parochial issue from the other side. Instead of asking when a parish must be split up, it asked: how many small parishes can be merged without doing violence to the "good-shepherd" ideal?[18]

Thus the Council left open the question concerning the maximum number of parishioners. But the guiding principle had been set forth: the good shepherd who knows his own and is known by them in return. "*Mandat sancta synodus episcopis, ut distincto populo in certas propriasque unicuique suum perpetuum peculiaremque parrochum assignent, qui eas cognoscere valeat et a quo solo* [Trent!] *licite sacramenta suscipiant.*"

3. *Later Ecclesiastical Statements.*

We find the first official mention of numbers in a brief of Pope Pius VI to Cardinal de la Rochefoucault dated March 10, 1791. The French National Assembly had made new arrangements in Church-State relations, redistributing parishes

[18] At that time Rome had approximately 160,000 inhabitants and 132 parishes. Only the prelates from Paris could have provided first-hand information on overcrowded urban parishes. But they were not present at these discussions.

and proposing that each should have about 6,000 members. In his letter the Pope asks: "How can one man take care of that many souls adequately? Who can deny that this number would overtax his strength? It must necessarily follow that many parishioners will be deprived of spiritual assistance."

Thus in an indirect way the Pope clearly indicates that 6,000 parishioners would be too much for one pastor to deal with in a personal way.

In 1824, Leo XII set out to reorganize the parishes of Rome. He proposed 3,000 as the average number for a parish, which would have assistant priests, of course.

Under Kaiser Josef II about a thousand new parishes and pastoral posts were erected in the Austrian empire. 3,000 was set as the upper limit for any given parish. The canonical validity of all this is not at issue here.

When the provincial synod met in Vienna (1858) to deal with the problem of urbanization, it set 10,000 as the maximum number of souls for any given parish. But this number could only represent the absolute limit, the point at which "any real pastoral ministry became impossible" (H. Swoboda).

4. *The International Catholic Institute* for Social Research on Ecclesiastical Matters (Geneva) puts the optimal ratio at one pastoral minister per 1,000 souls.

One cannot compute mathematically how many men can be cared for by one pastor. There is no way of formulating a proportion between the number of people to be cared for and the amount of time available to the minister for his various duties. This approach would be too mechanical.

It is rather a socio-psychological question. How many men can one pastoral minister really know, at least to the extent that he can judge the religious life of his parishioners and keep the *status animarum?* Various answers are given, but in general they range between 1,000 and 3,000. The question must take into account individual ability, capacity, and achievement potential. One cannot divide the number of parishioners by the number of pastoral ministers, not even in a parish with the large number of priests; usually the majority of practicing Catholics are well known to the pastor and his assistants too.

§ 6. *A New Danger: The Enlightenment*

The newly organized parochial ministry, still suffering from serious obstacles, was confronted with a new danger in the late seventeenth and eighteenth century. The Age of the (so-called) Enlightenment dawned over Western Europe. The separation of the Protestant sects from the chair of Peter had not affected their belief in the basic tenets of Christianity. In fact, the Reformation had introduced an excessive concentration on the supernatural (Fideism).

In the Enlightenment, revelation and supernatural realities were challenged by pure naturalism (England) and rationalism (the European continent). The most high-minded protagonists of the Enlightenment wanted to restore unity to a divided Europe on the basis of a new religion founded on reason alone. The theologians, who were at odds on essential questions, were of no use at all; indeed, their conflicting theologies had provoked the Enlightenment in the first place.

What were the main principles of the Enlightenment? 1. Human reason (*ratio*) is the guiding norm of human life and thought. All reality, including every religion, must be judged before the court of reason. 2. A religion of reason would have to preserve those principles common to all religions which had stood the test of reason. 3. In this "religion" God was the creator of the world, but He did not rule His creation (Deism). 4. This new rational religion would accept not only the reasonable elements of Christianity, but also the truths of other religions.

A popular philosophy, propounded with great wit and

skill by the Encyclopedists, sought to "convert" people to this new religion.

Next to the Reformation, the Enlightenment was the most serious breach in the spiritual environment of Western Europe, which had been basically Christian up to that time. Even though it attracted only an intellectual elite in the eighteenth century and was severely challenged by romanticism, it remained one of the strongest anti-Christian and anti-religious movements. It spread to the masses through the tenets of Marxism and was ever the implacable foe of Christian thought.

1. The spirit of the Enlightenment tolled the knell of a functional ministry. The Augsburg principle—"*cujus regio, ejus religio*"—had continued to maintain the link between Church and State. But now this link was broken forever, and religion became a private matter.

Henceforth the pastoral minister would have to seek out individuals to preserve their faith or reconvert them to it. A secularized atmosphere pervaded the public forum of life. Many pastoral ministers wore themselves out fighting against it. A person had to be truly mature in order to withstand these dangers. Local parishes in large cities and industrial areas became the domain of the "*pusillus grex*" shoring up their defenses against their anti-Christian environment. But this situation demands a separate section.

III. THE INDUSTRIAL REVOLUTION

§ *1. The New Challenge*

1. The following comments do not apply to country areas. The newly ordained ministry organized by Trent was now

confronted with another challenge, more earth-shaking than any previous one: the Industrial Revolution.

With unbelievable speed and thoroughness the hand gave way to the machine, the shop to the factory. The individual worker now became a member of the assembly line, repeating the same specialized task over and over again. Production rose to unheard-of heights, and prices dropped sharply. A new tension developed—between capital and labor. Over against the small elite of capitalists stood the countless proletariat of workers. They had no choice but to offer their services on the labor market and were a prey to the shifting economic cycles.

2. The impact on society and on the pastoral ministry was immediate and enormous. Factories sprang up everywhere and gave rise to industrial centers. In a few decades small villages and towns became huge cities. Their inhabitants became an uprooted proletariat with no past and no future, without home or rights. They fell prey to the erroneous principles of the Enlightenment, to radicalism and impoverished despair. Amid these gloomy circumstances the *Communist Manifesto* (1848) of Marx and Engels sounded a note of hopeful defiance.

To be sure, ecclesiastical agencies tried to alleviate the condition of the workingman. But the charitable resources available could not cope with the widespread misery. By the time such men as Bishop Ketteler and Pope Leo XIII began to analyze the labor question, the masses had already rejected the Church's leadership.

3. In a few short years the pastoral minister was confronted with problems which he could not handle. Most urban pastors found it impossible to reiterate the words of the good shepherd: "I know mine and mine know me." Parishes which once had only a few hundred or a few thousand souls, now had tens of thousands. The pastor did not know them person-

ally, and could not get to know them. The countless thousands could not attend Mass even if they wanted to, because the church was too small or did not exist.

The tragic result was that the people lost the concept of parochial identity. By the time the second generation had appeared, the loss of parochial contact was an accepted fact. One cannot accuse the ministers of failing to do their duty; it was an impossible task.

Into this spiritual vacuum rushed the principles of the Enlightenment, embodied in the concept of popular education. The visionary concept of progress captivated the upper classes and the bourgeoisie. Religious ideals ceased to exert any influence. People fastened on atheistic Marxism as the new gospel and philosophy of life. The community of the faithful became a forgotten concept for countless thousands, being replaced by the concept of class and the ties of racial nationalism.

The nineteenth-century Restoration was first regarded as a hopeful development by the sorely pressed pastoral ministers; in fact, some saw it as the answer to a seemingly hopeless situation. But in the end it came to be regarded distrustfully by those whom it oppressed. History had repeated itself once again.

The first one to survey the hopeless plight of the pastoral ministry—at a rather late date—was Heinrich Swoboda (*Groszstadtseelsorge*—1911). He gives us an idea of the size of parishes in some of Europe's large Catholic cities at the turn of the twentieth century. In Vienna there were nine parishes with 20,000 souls; thirteen had more than 10,000. In Munich there were twelve parishes with more than 20,000, four with more than 10,000. In Cologne there were two parishes with over 20,000 parishioners, and thirteen with 10,000 plus. Brussels had three parishes with 20,000 plus, twenty-two with 10,000 plus. Paris had three parishes with 90,000 plus, fourteen with 50,000 plus, thirty-one with 30,000 plus, fourteen with 20,000 plus, forty-six with 10,000 plus. Rome had twenty-seven with more than 10,000; Milan had two with 40,000 plus, six with 20,000 plus, and eleven with 10,000 plus. Swoboda's book was not only a cry of alarm, but a call to deep consideration and vigorous action. It was the forerunner of later works on this subject.

§ 2. *Defensive Measures*

1. The immediate pastoral reaction to the Industrial Revolution was to shore up the parochial defenses. An effective ministry to all the baptized parishioners had become impossible because of the numbers involved and the strength of the opposing forces.

The first step was to build new churches. But even then there were not enough to fill the need. Many towns had grown so rapidly that no building-sites were left. Churches were jammed: no one gave much thought to the countless numbers who no longer came to Mass.

Most pastoral ministers, with a few noteworthy exceptions, concentrated on the *pusillus grex* who had remained faithful. Their course of action was basically erroneous, but quite understandable. The churches were full of people even if they represented only a fifth of the parochial population. So they did as much as time and their ability permitted.

2. The daily schedule of the parochial assistant was taken up with religious instruction and Catholic organizations. The year 1848, which brought a large measure of freedom to many, also encouraged the establishment of various organizations. Revolutionary cliques took advantage of these organizations before the Church did. The first Catholic organization was founded by Josef Busz in Freiburg. By the end of the nineteenth century, Catholics—at least in German territory—had the strongest organizations among various classes of society and different age groups. The average city-priest spent so much

time with these organizations that the pastoral ministry seemed to be devoted almost exclusively to this work. But such organizations represented only one to five per cent of the parishioners, even though they occupied so much of the priest's time; as a result, the missionary aspects of the ministry were for the most part neglected. In contrast to the good shepherd, the parish priest now stayed with the one per cent of the faithful and abandoned the ninety-nine per cent which had been lost.

Membership in a Catholic organization was so closely associated with membership in a parish that a parishioner who did not belong to any organization could not take part in the Corpus Christi procession.

3. Those who did not belong to a Catholic organization and did not come to Church, were "the others": Liberals, Nationalists, those who did not read a Catholic paper or periodical. Political and semipolitical categories became indicators of Church affiliations. There was some justification for this, but it was a dangerous practice.

All of these people bore the indelible character of baptism on their souls and received the religious instruction prescribed in the elementary schools. Most of them had been confirmed, married in the Church, and wished to be buried as Catholics. This small measure of affiliation with the Church was all they wanted, and it represented the thin veneer of Christianity pervading many cities.

4. The latter half of the nineteenth century was marked by a strong interest in political parties and their potential effectiveness. The resources and powers intrinsic to the Church were disregarded. Christian political parties were formed to utilize the power of the vote. Politics took over the pulpit. The dominant influence was the centralized organization which operated in every parish of the diocese and controlled the

Catholic press. Instead of synods, the dioceses held huge meetings at which Christian politicians made speeches.

One can scarcely speak of a ghetto-Christianity in these decades. It would be more apt to say that Christianity lived in a fortress and that most baptized Christians, including excommunicated ones and outright enemies of the Church, sought admission only on the occasion of a baptism or a marriage.

§ 3. *Studying the Situation*

Around the turn of the century people began to devote serious attention to the contemporary situation. A few sharp-sighted men had done this at an earlier date, but they had been ahead of their time.

1. It was Heinrich Swoboda who called attention to the crying need of the time and re-emphasized the motto of the good shepherd; this, he said, was the pattern for all endeavors devoted to the salvation of men.

New churches were built everywhere. Large parishes were split into smaller ones, or divided into smaller areas headed by a priest who had to render account to the diocese. During the pontificate of Cardinal Innitzer more parishes were built in Vienna than had been built for the past one hundred and fifty years. It was much the same in other large cities. Men became aware of the people's spiritual needs, even in the densely populated suburbs of Rome which already had many churches. The French (Pierre Lhande) were the first to call attention to the needs of the people living in overcrowded sections of large cities.

Catholic youth movements joined with far-sighted priests to erect new chapels in barracks and unoccupied buildings. Religious communities took up the idea, and building societies sought to set aside one room which could be used for Mass and sermons. The established Catholic organizations found a new and rewarding field of endeavor. Today all these chapels have become parishes.

2. All these activities mirrored a new evaluation of the parochial community as a cell in the Mystical Body. Youth clubs studied and sought to realize the principles expounded in Holy Scripture and in the works of men such as Josef Scheeben, J. A. Mohler, Karl Adam, and R. Guardini. The principal work on pastoral theology during this period was Konstantin Noppel's *Aedificatio Corporis Christi* (Eph. 4: 12). The encyclical of Pius XII, *Mystici Corporis* (June 29, 1945) explained and confirmed the new spirit sweeping the Church. It was the crowning touch. Once again the parish was presented as the *community of God's people celebrating the mystery of our redemption, the place where God's word is preached.* A new emphasis was put on parochial life, and all religious and pastoral activities were centered around the altar and the pulpit.

3. Once again the parish became the starting point for the re-conversion of lukewarm and lost Catholics. Catholic Action called upon the help of the laity because the priest could not handle the job alone. This led to an emphasis on the implications of baptism and confirmation, on the missionary responsibilities of all the faithful. New vitality was injected into the Church by the Eucharistic reform of Pius X and later by the liturgical revival. The latter reform, which started as a specialized movement, found a wider audience through the efforts of such men as Pius Parsch. Social action spread out to encompass "the outsiders." Cardinal Joseph Cardijn set out to convert the workers by establishing personal contact with them.

4. However, there was still a shortage of pastoral ministers. The prospects for converting outsiders looked brighter. Many

new churches and parishes had been erected, and the laity had joined the ranks of Catholic Action. But the ratio of priests to parishioners was still disproportionate.

Some have compared the ministry to politics and called it "the art of the possible." But mathematical statistics tumble before the over-riding power of grace and love. In 1925, Jean Vianney was canonized and made the patron of parish priests. In his lifetime he proved that pastoral care is the art of the impossible. From his small parish of two hundred and thirty souls he exerted an influence on the world outside, and many thousands owe their salvation to him.

In short, numbers and statistics mean little in the kingdom of heaven. The small isolated parish of Ars did not prevent Jean Vianney from exerting an influence on the world outside. The priest cannot be frightened by large numbers or by the size of his parish. The noisy din and the existence of large organizations mean little. Holy priests and pious lay people can accomplish anything, even the improbable and the impossible.

The basic problem in pastoral work is still the minister himself. His maturity, his character, and his holiness will determine the extent of his influence. These factors will decide the fruitfulness of his ministry. The material environment of his parish must not discourage him, because its essential environment is suffused with Christ's pneuma.

IV. THE LAY APOSTOLATE

Here is the basic situation. The pastoral minister is a central figure in promoting the spiritual life which gives impetus to man's labors on behalf of the kingdom of God. There are quite a few pastoral ministers, but hardly enough to handle the many complex problems involved in the ministry. The priest needs outside help.

There is nothing new about lay people taking an active

part in the work of God's kingdom. But it may be news to many priests that this participation is a duty imposed on every Christian by their baptism and confirmation. The lay Christian is not just the priest's client; nor is he a lackey who lends a hand only in cases of dire necessity. To be sure, the lay person can play only a subsidiary role in the central duties of the ministry. Only the ordained minister, "*ut personam Christi gerens*," administers the sacraments and offers the Holy Sacrifice. (This point was stressed by Pope Pius XII in his Allocution of November 2, 1954.) But it is also true that there is a *common priesthood of the Mystical Body*. It is "a real priesthood conferred on every Christian with his baptismal and confirmation character" (Ludwig Koesters).

§ 1. *The Common Priesthood*

1. *Biblical Basis*

Undoubtedly the principal scriptural text is 1 Peter 2: 3–11. The apostle writes: ". . . Indeed, you have tasted that the Lord is sweet. Draw near to him, a living stone, rejected indeed by men but chosen and honored by God. Be you yourselves as living stones, built thereon into a spiritual house, a holy priesthood (*Hieráteuma Hágion*), to offer spiritual sacrifices acceptable to God through Jesus Christ . . . You, however, are a chosen race, a royal priesthood (*Basíleion Hieráteuma*), a holy nation, a purchased people."

Then St. Peter describes their function: "that you may proclaim the perfections of him who has called you out of the darkness into his marvelous light" (v. 9). They are now the new people of God: "You who in times past were not a people, but are now the people of God; who had not obtained mercy, but now have obtained mercy" (v. 10). See also 1 Cor. 12 ff.; Eph. 4: 1 ff.

One of the most important tasks of present-day homiletics

is to preach the basic characteristics of this priesthood as they are presented in Scripture. 1. Christians have been *chosen* by God from among pagans and called "out of darkness into his marvelous light." They have become "a royal priesthood, a holy (*Hágioi*) nation." And this divine call is, at the same time, a duty imposed on those who have been chosen. 2. All Christians are members of a holy community, "*living stones*" in a "spiritual house." They are "a holy nation." Membership in this nation is more significant than membership in any earthly nation, because Christians are "a purchased people." 3. Thus Christians enjoy an eternal participation in the priesthood of Christ (S. Th. III, q. 63, a. 3). 4. This concept was so deeply ingrained in primitive Christian thought that in Scripture (1 Pet. 2: 3; Apoc. 1: 6; 5; 10; 20: 6) and early Christian literature the word *priest* (*Hiereús, Sacerdos*) referred only to Christ or the Christian people as a whole. For ordained priests the words *Presbyteros* (*elder*) and *Epískopos* —or *Proestōtēs* (*overseer*) were used.[19]

2. *Its Duties*

a) The Christian priesthood must participate in the celebration of the liturgy. In its etymology and in Christian tradition the word *liturgy* (*Leiton Érgon*) means communal worship. As a member of the Mystical Body every Christian takes an active part in the unbloody sacrifice of Christ "in which he, through the hands of the priest, offers his pleasing sacrifice of praise and expiation for the Church's intentions" (Pius XI). The Christian community joins the ordained priest in celebrating the mystery of our redemption. The priest uses "we" in the orations at Mass; Holy Communion is a sacramental participation in the life of Christ's body; and excommunication bars the Christian from participation in the sacramental life of the Christian community.

[19] Cf. Stanislaus von Dunin-Borkowski, S.J., "Die Kirche als Stiftung Jesu," in *Religion, Christentum, Kirche*, III, 50–70 (Kempton 1923[5]).

b) This liturgical community is the supernatural basis underlying any legitimate lay apostolate. From it the missionary call goes out to the layman. If the priest forgets this fact, he will profane the layman's role and abuse his missionary potential. If, on the other hand, the laity are nourished in the supernatural life of the liturgical community, their words and actions will "proclaim the *mirabilia Dei*" to those around them.

c) There is one sacrament which only lay people administer to one another: matrimony. Much has yet to be said on the essential role of conjugal life and the family in building the kingdom of heaven.

§ 2. *Catholic Action*

1. Readiness to cooperate in the work of the kingdom is an essential attitude for every baptized person. Present-day circumstances underline the necessity of this attitude, and the complexity of contemporary problems calls for proper organization. This was the call sent out to Catholics by Pope Pius XI in his encyclical *Ubi arcano* (December 23, 1922). He pleaded for "the participation of the laity in the apostolic work of the hierarchy." The individual Christian, signed with the seal of baptism and confirmation and called to service in the common priesthood of the Mystical Body, must help to save souls enmeshed in the dangers of today's world. "The laity need no delegation from the hierarchy to participate in this mission. It is merely their response to the duties imposed on them by baptism and confirmation" (Statement of the French Bishops, February 28, 1945). In this work the laity are to follow the directions of the hierarchy, for they participate in the pastoral mission of the hierarchy.

2. "The lay apostolate has always been active in the Church.

It would be interesting and instructive to study the role it has played in the course of centuries" (Pius XII, October 12, 1951). Indeed, in Apostolic times the lay apostolate was already full blown. The epistles of St. Paul indicate how much use he made of the laity in his work. The first woman he converted on European soil was Lydia, "a seller of purple" (Acts 16: 14) in Philippi. One of these women, Phoebe, was to become the patron of women who assist in the ministry (feast-day, November 3). "But I commend to you Phoebe, our sister, who is in the ministry of the church at Cenchrae, that you may receive her in the Lord as becomes saints, and that you may assist her in whatever business she may have need of you. For she too has assisted many, including myself" (Rom. 16: 1–2).

3. The duties of those involved in Catholic Action were spelled out by the first international Congress of the Lay Apostolate (October 7–14, 1951, Rome).

a) *The contemporary background.* Most of mankind does not yet profess the Christian faith. Modern society has become extremely complex. Economics, politics, science, education, and the other fields of human endeavor demand specialized training. Only a fellow expert, a layman, can bring the message of Christ into these areas.

b) The universal scope of Christ's salvific mission ("Go, therefore, and make disciples of all nations . . .") was never so clear and compelling as it is today. And today, thanks to modern technology, there is greater hope of fulfilling this mission.

c) Lay participation in the apostolate is the crying need of the day. By reason of numbers and capabilities, priests cannot reach countless millions. Broad areas of human endeavors are closed to them. Technological science and its many branches are open to the specialist, and only laymen can gain entrance. Technology must become the servant of mankind, not his master; it must be given meaning and purpose. Only the qualified layman, living the life of faith, can do this.

d) This missionary task must be carried out in close conjunction with the ecclesiastical mission of the hierarchy. The lay apostolate is a many-sided endeavor, but it is orientated toward the single goal of all Christian endeavor, the building-up of Christ's Mystical Body (Eph. 4: 12).

e) The priest has a duty to make Christians aware of their missionary responsibilities. The motivating force behind the lay apostolate must be their own life in Christ.

f) One of the most urgent tasks is the establishment of a just social order in which man's inalienable rights are insured. Men have a right to conduct their life in accordance with their religious, moral, and intellectual principles. They have a right to obtain religious training and education, to worship God in the private and public forum. They have a right to engage in charitable activities, to marry and raise a family, to fulfill their marital obligations. They have a right to choose their state in life, to work, and to receive a just wage so that they may support their family.

§ 3. *Catholic Action in the Parish*

Every baptized Christian is called to participate in the work of the kingdom. But many, often the majority, are unwilling or unprepared to participate. They have not the time, the ability, or the desire. Christ's words are still valid: "Many are called, but few are chosen" (Mt. 20: 16). But the priest must continue to remind them of their obligation.

An effective program of Catholic Action calls for a new type of pastor, a missionary strategist who is the living embodiment of pastoral work itself. He must know the lay people working with him.

1. Directly under him: the executive officers, active workers in charge of some particular field of activity, drawn up, for example, according to age-groups.

2. These officers recruit a staff of workers who labor to carry out the monthly program.

3. These people recruit a staff of trusty helpers who understand the goals of Catholic Action and wish to promote them. These helpers, too, must be trained.

4. The helpers' main task is to spread the aims of Catholic Action far and wide and recruit sympathetic listeners who will join their organizations and add new life to the movement.

5. The mission field of Catholic Action is composed of those many souls who are not engaged in promoting the works of God's kingdom—apathetic and tepid Catholics, thoughtless Catholics, and those who have fallen away from the Church, those who do not yet know the Church or are actively opposed to her.

§ 4. *The Parish Council*

The upper echelons of these parochial workers may also be the prescribed parish council with which the pastor has to discuss all important pastoral undertakings. If this is not the case, we may set down the following guide-lines with regard to the parish council:

1. The abolition of the old system whereby different organizations send "observers," not workers, to represent them and report back.

2. To be sure, the above-mentioned leaders can be chosen by

the groups themselves. But it is best if they are chosen by the pastor. The bishop is to confirm the choice.

3. If the parish council is identical with the central committee of Catholic Action, then there is no doubt about its vitality and capabilities. If this is not the case, the efficiency of the council must be preserved in some way. Thus, for example, older members who can no longer work too hard might be given "honorary" posts.

4. It is important to remember that they are really co-workers with the pastor. As a speaker once remarked, they are clinical assistants, not patients.

§ 5. *Traditional Lay Functions*

1. The sexton (*mansionarius*) has a long history and goes by many names, corresponding to his various functions: custodian (*custos*), sacristan, bell-ringer.

a) He directly assists the priest in his sacred functions, performing the tasks once carried out by deacons. When so commissioned by the priest, he takes over the functions once performed by those in Minor Orders. Ever since the time of Gregory the Great, and most recently at the International Congress of Sacristans (Vienna, July 22–24, 1959), some have expressed the hope that the post might be elevated to a distinct office in the Church. The prospective candidate could obtain proper training in a school for sacristans and then receive Minor Orders. He should also be trained for catechetical work.

b) This training would point out the dignity of this office and inculcate proper attitudes in the candidate. For it is a training acquired by rendering service to the pastor, and such service is exemplary. In any case, the office calls for more than knowledge alone.

c) The sacristan should receive a fixed salary and not have to depend on "tips." These remarks also hold true for other posts connected with the altar or the rectory. Some pastoral institutes have training programs for would-be sacristans. They conclude with a final examination and the conferral of a passing certificate.

2. The acolytes (altar boys) also assume tasks which the priest assumed as an ordained acolyte and ostiarius. This fact alone, plus the kind of service involved, should prompt an attitude of dignified reverence, insofar as this can be expected of growing boys. Pious poses are out of place. The altar boys should be boys, good boys. But in large cities one can very easily get adults to serve Mass as well.

The dignity of this function calls for proper training and preparation. It is no small matter that the server's responses represent the whole community. Canon 813 prescribes that a priest cannot celebrate Mass without a server. The liturgy is essentially communal worship. In a private Mass there must be at least one server to represent the community.

The dignity of this office calls for a corresponding awareness on the part of the server, even if it be on a child's level. The pastor must choose suitable candidates. Some pastors stick to a given number (e.g., twelve), even though more candidates are standing in line. The admission of new altar boys should be attended by a certain degree of ceremony. And during their "time of service" they should be looked after. In diocesan cities all the acolytes were presented to the bishop once a year. Other meetings of sacristans from all over the world in some place of pilgrimage have had a salutary effect.

3. The *regens chori* is usually an honorary post in country

areas. But in city regions he often is paid to direct the choir. Our present-day choirs go back to the *schola cantorum* which was composed of clerics in its early days. The choir master must be more than a good musician, organist, and director. As an assistant in the liturgical service, he must have liturgical training. He should be a devout Christian, because he can perform his duties worthily only if he has deep faith. Various pastoral institutes have provided supplementary training for choir masters with great success.

4. For decades now, especially in large cities, women have held the post of parish sister.

a) Frequently the women are Religious Sisters, and some Orders have been founded specifically for this work. When there are several Sisters in one parish, they live a communal life. The function is so important that the Congregation for Religious in Rome was delighted when a group of teaching Sisters switched over to this work (directive dated May 29, 1930).

b) We might lay down the following principles regarding their work in the parish: 1. They are help-mates in parochial work; they cannot initiate pastoral projects on their own. 2. They assume tasks which the pastor cannot carry out for some reason, e.g., lack of time. 3. They cannot take the place of a priest or a pastoral minister. They perform tasks which are suited to their station and their capabilities. Thus, for example, they should not take charge of pre-marital instructions. 4. The pastor is responsible for their activities.

c) In recent years training schools have been set up in various countries. They provide not only specialized training, but also a certain measure of theological background. The candidates are tested in examinations. Thus they obtain a thorough moral and religious training, and can judge whether, as human beings and Christians, they are suited for this important work.

The training program concludes with a religious ceremony in which the diocesan bishop usually hands out diplomas. Steps are taken to insure further religious and moral development. Sometimes additional training in parish work itself is also provided. This vocation should occupy all the energies of the candidate. In accordance with 1 Cor. 7: 34, she should not marry as long as she fills the post. And the training program should make clear what kind of work she is suited for. A particular job may not be right for everyone. Such decisions are best made during the time of training. Only love of God and zeal for His kingdom should prompt one to assume this office. But the candidate should get a decent wage and be paid punctually. These workers should not be overtaxed with work. Everyone has a right to a vacation and time-off.

d) The experience of the past few decades has given us a fairly accurate picture of the duties proper to this office:

α) Keeping the parish records and other supplementary files. These records must be up-to-date and open to examination at all times. Obviously this calls for a staff of helpers who will note down pertinent pastoral data.

β) To this end they must visit houses and do as much as they can to bring back lukewarm and fallen-away Catholics.

γ) Preparing people to enter or return to the Church.

δ) Reporting to the pastor about those tasks which can only be handled by a priest.

ε) Lending a hand in charitable activities.

ζ) Taking part in the pastoral care of certain age-groups, e.g., training young boys and girls and visiting the elderly.

η) Preparing the parishioners to participate fully in the liturgy.

5. The most important co-workers of the parish sister in maintaining the parish records are the house visitors. In large urban parishes they are indispensable. However, a pastor usually

considers himself fortunate to have one qualified visitor for a given street. Their duties are two-fold:

a) They keep the parish records up-to-date by making house visits and reporting what they find. The two tasks are obviously interrelated. The visitors report new arrivals and departures in the records, as well as births and deaths. They note how the different families attend to their religious duties, whether the adults attend Mass, how many children there are, whether they attend classes in religious instruction.

If possible, incoming parishioners should be greeted with a letter from the pastor informing them about the location of the parish church, the schedule of services, and so forth.

b) The visitors report all cases of serious illness and dire need. They should feel a personal responsibility for these people and lend assistance when it is sorely needed. They also are to report on those who have fallen away from the Church; if it can be done tactfully, they should try to find out the reasons for these lapses.

§ 6. *New Apostolic Movements*

The call to the work of the apostolate has led to the formation of other organizations and institutes (besides Catholic Action) which have exerted an influence on Christian life.

1. Schools for women engaged in ecclesiastical activities.

2. Social Action schools for men and women.

3. New religious congregations such as those founded by P. J. van Ginneken, S.J., for the home mission (Holland). The "Women of Nazareth" (1901) and the "Women of Bethany"

(1919) work in the world and do not wear a distinctive religious habit.

4. The Legion of Mary is a lay movement founded in Dublin by Frank Duff in 1921. It has strict rules for admission and a well developed system of self-government. There are local centers in about four hundred dioceses. The main praesidium is the de Montfort House in Dublin.

5. The Apostolic Constitution *Provida Mater Ecclesia* (Pius XII, February 2, 1947) approved the establishment of *Secular Institutes*. They are pious communities which take the vows of poverty, chastity, and obedience. But they do not wear a religious habit and they work in the world to further the kingdom of God.

6. France has been a fertile ground for new apostolic movements. On February 6, 1955, Bishop Brot spoke to the communities of nuns gathered in the crypt of Saint Odile in Paris. Following the desires of the French Cardinals and the example of Pope Pius XII, he called upon them to recognize the pressing needs of the present day: "You have no right to remain passive in the face of the de-christianization process at work in the world. Ask yourself what you must do to counteract this activity. Any nun today who sees no problems connected with her apostolic commission, betrays her vocation. You cannot live outside the world, aloof from it. For you are the salt of the world, and salt must be shaken out, if it is to be of any use. Step out from your ghettos!"

Many religious congregations of women have adapted themselves to apostolic works since then. They go out to visit women's prisons, homeless people, and poor families in which the mother is sick. The "Little Sisters of Charles de Foucauld," for example, work in factories during the day to render silent witness to Christ. On February 11, 1950, there appeared another society of women devoted to the cause of neighborly love—the Missionary Workers of Mary Immaculate. They carry on their noble work in factories, slums, hospitals. All these new congregations represent a radical departure from the older mission activities. They call the Christian to live out in the world, sharing the poverty of his fellowmen.

7. On February 10, 1952, and again on October 12, 1952, Pope Pius XII gave his blessing to Father Riccardo Lombardi's "Movement for a Better World." It is directed principally toward bishops and priests. But its full program involves lay participation.

8. The Young Christian Workers (Y.C.W.) founded in 1912 by Cardinal Cardijn has its own distinctive program and *modus operandi*. It involves actual contact with individual workers and a program of action ("see, judge, act"). In 1925 he told Pope Pius XI: "Holy Father, I wish to go out and save the masses of workers." And he and his co-workers have set out to do this on a person-to-person basis. Y.C.W. has grown into a world-wide organization. Its leaders and helpers have hundreds of thousands under them. They represent one of the most vital lay factions in the Catholic world. Local branches are composed of "cells," each containing twelve men. Each cell meets weekly to review the work already done and to plan future projects. The meeting is programmed into several steps: 1. prayer, 2. a reading from Holy Scripture followed by a brief explanation, 3. a review of the projects undertaken in the past week and their results (why did they succeed or fail?), 4. choosing the projects for the coming week after considering the needs of the moment, 5. "newsreel": the most important events in the working world, 6. questions and answers. Y.C.W. is run by the workers themselves. The priest only acts as spiritual advisor and co-worker.

9. It is noteworthy that since the two world wars there has

been an ever increasing number of lay people involved in catechetical work throughout the world.

10. The Crusade for Souls was proclaimed in 1951 in the United States. It encountered very few of the problems which seem inevitable in Europe. It began with prayer, and prayer was a constant during the campaign. Calmly, resolutely, and confidently an army of 32,000 Catholic men and women traveled from door to door for a solid week. 1. They wanted to know whether those who received them were practicing Catholics or not. 2. Practicing Catholic families were invited to religious gatherings in the parish. There pamphlets and leaflets were distributed. The bishops soon discovered that seventy-two percent of all American Catholics were never invited to attend Church services by their fellow Christians and neighbors. Furthermore, the majority of those interviewed who practiced no religion (75 million in the U.S.) expressed a desire to join the Church or some religious body. But they did not know how to go about it. Every one of the 32,000 lay volunteers pledged to introduce interested persons to the Church's life and doctrine. Three hundred thousand circulars entitled *Finding Christ's Church* were distributed. Summing up, the volunteers made the following comments. 1. They were well received by all the families they visited. 2. Many people interviewed wished to become better acquainted with the Catholic religion by attending courses of instruction and church services. 3. A large number of non-practicing Catholics expressed a desire to take part in the life of the Church once again. 4. The workers themselves felt blessed by God Himself for having had an opportunity to take part in the Crusade.

11. The street preaching of Johannes Leppich, S.J., seemed to be a strange and futile kind of apostolate in this day and age. But it has shown what one priest can accomplish when he devotes his full energies to a project. His talks on city streets

and squares reached hundreds of thousands who would never have come to Church—neo-pagans, non-practicing Catholics, and non-Catholics. And thousands were moved to action. Leppich knows how to present the Sermon on the Mount to the man on the street, although his street sermons would have to be modified before they could be delivered from the pulpit.

He was soon joined by others. He asked that they 1. read Sacred Scripture daily, 2. heed the divine commands encountered therein, and 3. engage in corporal and spiritual works of mercy.

Since 1958 the movement has developed a more tight-knit organization. Teams of about twelve men from the nucleus of the group. An attempt is made to have the men in each team represent as many different social strata as possible. Every month Father Leppich presents the program of action to them. 1. Their evening meetings begin with a consideration of Holy Scripture. This lasts for twenty minutes and is meant to strengthen the spiritual fibre of the team. 2. Then there is a brief instruction period in which the members are quizzed on their religious knowledge. 3. Next the program of action is discussed and tasks are assigned to the various members. 4. In a similar way they discuss and plan charitable activities on behalf of the poor, the sick, the needy. Spiritual exercises contribute to the further development of the religious life of the members. This movement represents another working model of the apostolate, contributing to the spread of the kingdom of God.

§ 7. *Fields for the Lay Apostolate*

The following comments apply mainly to urban areas and industrial districts.[20]

1. Promoting the spiritual welfare of *young children*.

[20] Cf. *Die Seelsorge*, 1924, 2 Jg., 5, 137 ff.

a) They report recent births to the registrar's office and visit parents if it is feared that they will not have the baby baptized.

b) They maintain contact with maternity wards so that babies can be given emergency baptism in a case of necessity. To that end they make sure that those involved know how to administer the sacrament. Those who know something about prenatal care offer help and advice. Others can establish contact with the proper welfare agencies and social services, if help is needed.

c) They can provide information about day nurseries, kindergarten schools, orphanages, camps, adoption agencies.

d) They can help to prepare school children for First Confession and First Holy Communion, and provide them with the proper clothes.

e) They can work together to erect and maintain Catholic schools, and exert their influence on local P.T.A. boards. They might also show an interest in juvenile courts and other offices of this sort.

f) They can help to provide vocational guidance to school drop-outs and perhaps even offer apprentice training.

g) It should be remembered that children can also help in this work. But tact and due respect are necessary.

2. Helping older youths.

a) In every city some people must devote their attention to the problems of juvenile delinquency. They must investigate the causes of these problems and note the trends in the city. "Religion pure and undefiled before God the Father is this: to give aid to orphans and widows in their tribulation, and to keep oneself unspotted from this world" (Jas. 1: 27).

b) An atmosphere of genuine faith, suited to the needs of

young people, must be provided for those who lack it. Parish organizations and clubs should be established.

c) Sound instruction should be provided on important problems and difficulties. Experts should be brought in when their help is needed. The dangers of alcoholism and dope addiction should be pointed out.

d) Attempts should be made to deepen their religious formation, by extending their knowledge and developing their sense of parochial identity.

e) Potential vocations to the religious life should be fostered.

f) Contact with diocesan youth organizations should be maintained.

3. Promoting the spiritual welfare of the family.

a) Preparing for marriage in a thorough way through pre-Cana conferences.

b) Keeping separate files on mixed marriages, purely civil marriages, common-law marriages.

c) Spreading good family reading material and visiting houses to encourage attendance at Mass.

d) Keeping informed about housing problems and working out possible solutions. Knowing about separated couples, teen-age marriages, boarders.

4. Participating in church work itself.

a) Helping to care for the Church itself and its furnishings.

b) Lending a hand in the publication of the parish bulletins.

c) Taking part in parochial reading groups and discussion clubs.

§ 8. *Types of Organizations*

It is important to distinguish between two types of lay organizations—ecclesiastical organizations and lay organizations.

1. *Ecclesiastical organizations* (according to c. 686, 1) are erected, or at least officially approved by the Church. Three types may be noted.

a) *Third Orders* (*Tertiarii saeculares*) are organizations of pious lay people who seek perfection in the ideals of some Religious Order "in a manner adapted to their life in the world and according to the rules laid down by the Holy See" (c. 702), e.g., the Third Order of St. Francis, the Benedictine Oblates.

b) *Confraternities* (*Confraternitates*), or *Sodalities*, are meant to promote self-sanctification and some form of public devotion. In the Middle Ages they were a dominant spiritual force in lay circles. Today every large parish has a Rosary Society and/or a Sacred Heart League (c. 707 ff.).

According to canon 711, 2, every parish should have a Confraternity of Christian Doctrine (CCD) and a Confraternity of the Blessed Sacrament. In countries where catechetical instruction is already provided for by some other organization, CCD need not be established. (Response dated July 21, 1905.)

c) *Pious Unions* (*piae uniones*) need only the bishop's approval. According to canon 707 the term applies to any lay organization erected by the Church for works of piety or charity. The various Marian sodalities make up the bulk of this group.

All three types should recognize the needs of the hour and lend a zealous hand in pastoral activities. Such actions would revitalize their own organization. The various Third Orders could be an extension of the pastoral activities proper to the Orders themselves. The pious unions have always realized this.

d) The Secular Institutes do not fall under this classification. Strictly speaking, they represent a type of Religious Order with its own peculiar rule of life. But we mention them here because their members live and work in the world without wearing a distinctive religious habit.

2. *Lay Organizations* are approved by the Church. But they differ in several respects from *ecclesiastical* organizations.

a) They are founded by lay people, not by the Church. In many cases, however, they owe their beginnings to some priest or to ecclesiastical inspiration.

b) They are recognized and approved as legitimate Catholic organizations by the Church because of their guiding principles.

c) They are subordinate to the Church and its official representatives (the bishop, the pastor) in accordance with the general norms of c. 336, 2, the directives of c. 469 (the pastor must see to it that no doctrine contrary to faith or morals is taught in his territory), and canon 1505 which guarantees the bishop certain rights as executor.

d) The title "Catholic" or "Christian" can be approved, rejected, or removed later by the bishop.

e) The lay officers run the official business of the organization. In this respect the priest-moderator takes a back seat. His main concern is the spiritual welfare of the organization and its adherence to Catholic principles.

f) These organizations must also have state approval if they are to exist as a legally constituted body.

3. If we examine the history of church organizations over the

past hundred years, we can distinguish three types based on the size of membership.

a) The older organizations tried to recruit and hold as many members as possible. But the individual member was neglected for the most part.

b) More recently small cells of elite were established. Few in numbers, they glowed with missionary zeal.

c) Between the two stands a third type in which active workers seek to strengthen their own organization by looking out for the general membership as well. The experiences of the past hundred years would seem to give the nod to types b) and c).

V. CHARITY IN THE MINISTRY

§ 1. *The Great Commandment*

Love of God and neighbor is the first commandment for the individual Christian in his dealings with others (Mt. 22: 37–39). So it must also be the goal of the Christian community as a whole. Love for all is the distinctive trait of His disciples and the touchstone of their fellowship with Him. "A new commandment I give you, that you love one another: that as I have loved you, you also love one another. By this will all men know that you are my disciples, if you have love for one another" (John 13: 34–35). Mutual love does more than the spoken word to build and unite the Christian community. Tertullian (*Apologeticum*, c. 39) tells us that in the days of the persecution the pagan onlookers used to cry out: "See, how they love one another!" Such a love was a new experience for them, because hate pervaded the atmosphere of pagan society.

So, too, in our day hate for one's enemies was considered a virtue by neo-paganism. No amount of faith can take the place of love. "Even the devil believes, but he does not love" (Augustine).

§ 2. *Charity*

1. The word itself comes from the Latin *carus* (*costly, dear*). *Caritas,* first of all, meant *high price*. Hence it came to mean affection, love, esteem. It did not come from the Greek word *Cháris* (which meant *favor*), but rather was the Latin translation for the New Testament word *agápe* (*love, love-banquet*—the Eucharistic banquet). It is the word used to designate the Christian concept of supernatural love, love for God who first loved us (John 31: 3), and love for our neighbor because God loves him ("*amare in Deo*"—Augustine).

2. In scholastic theology the word was applied to the "*virtus infusa*" of supernatural love and the moral virtue of love for God and our neighbor which expresses itself in good deeds.

Today it is used as a general term for all actions motivated by Christian love, for charitable projects of all sorts, and for charitable organizations themselves.

§ 3. *Christian Charity in Action*

It begins with the primitive community in Jerusalem.

1. "And they continued steadfastly in the teaching of the Apostles and in the communion of the breaking of the bread and in the prayers . . . And all who believed were together and held all things in common" (Acts 2: 42–44). Thus this charitable activity was a communal one from the very beginning. "Now the multitude of the believers were of one heart

and one soul, and not one of them said that anything he possessed was his own, but they had all things in common . . . nor was there anyone among them in want" (Acts 4: 32–34).

This so-called "Communism" was not a collective system enforced through dictatorial means. It was the spontaneous expression of a selfless love for one another. The right to private property remained unimpaired, as the case of Ananias and Sapphira shows (Acts 5).

2. Eventually this charitable activity had to be organized. The order of the diaconate was established to free the Apostles for preaching. But this generosity made everyone poor. For the next few decades the Jerusalem community had to be supported by collections from other communities.

3. Throughout the following centuries the Church and the many Religious Orders labored unceasingly to alleviate the condition of the sick and the poor, the aged and the orphaned, the pilgrim and the traveler.

§ 4. *Charitable Organizations*

The problems of the needy became too complex and extensive to be handled by individuals as such. Yet the commandment to help one's neighbor still remained. So the Church began to organize her charitable activities into a more tight-knit structure, usually along diocesan lines.

1. The essential duty incumbent on all the Church's charitable organizations has a threefold aspect.

a) Advertisement. Using concrete data, they must point out the urgency of the problems involved and offer workable solutions. They must awaken a sense of responsibility in the individual by utilizing the mass communications media.

b) Organization. They must utilize the available resources to the best and fullest extent, directing them where they are most needed. They must also train competent workers.

c) Research. They must gain precise knowledge about the temporal and spiritual needs of a given area. A staff of workers must be recruited to make surveys and gather statistics. An attempt must be made to root out the underlying causes, so that in the future certain problems can be nipped in the bud. Catholic organizations must cooperate with national and international organizations, and attend conferences on these world-wide problems.

Obviously these tasks cannot be accomplished by lone individuals or localized communities such as the parish.

2. Fields of Activity:

a) the poor, the sick, the aged.

b) the care and education of children: orphans, handicapped children, foundlings. The erection of day nurseries, recreation centers.

c) The protection and rehabilitation of people with moral problems: delinquents, ex-convicts, dope addicts.

d) the welfare of various social groups: students, businessmen, teachers, unskilled laborers, the unemployed.

3. It is quite obvious that present-day procedures in this whole area involve too much red tape. The only effective help is *prompt* help.

§ 5. *The Role of the Parish*

1. Fundamentally, the parish represents the Christian community in a given area. It is the living embodiment of Chris-

tianity and its principles—not the least of which is charity, the distinctive trait of Christ's followers.

2. Hence it is to be desired that the charitable activities of large agencies should be conducted on a parochial basis. But this can be done realistically only in parishes with their own charitable organizations (e.g., in the U.S.A.). So the best working arrangement would seem to call for cooperative action between the parishes and the large agencies.

3. In large cities and industrial areas the older charitable societies are still doing fine work on a parochial basis. Such groups as the St. Vincent de Paul Society provide shelter and living expenses to deserving poor people.

In many countries social legislation (social security, workingmen's compensation) has alleviated the Church's burden in this area. But the basic task still perdures, no matter how many laws are passed. Christ's commandment and man's needs remain constant.

PART FOUR: THE PAROCHIAL MINISTRY TODAY

The origin and historical development of the localized ministry—the parochial ministry, as we would say today—has already been sketched in outline form. In this section we shall examine the parish as a total unit from a synchronic viewpoint.

I. TOWARD A THEOLOGY OF THE PARISH

§ *1. The Parish as a Canonical Entity*

1. Ever since the division of the Church into dioceses under the direction of a bishop, there has been little doubt that parishes, as diocesan sub-divisions, are subordinate to the bishop canonically and pastorally.

The proponents of Gallicanism were the first to challenge this view. A decree issued by the French Parliament on April 29, 1665, proclaimed the parish to be an entity established *de jure divino*. A few theologians expressed the same view. And the Synod of Pistoia (1786) concluded that the bishop only indirectly exercised pastoral influence on the individual parishes. This view was condemned by Pope Pius VI (Denz. 1509 ff.).

The existence of an authentic parochial ministry forces us to re-examine the theology of the parish. Karl Rahner adopts this starting point: "It is quite clear that one cannot regard the parish and the pastor as *jure divino* institutions like the Church, the Papacy, and the Episcopacy."[21] For him the

[21] *Die Pfarre* (Fr. in Br., 1956), p. 27.

basic principle is this: "The Church, as a living organism, is necessarily encountered on the local level—as a local community."[22] The individual "fully perceives the Church as a visible entity only when he experiences it as the community of the faithful, as a Christian collectivity."[23] "In the deepest core of her being the Church is the enduring presence of the Incarnate Word in history and time. And so her presence is most keenly felt where Christ, the risen Redeemer, is rendered present through the words of Consecration."[24]

The theology of the eighteenth century was dominated by the concept of a Church mechanically parceled into distinct units. But "the parish church is not an atomistic subdivision; it is the foremost representative of the universal Church, the living cell in the mystical organism. In this connection one must realize that the Episcopacy is a *jure divino* office."[25] The parish priests belong to the bishop's company.

From all this Rahner concludes: "The parish is the foremost embodiment of the living Church.[26] It is primarily a local community, because it is founded along territorial lines."[27]

2. The parish, as the assembly of the faithful under the guidance of a pastor, is not a moral person in the eyes of Canon Law. Hence it has no rights, and may not even have any say in the appointment of the pastoral minister or the determination of his mission. According to Canon Law the moral persons are:

a) the benefice (*beneficium*) supporting the pastoral minister (c. 1409);

[22] *Ibid.*, p. 29.
[23] *Ibid.*, p. 31.
[24] *Ibid.*
[25] *Ibid.*, p. 33.
[26] *Ibid.*, p. 34.
[27] *Ibid.*, pp. 36 f.

b) the church plant (*fabrica ecclesiae*) with its own income which provides for church maintenance (c. 1356, 1; 1183; 1184).

3. Parishes are established by the diocesan bishop (c. 216, 1–3). He divides his diocese into "*partes territoriales,*" pastoral areas usually with fixed limits. Each parish should have its own church, its own priest, and its own parishioners ("*cum populo determinato*").

4. Each parish should have its own permanent and adequate endowment ("*stabilem et congruam dotem*").

a) The endowment is considered sufficient, if it enables the pastor to devote his full attention to pastoral work.[28]

b) However, Canon Law provides for the erection of needed parishes, even when there is no permanent and adequate endowment. In such cases the bishop accepts responsibility for the pastor's maintenance (c. 1415, 3). Only in this way was pastoral work able to be continued in the burgeoning cities and industrial areas.

c) Religious Orders of men may accept and run parishes in their churches; but parishes may not be set up in churches belonging to the Religious Orders of women (c. 619, 2).

d) With papal permission non-territorial parishes (e.g., national parishes) can be established (c. 216, 4). The traditional practice of maintaining such churches in the military corps is acceptable (c. 251, 3). It is permissible to erect parishes of different rites in the same territory. In such cases the ones who make the proposal provide the endowment.

[28] *Lehrbuch des Kirchenrechtes* (ed. Eichmann), II, 3, 238.

§ 2. *The Parish and Its Pastor*

The personal qualifications of the pastor were discussed in a previous section. Here we shall repeat certain important points and elaborate on others.

1. *The Pastor's Appointment*

a) A parish can have only *one* pastor; his main duty is the pastoral care of the faithful under him.

b) A pastor can have only *one* parish "in titulum." But today there is a serious lack of priests. So in many areas a pastor supervises the affairs of several parishes.

c) Pastors are appointed on a permanent basis (c. 4547).

d) Canon 458 stipulates that a vacant pastorate be filled within six months, presupposing that there are enough priests available for all the parishes.

2. *Parochial Identity*

a) This is usually realized by maintaining residence (*domicilium*) within the parish boundaries (c. 216, 4). In European rural areas the sense of parochial identity has always been strong. Pious custom and local tradition bind the people together and strengthen pastoral ties. In olden days it was customary for the pastor to sprinkle water on the local graves at the *Asperges*.

b) In large cities the sense of parochial identity often is nonexistent. It is a canonical fact, nothing more. The individual does not feel any personal tie with his parish. So the first task is to instill a sense of parochial identity in the parishioners. Churches run by Religious Orders lend valuable assistance, but they often dull the sense of parochial identity. The same is true of many Catholic organizations which extend beyond parish boundaries. Many people living in a given parish attend another church regularly because it is closer to them. Others have a confessor or spiritual director outside their parish. And only rarely does a city parish have its own cemetery.

c) No longer in force is the old canonical interdict whereby the parishioner had to fulfill all his religious duties in the parish church. Now he can confess to and receive Communion from any priest.

However, the pastor does retain certain privileges proper to him alone: the administration of the sacraments noted in the parish records—solemn baptism, confirmation in a case of need, officiating at a marriage (c. 1094). He also has the right to publish the marriage banns (c. 1022) and perform the obsequies of his parishioners. But on these matters too there are general (c. 397, n. 3; 514; 848, 2; 938) and particular (c. 462) canonical exceptions.

The pastor has a clear right to confer any blessings to which some public ceremony is attached (e.g., blessing houses, hospitals, statues). And he alone has the right to hold processions within his territory.

It is recommended that the Easter duty be fulfilled in the parish church, but it is not obligatory (c. 857, 3). At least the pastor should know which of his parishioners have fulfilled it. If he is sure that a certain person has not fulfilled this duty for many years, he can regard him as a public sinner and refuse Christian burial (c. 1240).

d) Parochial identity should be more than a canonical concept. Ideally it should mean that the parishioners are united in faith, hope, and charity and work together to grow in virtue. The pastor is the father of the parish family, as the title "father" would indicate.

3. A *Mystical and Eschatological Community*

If we trace the word *parish* back to the word *paroikia*, then *parishioners* would be those who encamp around God's house. God has His own residence, and the parishioners have settled near it. Every baptism enrolls a new member in the divine colony; every burial celebrates the departure of a settler "signed with the seal of faith" for his eternal home, "a place of refreshment, light, and peace" (*memento mortuorum*). The parish is a cell in the Mystical Body united to the universal Church through communal worship and the reception of the sacraments. "For more than a thousand years an uninterrupted stream of sacramental grace has flowed out on our people and our country [Germany]. Should it not have stamped an indelible character on our people even when they were not willing to receive it?"[29]

These words hold true for the Church as a whole, for every people belonging to her, and for every parish in which this sanctifying power is actualized. In practice, people experience the living Church as a local reality—ecclesia, in St. Paul's sense of the word.

b) The word *paroikia* also means *hostel*. Parishioners are pilgrims in this world, men "in via." "Beloved, I exhort you as strangers and pilgrims to abstain from carnal desires which war against the soul" (1 Pet. 2: 11). The other communities of God are also pilgrims living in distant lands.[30] The various parish communities are bands of pilgrims. Each one by itself is a "heavenly colony planted on earth" (K. Noppel), and all are linked together in the Christian mystery, separated from the temporal world.

4. *A Sacramental Community*

This is just another way of expressing what was said above.

[29] Werner Bergengruen, "Die Antwort der Geschichte," in *Die Stunde des Christentums* (Berlin, 1937), p. 21.

[30] Konstantin Noppel, *Die neue Pfarre*, p. 180. Two letters from Apostolic times testify to this. The first letter of St. Clement to the Corinthians begins with the salutation: "The Church of God living in exile in Rome, to the Church of God living in exile in Corinth." The letter of St. Polycarp to the Philippians begins: "To the Church of God living in exile at Philippi."

a) The pastor must be an ordained priest (c. 453, 1). This requirement eliminates an age-old abuse. A man would receive tonsure just to be eligible for a parish, or, more exactly, for a benefice.

At his ordination the pastor received the power to offer the sacrifice of the New Law. It is his primary duty. "*Sacerdotem oportet offerre.*" He must reiterate St. Paul's questions to his parishioners: "The cup of blessing that we bless, is it not the sharing of the blood of Christ? And the bread that we break, is it not the partaking of the body of the Lord?" (1 Cor. 10: 16) Every Sunday and Holyday of Obligation he celebrates the mystery of salvation, surrounded by his parish community. If they fully realized this, it would not be necessary to stress that attendance at Sunday Mass is a commandment. In earlier times participation in this mystery was regarded as one of the rights of the faithful. We must instill this attitude in the people once again.

b) The primitive attitude later led to the enactment of a law (no longer in effect). The people were obliged to attend Sunday Mass and fulfill their Easter duty in their own parish. *Communio* (*Koinonia*) involves more than personal union with the Lord. It is the union of the whole community, as a group, with their Lord through the breaking of bread. Excommunication cuts the Christian off from the sacramental life of the Church.

Today, however, the Church is calling for more than mere passive attendance at Mass. She wants the laity to participate actively—*actuosa participatio*—in the celebration of the liturgy (Pius XI, *Divini cultus*). In his encyclical *Mystici Corporis,* Pius XII stated the underlying reason. "The spotless offering is made present on the altar only through the words uttered by the priest. But the *faithful themselves* unite with him to offer it to the eternal Father through his hands."

The parish church is the site where grace is conferred

through the sacraments. Only there can one find the baptismal font, where individuals are reborn to newness of life, where the parish is constantly revitalized. And all the other sources of grace are linked to this first sacrament, baptism. In the parish church the mystery of our salvation is fulfilled—in its threefold aspect. 1. As a *cultic* activity, "a sacred drama which renders present the salvation-reality. The community takes part in the liturgy and participates in the salvation-reality. And thus it obtains salvation."[31] 2. As a *gospel* mystery, the mystery of faith is proclaimed from the pulpit in all its depth.

3. Finally, as a *dogmatic corpus*, the historical truths of the salvation-mystery—the life, death, and resurrection of Jesus—become living realities for the person reborn in water and the Holy Spirit. This fact is expressed in the "Unde et memores" immediately following the Consecration.[32] The parishioners unite with the priest sent to them by the bishop in celebrating the liturgy. And thus they participate in the mysterious life of the Church and share in the mystery of salvation. The supernatural life of the individual attains its full measure and maturity through the graces of the sacraments. Grace gives us the strength to persevere in our efforts to do good.

c) Only in this community of living faith and active grace can one appreciate the "new commandment" of Christ, the call to brotherly love (John 13: 34). Only here can it become a visible reality marking off Christ's disciples from other men and proclaiming the truth of His message. "And if one member suffers anything, all the members suffer with it, or if one member glories, all the members rejoice with it" (1 Cor. 12: 26).

[31] Odo Casel, *Das Christliche Kultmysterium*. Trans. *The Mystery of Christian Worship* (Newman, 1962).

[32] Noppel, *op. cit.*, *Die neue Pfarre*, pp. 99 ff.: Gottlieb Soehngen, *Der Wesensaufbau des Mysteriums* (Freiburg, 1938) p. 82.

II. THE PARISH–A CENTER OF PASTORAL ACTIVITY

In large metropolitan cities and in many industrial areas the huge parish is an accepted fact. The priest who has the courage to accept such a pastorate must draw up a comprehensive strategy for his pastoral activity. If he does not do this, he will soon be longing for a smaller parish which he can handle more adequately. "I would be the most contented priest in the world, if I were not haunted by the thought that I must render an account of my pastorate before God."[33] Jean Vianney wanted to run away on two occasions, and he had only 250 souls to care for. To be sure, hundreds of thousands came to confession, but they were from outside his parish.

Every pastor, even those sent to large urban parishes by their bishop, must imitate the example of the good shepherd: "I know mine, and mine know me" (Jn. 10: 14). In order to accomplish this, the new pastor will waste no time in drawing up an overall survey of his parish. This will serve as a means of orientating himself and his assistants. And it can be used as the basis for future pastoral activity.

§ *1. The Religious Structure of the Parish*

The following sketch of parish structure is based on the yardstick of faith, i.e., to what extent the parishioners participate in the Christian message and the Christian mystery. In the center stands the source of Christian holiness, the celebration of the salvation-mystery accompanied by the preaching of God's word. And the parishioners are grouped in concentric circles around this center according to the measure of their participation.

Other norms could be used to delineate or subdivide these

[33] Francis Trochu, *Der heilige Pfarrer von Ars* (Stuttgart, 1930), p. 564. Trans. *The Curé D'Ars* (London, 1949).

groups. But this overall sketch provides a good general orientation for future activity. Here all the groups are represented by lines of equal width. If this sketch represented a particular parish, then the width of these circles should represent the approximate percentage of people belonging to a given group.

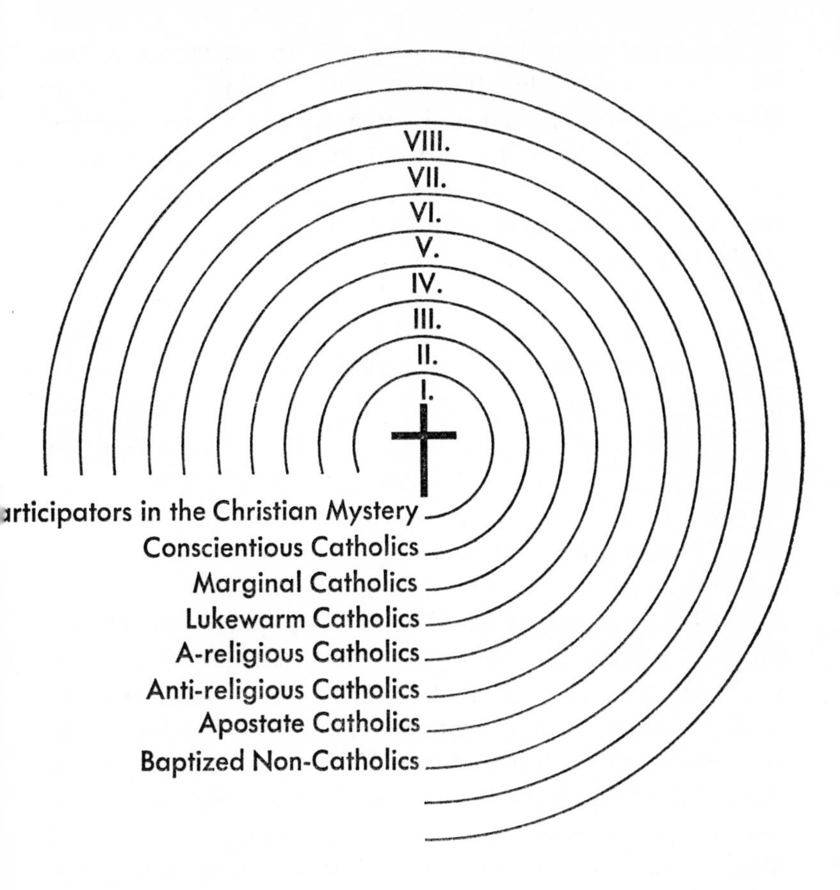

1. *Those who live the Christian message and the salvation-mystery.*

This group may be quite small numerically (Lk. 12: 32). Calmly and courageously they grow in faith and participate in the Eucharistic life. They hunger and thirst after justice (Mt. 5: 6), faithfully fulfill their Christian duties, and share in the life of the Church and the parish. They are ready to work zealously for the kingdom of God because they have responded to Christ's call: "Seek first the kingdom of God and his justice" (Mt. 6: 33).

a) The pastor will recruit his lay apostles from this group. And from them he will select the most zealous and most capable to take charge of some apostolic activity, using men, women, and young people in the areas where they can do the most good. It is up to the pastor to judge how, when, and where they can be used most effectively. From this elite he will appoint the "parish council."

With the help of the parish priests these leaders will collect a group of active co-workers to plot the goals of their activity and formulate plans of action.

b) Even among this group of zealous souls who participate in the Christian mystery, there are many who will not or cannot involve themselves in the lay apostolate. Why?

Some of them are lone wolves who concentrate on personal piety. Yearning for solitude and a peaceful atmosphere, they shun organizations and the noisy crowd. They may be Christians without a sense of social responsibility, introverts (C. G. Jung) or individualists who prefer to work alone for one reason or another. They say that there is nothing they can do.

In such a case their confessor or spiritual director is confronted with a ticklish problem. He must try to show them their responsibilities in this area and utilize them as best he can. To do this right, he must have a fair appreciation of human nature and know how to deal with various temperaments.

But some of these people will really have no time for this work. Mothers may have to devote their time to their small children; fathers may already be loaded down with work. Students may be occupied with school work and part-time jobs. In such cases the priest must use the pulpit and the confessional to remind these people of the duties imposed on them by their baptism and confirmation. They must have good reasons for not taking part in apostolic work. And they must still take part in the apostolate of prayer and good example.

2. *Those who fulfill their religious duties.* The majority of these are what J. H. Fichter[34] calls "average parishioners." The common term "practicing Catholics" is quite misleading because more than mechanical activity is involved. These people conscientiously fulfill their basic duties. They attend Mass, abstain on Fridays, fulfill the Easter duty. They also may attend Mass on special feast-days and receive the sacraments fairly often. Their family life and their general conduct are in accord with God's laws, and they read Catholic publications. This group forms the nucleus of the parish. They are ready to contribute to the welfare of the parish and may even offer some active support in apostolic work. Lay leaders in the apostolate will recruit assistance from this group. Often these people will readily join parish societies and other organizations. When they represent a large portion of the parish membership, they shape the parish environment and contribute greatly to the pastoral activity of the priest.

Thus they strongly influence the attitude of non-Catholics toward the Church. They can cause great harm if their Catholicism is merely a question of pious custom or mechanical observance, if it is prompted by social pressure rather than by divine and natural law. Though they may remain faithful to the parish, one cannot be sure that their children will do the same.

On the outskirts of this group are those who prefer to remain anonymous. It is difficult to get them involved in anything, but in times of crisis they can be relied on.

[34] J. H. Fichter, *Social Relations in the Urban Parish* (Chicago, 1954).

In country areas these first two groups are represented mainly by farmers; in city areas, by middle-class people. Intellectuals exert little influence numerically, but their ideas may be quite influential. The respect of all these people for the priest may be as marked as their distance from him. Family prayer and devotion are becoming rare among them, but they support the church as a matter of course.

3. *Marginal Catholics*

Father Joseph H. Fichter uses this term to describe the next group and explains it in sociological terms. We follow his treatment here.[34] Three basic sociological principles are involved:

a) One of the primary functions of institutions is to set up models and norms for individual behavior. The "ideal" is embodied in the conduct of the groups already mentioned in varying degrees. Everyone is measured on the basis of this ideal.

b) Men oppose this process of religious standardization in many different ways. Precisely because they stand on the outskirts, they are exposed to the influence of other social institutions.

c) There is a dynamic interaction between the various institutions, especially between the sacral and non-sacral. Thus some people find themselves harboring a curious mixture of uncertainty and doubt. This manifests itself socially in a certain alienation from the Church. Their sense of values and behavior patterns are a curious amalgam of conflicting principles. Gradually they lose sight of the discrepancies involved and feel no psychological discomfort. One of the trademarks of this attitude is a certain moral relativity. The goodness or badness of an act depends on the circumstances in which one finds oneself. This is the principle used especially in matters of sex and marriage. They feel that the opposition to contraceptive devices is a personal quirk of the Church and her celibate clergy, that God understands their position. They would never question the validity of Catholic doctrine, but they remain unmoved by it.

Another trademark of this viewpoint is a certain opposition to authority. They feel that priests should attend to sacred functions and not interfere with their parishioners in other areas.

In Europe this kind of Catholic insists that he is "a good Catholic" opposed to extremist measures and religious fanaticism. He attends Mass and religious services, rears his children as Catholics, and contributes to the support of his Church.

4. *Lukewarm Catholics*

We might sketch the following portrait of this type. They were born and raised as Catholics, and consider themselves to be Catholics. They marry in the Church, raise their children as Catholics, and hope to be buried from the Church. They also contribute to the support of the Church. In past decades they often were quite friendly with the local clergy; today they usually do not even know them.

They do not attend Mass or fulfill their other religious obligations. For them the Church year is summed up in spending Christmas Eve by the lighted Christmas tree and visiting the cemetery on All Souls' Day. They may also come to church to witness a marriage. But that is all. And yet they feel no pangs of conscience.

We cannot single out any one factor to explain the behavior of this group. Perhaps they grew up in a family of the same type and inhaled the same atmosphere. Their religious training made no deep imprint on them. When they received First Holy Communion, they were only impressed by the external trappings. And this superficiality was nurtured by the poor religious atmosphere at home. Interestingly enough, the result may be much the same even if they are educated in a

Catholic school. The educational value of these schools is appreciated even by tepid Catholics. But it has no lasting effect.

Their attitude may also derive from unresolved moral conflicts or religious doubts. At first they feel a certain uneasiness. But soon they become accustomed to this feeling, and eventually lose it. They sleep well, untroubled by pangs of conscience. Of course, the un-Christian environment of today's world tends to put them at ease. They may even adopt certain erroneous modern practices without a second thought, divorcing and remarrying civilly. And so they spend their lives in an invalid marriage, calling themselves Catholics and forgetting the serious consequences this may have for themselves and their posterity.

It is not easy to make an impression on these people. And over them hangs the threat uttered against the Church of Laodicea: "Thou art neither cold nor hot. I would that thou wert cold or hot. But because thou art lukewarm, and neither cold nor hot, I am about to vomit thee out of my mouth" (Apoc. 3: 15–16). The very crux of their malady is that it is hard to set them right and bring them to make a decision of either-or. Temporal misfortune may be the only thing which will lead them back to salvation. In the depths of their soul they still feel that they belong to the Church; if they accept misfortune in the right spirit, it could be a turning point in their lives.

5. *A-religious Catholics*

In urban and industrial areas there are many people in this group. These, too, identify themselves as Catholics in census reports, though they may have some misgivings about it. But they have no real contact with the Church. They have been baptized, and may even contribute to the support of the Church. Since these people are often fairly well-to-do, their contributions may be quite sizable. They, too, received religious instruction in their childhood. And it is worth noting that this instruction often confirmed them in the erroneous belief that Christianity was a doctrine only, not a way of life. They have always received "good marks" in religion and have learned a great deal about God. But they have never experienced divine realities or their own sinfulness. When confession was a school exercise, they put on a good show. And their later development is summed up in the words of Emmanuel Mounier: "Neglect breeds forgetfulness; forgetfulness breeds rejection."[35]

Why do not they leave the Church entirely? Very few reasons can be adduced which will apply to every case. The reasons vary from one individual to the next.

Many hesitate to take this step out of respect for family traditions. Their family has been Catholic for many generations, and they do not want to betray this tradition. Others, in a similar vein, are reluctant to take this drastic step and make a formal break with the Church; so they do not.

Many of them are philosophers in one sense or another. They grew up in an agnostic environment or became agnostics later on. The "born" agnostic is harder to reach than the agnostic who has been driven to this position by doubts. There is no basis for a meaningful dialogue. They have an aversion for every kind of intolerance and injustice, for religion and its principles insofar as they know them. They also are opposed to anti-religious feelings. The basic religious questions seem to be unanswerable, and the consequent disputes and separations absurd. This attitude is nicely summed up by Ludwig Wittgenstein: "Questions that cannot be answered philosophically, should not be asked." He himself remained in the Church all his life and respected every religious conviction.

These people see good in all religions and regard them as sincere attempts to solve the riddle of life. As Catholics, they

[35] *Angst und Zuversicht der 20 Jahrunderts* (Heidelberg, 1955), p. 96.

consider the Christian faith to be the best of all. Many have a deep respect for Christian art and culture. To them the Church is the greatest museum of all time.

Frequently they come from families with liberal ideas which extend beyond their provincial environment. And they oppose the Church on political grounds.

Others are disillusioned with the Church for some reason. They feel that the Church failed to live up to her responsibilities at critical moments in history, e.g., in the early days of the labor movement. They still have a deep respect for Christ, erroneously regarding Him as the first defender of the proletariat, the poor masses. For them this is the road to true faith. And they erroneously believe that the Church would side with the capitalists in a showdown.

It is even more difficult for the priest to meet people who refuse to accept the Church for "religious" reasons. Schiller, for example, refused to belong to any religious sect for this reason. Other men, who had great respect for the Church, never entered her portals. The Christian way of life, as they saw it, held no attraction for them. Some were repelled by the church-goer whom they encountered. Others were repelled by the external pomp of processions, the mediocre sermons, and the excessive concentration on non-essentials. In short, they found no answer to their deepest questions concerning religion. It seems paradoxical that books on religious questions sell so well, and yet the Church and the parish remain foreign to the readers.

If these people are part of the common folk, they are, for the most part, victims of the materialistic atmosphere on both sides of the iron curtain. They are speechless before the wondrous achievements of modern technology. The Church seems to be a relic of yesteryear, with nothing more to contribute. She still deserves their respect, but not their attention.

But modern technological society causes conflicts for the individual and induces neuroses and complexes (C. G. Jung goes so far as to consider the atheism of urban areas as a neurosis[36]). Even when the conflicts involve moral or religious issues, the people do not go to the parish priest or to the confessor. Instead they go to psychiatrists, psychoanalysts, and counselors. Or they may even go to astrologists, graphologists, fortune tellers.

6. *Anti-religious Catholics*

Anti-Catholic feelings are no longer general and widespread. Where they do exist, they are usually conditioned by political factors or personal animosities.

It may seem strange that these people are included in the parish set-up. But technically they do belong to it. For even though they are hostile to the Church, they have not openly withdrawn from her. They are still in the fold.

What kind of people are they? Is not their life one big contradiction? So it may seem, and yet we find the same contradiction in other areas. We find children who hate their parents, but cannot bring themselves to break the family tie. Even so, there are families who have harbored anti-clerical feelings for generations, but still decline to leave the Church. Some of the reasons behind this attitude have been discussed in the previous section. At any rate, the antipathy is passed down from generation to generation and gradually hardens. Frequently the people in this group are the descendants of Marxists and free-thinkers who were a-religious. But they never renounce the Church irrevocably. Each generation instills anti-Catholic attitudes in the younger generation, but fails to realize where the attitudes come from.

Certain historical works are imbued with a marked antipathy for the Church. They read these versions of history and sometimes are brain-washed by them. Though they still remain Catholics at heart, they oppose the "visible" Church and her influence in the public and private sphere. For them

[36] *Psychologie und Religion* (Zurich, 1942) pp. 64, 80 ff., 155 ff. Trans. *Psychology and Religion* (New Haven: Yale U. Press, 1938).

the Church is only a spiritual entity. In this connection one is reminded of the anti-clericalism which has been prevalent among the Italian intelligentsia since 1870. At one time it was so virulent that trains would not leave the station if there were priests on board. But even these people never thought of leaving the Church.

Time and again people have set up a sharp contrast between Christ and His Church. They love Christ, but despise the Church. "Jesus, the bright ray of sun, cannot be completely forgotten by anyone who has seen His light. He may be overlooked or even rejected, but He still lies buried in the depths of the human heart, ready to rise at any moment. But the Church is affected by the poison of these denunciations."[37]

The whole range of education, especially at the upper levels, had an anti-religious tinge in the nineteenth century; and the reverberations are still being felt. It was cloaked under the guise of a somewhat haughty judiciousness. Rationalism and nihilism found many adherents. While people developed their knowledge in other fields, their religious education remained fixed on a childlike level. Educated people came to regard the Church as a myth, and Christianity as a flight from reality.

In many cases, the anti-religious feelings developed as the result of some unpleasant encounter with a priest or a religion teacher. The aggrieved party focuses his resentment on the Church. Or the individual may despise the Church for her "intolerance," her opposition to "life," or her strict laws. The secular atmosphere of modern life poisons their outlook. "The essential characteristic of the modern mentality is its a-religiosity" (Joachim Bodamer).

We must also remember that some anti-Church sentiment is based on religious motives. To some people the Church is more like a political organization than a religious body.

[37] *Hans Carossa, Kindheit und Verwandlungen einer Jugend,* p. 327.

Charles Peguy, for example, loved Christ, but had strong dislikes for certain aspects of the Church. Many of these people, disappointed with the Church, join some sect which caters to their own particular views and predilections. But the Church is *catholic* in the full sense of the word. She cannot cater to certain cliques. She will always be a Church composed of sinful men, even though this may scandalize some people.

7. *Apostate Catholics*

Here we are speaking of those who formally withdraw from the Church. Are they still members under the care of the priest? Yes, for even though they have rejected the Church openly, they still bear the indelible character imprinted on their soul by baptism.

In this century two significant movements, Fascism and Communism, have advocated apostasy and encouraged open breaks with Rome. Many of the people who swallowed this propaganda at first, returned to the Church later.

However, every year a fair number of people join the ranks of the apostates. Many priests tend to say "good riddance" and make no effort to bring them back into the fold. They find justification for their attitude in the words of Heb. 6: 4–6: "For it is impossible for those who were once enlightened, who have both tasted the heavenly gift and became partakers of the Holy Spirit, who have moreover tasted the good word of God and the powers of the world to come, and then have fallen away, to be renewed again to repentance." But the apostate does not appreciate the gravity of his action. Every priest must realize this and try to impress this fact upon the apostate. On one occasion a man came to his parish priest for a certificate verifying his withdrawal from the Church. When asked what it would cost, the priest replied, "Your eternal happiness."

8. *Baptized Non-Catholics*

It is very important for the pastoral minister of today to know a good deal about the doctrines and the rites of the various Protestant sects. This involves more than mere apologetics. The priest must know what attracts people to these sects, if he is to re-convert them to the true Church.

Baptized Protestants also are under the care of the priest, for there is only one Church and one baptism. Canon Law obliges the pastor to keep them in mind "*commendatos sibi in Domino habeat*" (c. 1350, 1). According to an instruction of the Holy Office dated March 1, 1950, the care of baptized non-Catholics is "one of the chief duties of the pastoral ministry." And canon 1351 emphasizes the fact that entrance into the Church must be a voluntary act based on personal conviction. In any case, the priest must carry out this duty with great tact.

* * *

Any good parish survey will account for these eight groups and distinguish carefully between them. Supplementary surveys from different viewpoints may also be valuable, e.g., a sociological survey based on occupation and profession.

During the year the pastor should make repeated attempts to recruit new members for the lay apostolate.

§ 2. *The Parish in Its Environment*

The newly appointed pastor must ascertain the religious condition of his parish as soon as possible. The structural survey described in the previous section will be of great help. But besides knowing the relative size of each group, he should be able to judge its relative influence on the parish atmosphere. The number of apostates, for example, may be quite small. But if they have a great effect on the parochial climate, then the pastor must take decisive steps to combat their influence.

This important consideration is the basis for another type of analysis delineating the general atmosphere of the parish and its influence on the surrounding environment.

1. In some parishes the general atmosphere is created by pious Catholics who belong to the innermost groups described above. In numbers and in impact they are the dominant force. Many go to Communion daily and fulfill their religious duties as a matter of course. There is an active lay apostolate; and the few people who do leave the fold are censured, silently at least. In short, an atmosphere of deep faith pervades the parochial community.

Such an atmosphere can be found in some small communities where the majority of inhabitants are good Catholics. But it can also happen that in such areas Catholicism is taken for granted, and the people forget that they must deepen their faith and their sacramental life. There may be troubled days ahead for such localities, unless the priest utilizes his time to strengthen the religious life of his community.

2. In some parishes there is a strong concentration of good Catholics, but also a large percentage of lukewarm and marginal Catholics. Catholicism is a force in the community, but it is only one among many. Political cross-currents, movies, newspapers exert an influence on the community, and contradictory outlooks exist side by side. In such communities the good Catholic must remain vigilant and should not need much urging to participate in parochial life. Close observation, careful planning, and vigorous action are called for.

3. In some areas the parish community represents a minority living in an a-religious atmosphere. It is the "*pusillus grex.*" No longer does it exert a strong influence on the surrounding environment even though its rights are respected. The faithful themselves have a strong sense of parochial identity, but it is

somewhat provincial. They tend to forget the missionary ideals which are so necessary in this kind of parish.

4. In some areas the number of good Catholics is quite small, and the surrounding atmosphere is anti-religious. The parish is very much on the defensive. Other people regard it as an outdated organism, a foreign body. In times of persecution many parishes have experienced this fate. Today this is often the case in Communist lands. The parish endures great trials, and courage is a dangerous virtue. The people are confined to the church and the sacristy, if such still exist.

But this can instill a new spirit in the faithful, a spirit akin to that which prevailed in the early days of Christianity. The blood of martyrs has always been the well-spring of new life in the Church. The small band of faithful, gathered around their shepherd, pray for the persecuted and their persecutors; and their life becomes a silent force for good amid their difficult surroundings.

5. In some areas the parish is really an atrophied community. It is lucky to have a pastor, a dilapidated church, and a few pious souls. Such parishes may even be found in countries which are considered Catholic. If we can believe the reports of novels and travel journals, there are areas in France where one pastor oversees four or five parishes; and the number of people who attend Mass can be counted on one hand. The pastor often must celebrate the Eucharistic sacrifice alone because there is no community of the faithful to participate in it.[38] In parts of South America the situation is even worse. In such parishes the situation eventually becomes intolerable for everyone and cries out for redress.

6. Some parishes are still in the process of formation and do not yet have a well-defined atmosphere. The community itself

[38] Henri Queffélec, *Unter leerem Himmel* (Graz, 1953); even more pessimistic, Bruno Gay-Lussac, *Bitterer Wein der Nacht* (Munich, 1954).

may still be taking shape. The new pastor is really starting from scratch—no foundation to build on, no mistakes to correct. Unhandicapped by past history, he can establish contact with his new parishioners and come to know their attitudes. A deep inner life and an optimistic outlook will be his foremost weapons.

§ 3. *Statistical Surveys*

1. *Uses and Limitations*

An accurate statistical survey of the active and inactive members in a parish can be of great value to a pastor and his assistants. But there are many problems involved in taking such a survey, since it is almost impossible to hire the services of a professional organization.

The International Catholic Institute for Social Research (Geneva), with branches in many lands, proposes one method which greatly simplifies the process. It is worth mentioning, even though some people object to it on the grounds that it disturbs the liturgical ceremony and offers little information of real value.

On a given Sunday the survey is conducted at every Mass. After the sermon a group of workers distribute cards to everyone present. The priest explains the purpose of the survey and reads out the questions. The people fill out their answers on the cards which are then collected once again. The whole process need take only ten minutes. It should be conducted on a typical Sunday.

On the cards are questions about the following items: date and place of birth, sex, marital status, name, address, occupation. Through these questions the pastor can find out 1. how many attend Sunday Mass, 2. how many attend Mass more often, 3. how many belong to the parish and how many come from elsewhere, 4. the relative number of men and women in attendance and their average age, 5. the marital status of the parishioners and their occupations.

This purely statistical survey provides little information on the religious structure of the parish. Other vital items are also beyond its scope.

2. *Representative Types*

a) Denominational surveys on the number of Catholics, Protestants, and non-sectarians in the parish. This would include a record of the various sects. Such surveys give the pastor a good idea of the environment in which his parishioners live.

b) An accurate count of those who enter, re-enter, and leave the Church each year; if possible, this should be supplemented by a record of the reasons which led people into or out of the Church.

c) A list of the regular church-goers (*Dominicantes*) with notations on their sex and age-group.

d) Statistics on the reception of the sacraments, and on the number of births and baptisms in the parish. How many belong to Catholic parents? How many are children of mixed marriages? Statistics on those who fulfill their Easter duty, on regular and daily communicants. How many dying Catholics received the Last Sacraments? In what state were they—conscious or unconscious? How many people were married in the Church? How many mixed marriages? How many went through a civil marriage? How many divorces were there; how many could be righted?

e) Frequent Sunday inspections can give the pastor a good idea of the number of those who attend regularly, occasionally, or only infrequently.

f) Opinion polls have also been conducted on religious questions. In one cross-sectional poll the people were asked, "Do you believe in God?" The answers were grouped according to age-group, sex, social status. Forty per cent said "yes" in the full sense of the word; forty-four per cent said "yes, I guess so"; ten per cent said "How can one be sure?"; six per cent said "no." In spite of all precautions, such surveys always have loopholes.

g) It would seem that it is relatively easy to insure the attendance of children at classes of religious instruction. One survey conducted in Germany revealed that most adults wanted their children to receive religious instruction, even if they themselves were not good Catholics.

§ 4. *Pastoral Planning and Initiative*

1. Every priest who accepts the office of pastor must seriously ask himself whether he is really equal to the demands of the particular assignment. It is a grave question and cannot be answered lightly. The pastor will be able to answer it more easily, if he has an accurate survey of the parish in front of him. If such a survey does not exist, then he must make up a provisional one. The gravity of the pastor's responsibilities was emphasized time and again by the Curé of Ars.[39]

The question cannot be answered too quickly, especially in critical areas where a prompt answer is called for. Human existence, of its very nature, poses a challenge and calls for many personal decisions. Difficulty itself is often a spur to courageous hearts. But if a pastor realizes that the task is too much for him, he is bound in conscience to give up the post. No ulterior motive should alter his decision. There is no disgrace in switching from one post to another, from a larger parish to a smaller one.

2. If the pastor honestly feels that he is qualified for this

[39] See footnote 33.

particular assignment, he must ask himself further questions. Do I have a clear pastoral plan drawn up? Can I handle the work alone? Even in small rural parishes these questions are quite important today. In large parishes he must answer several other questions. Can I and my assistants handle the work alone? What other help is available to us? How and where can I enlist the help of the laity? In every case he must ask himself this important question: "What are the most pressing pastoral problems in this area?"

Assisted by an inner circle of helpers the pastor will then draw up a plan of pastoral action. There is no reason why "five-year plans" should be restricted to the economic sphere. "*Omnis agens agit propter finem.*" No matter how active a person may be, he will accomplish little if he does not set goals for himself. So the new pastor should ask himself: "What can we accomplish in five years?—in the first year, the second year?"

Today pastoral accomplishment is usually measured in terms of conversions or re-conversions. Many large urban parishes are planted in what amounts to a mission area. Pastoral activity must be aimed at introducing people to the Church once again. Certain specialized tasks will require the assistance of specific apostolic groups. All these groups must remain under the pastor's direction. And he must see to it that they remain true to their ideals by holding monthly meetings and providing spiritual direction.

The basic task of the apostolic parishioner is to induce others to come to Mass and to the sacraments. The pastor must try to give him a clear idea of his role as an apostle, and listen to his proposals in return.

III. THE MODERN ENVIRONMENT

Pastoral activity and parochial life do not exist in a vacuum. They go on in a particular locality and are influenced by the intellectual cross-currents of the day. We can only appreciate the modern environment if we take account of the technological atmosphere which has spread everywhere. To be sure, there are pockets here and there where people, wittingly or unwittingly, are shut off from this atmosphere. But here we are concerned with the over-all picture.

§ 1. *The Role of Religion*

To begin with, religion is no longer the dominant force in public life. It does not determine political issues, international relations, or economic policies. In some countries with huge populations God's name cannot be spoken in public, and religious worship is under strict state control. Laws and regulations make it impossible for religion to exert any appreciable influence on education, family life, or the public forum. Even outside totalitarian countries religion exerts relatively little influence.

The astounding technological advances of recent times have changed the face of the earth; and their impact has been felt in every city, street, and home. The wonders of God's creation, which once led man to God, have been overlaid with the wonders of man's creative genius. Man has come to exalt his own Promethean prowess, and atheism has resulted. In such an atmosphere churches seem to be relics of a bygone day. And young people easily fall under the spell of this atmosphere.

The deism of the eighteenth century recognized God as the creator of the world, but sought to minimize His influence over it. Atheistic materialism denies even His existence and points to the wonders of technology instead. Its influence reaches everywhere because of the mass communications media. Every new technical achievement proclaims man's omnipresence and omnipotence to the world. Unfortunately this spirit is most prevalent in nominally Christian countries, because they are also the most technically advanced.

These technological wonders automatically shape the thinking of "primitive" men in every country. They breed an indifference to metaphysical questions and supernatural realities, a preoccupation with the here and now. Millions of people fall prey to this spirit, and even good Christians are not unaffected. We find a peculiar type of human being, who has completely forgotten about his relationship to his Creator, who never suffers from religious scruples or pangs of conscience.

This type of man, a contemporary and a neighbor of the Christian, exerts an influence on those around him. His presence is taken for granted; and his tolerance toward one and all only increases his influence. The confessor will have to reckon more and more with this influence. There is often a connecting link between him and those Catholics who no longer participate in the fullness of the Christian mystery—lax Catholics, a-religious Catholics.

This modern attitude has not been propagated in an aggressive way. Nor is it the result of philosophical speculation. It has grown up almost overnight and maintains itself with the tenacity of a weed. It has no professional promoters, no full-time apologists, no propaganda machine. Yet, even though the modern worker is no longer impressed by the Marxist slogan ("Religion is the opiate of the people"), he is easily won over to this contemporary attitude.

But there are antibodies for every germ. And the modern worker can see through the insidious a-religious trappings of his environment. The rapid growth of atheism has also rekindled man's awareness of God and His existence. Such movements as Y.C.W. are the hope of the Church in many areas, counteracting the appeal of atheism.

The modern brand of atheism is not hostile to the Church or to the faithful. It prizes the Church for her past achievements and cultural contributions, seeing her as a patron of the arts, a valuable tourist attraction, or even a force for law and order. As a large institution in the world community, the Church is something to be dealt with. Even godless forces have good reasons for maintaining contact with her.

The local pastor is in close contact with these people, and his presence stirs pity in their hearts. They wonder how any man could choose such a calling. It is all the more reason to leave him in peace. Anti-clericalism is not one of their vices; indeed, it often seems to be more prevalent among practicing Catholics. These people would never think of spreading scandalous stories about priests, as was often done in the past. In the first place there is no room for moral indignation in a world where there are no moral standards. Instead one pities the poor creature who is still bothered by moral conflicts and scruples.

Such an atmosphere can only be counteracted by the living faith and the spiritual courage of godly men. Living and working in the midst of the world, they alone can restore the divine imprint to the face of modern civilization. This is the responsibility placed on the shoulders of the individual Christian and the community of the faithful.

It is quite clear that the average Catholic and the outdated trappings of the Church have not succeeded in this task. While it would be wrong to advocate the abolition of all pious ceremonies, one must not rely too heavily on huge processions and public demonstrations of faith. Press coverage of such events does not prove that they are having any real impact on the minds of men. The crowds disperse; the churches empty out; and life goes on as before. The sea of a-religious thought continues to eat away at the islands of faith.

If the pastor is a sober realist, he will pick up where he left off before the public celebrations. The feeling of pastoral unrest will still remain. Often he will feel that these ceremonies have accomplished very little and have used up valuable time. But we do not intend this to be a condemnation of public ceremonies. Often they are the only way in which outsiders can come in close contact with the Church.

§ 2. *The Attitude of the Priest*

The priest's reaction to this environment can vary greatly. Much depends upon his own temperament and the circumstances in which he finds himself.

Some priests take note of the a-religious atmosphere and exaggerate it. They rant and rave from the pulpit and abandon the world to the devil, justifying themselves by referring to Our Lord's own words.

Some priests fear for their flock and urge them to keep aloof from the world. They concentrate on the small band of faithful to whom, in their opinion, our Lord addressed these words: "Do not be afraid, little flock, for it has pleased your Father to give you the kingdom" (Lk. 12: 32).

However, the Son of Man has come to save the world, not to judge it (Jn. 3: 17). And this means the modern world as well. Yet some priests use the pulpit to complain about those who are not attending church. And those who do attend gradually fall prey to a pharisaical self-righteousness. Others place all their confidence in the mechanics of ritual observance. They feel that they have done their best. The rest is up to God.

It is even more deplorable when the priest gives up with a sigh of resignation—"It's hopeless!" He follows the book, fulfilling his daily routine mechanically. He is equally immune to hope and disappointment, and has given in to the despair around him. To him the Church is an impregnable fortress shut off from the perilous world outside. He finds comfort in the words of our Lord: ". . . the gates of hell shall not prevail against it" (Mt. 16: 19). All his hope is focused on the Last Judgment, when God will reveal His omnipotence.

Or he may look for changes on the political scene—new concordats.

These hopes are not objectionable in themselves. But they must not become a substitute for missionary zeal. It would be a shame if even one priest gave in to this temptation.

Some priests are convinced that great public ceremonies are the appropriate means of displaying the power of the faith to non-believers. They are the showmen of God, using their time and energy to organize lavish spectacles. The constant hustle and bustle allows no one time for quiet reflection. They feel that something must be going on all the time. And eventually even the best parishioners get tired of the constant activity.

Some priests work on a policy of counter-attack. In many cases this is a good idea. But today the priest must know a great deal to do this effectively. When the Church is openly attacked, a counter-offensive can be launched against the hostile doctrine. But when the enemy is an insidious foe which does not attack the Church openly, the problem becomes more complex. The priest can do great harm if he does not know the real enemy, or if he is not well informed about it. And it takes time and effort to become well-informed.

In the nineteenth century countless apologetic works were published. Today there are relatively few to answer the insidious attacks against the Church. This may be due in part to the realization that actions speak louder than words. But some such works are needed. They must be written in the spirit of Christian charity and provide a sound critique of the merits and defects of opposing doctrines.

Some zealots rivet their attention on those within the Church. They see enemies everywhere and denounce everyone whose views differ from theirs. They call for stricter censures and an expanded Index. It is this type of minister that the world seems to notice. And unfortunately he does not provide an example of charity in action.

Love is still the distinctive mark of Christ's disciples (Jn.

13: 35), a vital force in a world deprived of love. If we fail to set an example of fraternal love, we hinder modern man's search for God and the Church. Jesus Christ, our Redeemer, is still the one men seek in the depths of their heart. We must not drive them away from the Church by our example and force them to look elsewhere. Let us also hope that pious Catholics will not find a sharp contrast between the Lord's words and the priest's behavior.

We would do well to read the words of those who loved the Church deeply, yet found much fault with her, e.g., Bernanos, Bloy, Péguy. And there is much food for thought in the behavior of someone like Simone Weil. She was fully convinced that the Catholic Church was the true church. Yet, for religious reasons, she declined to enter it. All these people may have been guilty of some misconception, but it is not for us to judge them. Instead, we must pray that we are not guilty of scandal, that we are not held responsible for someone's refusal to accept the Church. The sincerity of these people cannot be disregarded.

§ 3. *The Challenge of the Hour*

At this moment in history we priests must ask ourselves whether we are equal to the challenges which confront us.

A paradoxical situation exists today. It seems puzzling at first, but rightly understood it gives us grounds for new hope and intensified effort. On the one hand, we find books on religious questions topping the best-seller lists. They are bought and read avidly. Apparently people are consumed with a real spiritual hunger. Yet, on the other hand, people seem to have a marked distaste for the formal worship embodied in church services. At close range the Church seems to them to be a business organization rather than a religious entity. Her ministers seem to be clerical functionaries, mechanical in their performance of the liturgy, deaf to religious questions or glib in their answers to these questions. The Church seems to operate along the lines of a large corporation.

Now we all feel that this is a rather one-sided view, that the view from within is quite different. But at present this is the only view they can get. They are looking for the holy Catholic Church, and cannot find it. Perhaps there is some guilt on their part. But, at any rate, at the church door they find a man who looks dapper, innocuous, and somewhat strange. There seems to be little hope of starting a meaningful dialogue with this creature: and many people with deep religious convictions wander away to join one of the countless religious sects.

Many join a sect which caters to their own psychological and religious temperament. Some join a sect which seems to take the greatest commandment seriously. Others join sects which seem to correspond more closely to the ideals of primitive Christianity.

We must always remember what distinguishes the Catholic Church from all these sects. She never can and never will cater to one facet of the truth alone, to one human desire or to one type of human being only. She remains a Church of saints and sinners, a Church for all men.

But these sects can remind us of certain elements of Christian existence which have been depreciated or neglected in the Church. The Quakers, for example, preach a doctrine of private worship alone. Man speaks to God in the silence of his heart. Such a doctrine cannot be accepted in all its ramifications. But we might come to appreciate once again the value of silent conversation with God, even during communal services.

The early Christians lived with an air of great expectancy, anxiously awaiting the second coming of Christ. Today we give no thought to the parousia. Our eschatology is restricted to a consideration of death and the particular judgment. The fullness of Christian eschatology is not considered at all. Very often the Sermon on the Mount and the great commandment are reduced to a set of moral injunctions. Many parishes are anything but living communities of the faithful. At best they are a collection of church-goers. A living parish community would eliminate many of the problems which we now try to solve by organizational techniques.

In many parishes Sunday Mass is hardly a communal service. Each individual church-goer is only concerned about fulfilling church law. The Sermon on the Mount seems to have little relevance in the affairs of daily life. It takes a Mahatma Gandhi to show us how it can become the basis of a practical political philosophy. We have watered down the harsh paradoxes of Christianity and compromised our Lord's call for a personal decision.

Our brand of Christianity lacks daring and initiative. Yet human life and authentic Christian existence are shot through with the risks and dangers involved in spiritual liberty. We shake our head over the daring of someone else. Whatever our final judgment on the French worker priests may be, we must realize that they set a shining example of living faith for the world at large. Despite some of its unfortunate consequences, the movement brought countless souls back to the Church.

This world, which seems so foreign to us, cannot be reached with outdated techniques, however "tried and true" they may be. We must accept the challenge it hurls at us and confront it boldly. There is no turning back. We live in this particular moment of history, and we must spread the kingdom of God in it. Besides using the mass communications media, we must prepare for our task by prayer and study. Only then can we initiate a real dialogue with the modern world.

When one takes a long, close look at the a-religious atmosphere of our time, he finds a certain strain of falsity in it. In many instances it seems to suffer from a guilty conscience. Some psychoanalysts single out the loss of God as the cause of certain neuroses.[40] Modern man is beset with an intolerable anxiety because he no longer has any sense of purpose. He finds himself alone in an absurd world. As Albert Einstein said: "We live in an age where man has countless resources at his disposal, but no goals to strive for." *Homo faber* is no longer the master of his own inventions. They seem to live a life of their own, sustained by some demonic force.

We, however, must not approach the world with pat phrases and glib answers. We only sound foolish when we stand on the pulpit and say: "I told you so." Glib treatises, for example, on the "theology of the atom bomb" are downright ridiculous. It may take years for us to formulate an answer to some problem weighing on the minds of men. We must wait and pray to God until He enlightens us.

Today the world—both East and West—seems to be shaping the image of a human collectivity, mass man with his collective psyche. But, in the very last analysis, every individual must find his own way to God; all we can do is help him in this search. There comes a moment—perhaps a terrifying moment—when he finds himself confronted with the reality of God.

[40] Cf. C. G. Jung, *Psychologie und Religion*, pp. 64, 147 ff. Trans. *Psychology and Religion;* Viktor Frankl, *Pathologie de Zeitgeistes* (Vienna, 1955); Joachim Bodamer, *Der Mensch ohne Ich* (Freiburg, 1958), p. 119 ff.

BOOK TWO

The Pastoral Client

PART ONE: HUMAN DEVELOPMENT

I. LIFE AND GROWTH

All living things, plants and animals included, differ from nonliving things in an important respect. They are guided by certain teleological principles; they grow and develop according to certain intrinsic laws rooted in their nature. From a seed they mature into a full blown organism, each part contributing to the development of the whole. And the final end of the organism is already contained potentially in the seed itself. They grow, blossom (literally or figuratively), bear fruit, age, and die. Every individual living being in the world comes to experience that last stage—death.

This cycle of immanent growth is punctuated with the rhythms of time. The development of the organism is, to a greater or lesser degree, bound up with the passage of time and the fortunes it brings.

Each stage of the organism's development has its own proper and peculiar function. Man can contribute to this development only by respecting the nature of the organism and its final end, by doing the right thing at the right time. If man steps in too early or too late, he only threatens the future of the organism. Every farmer knows there is a time to plant and a time to uproot, a time to sow and a time to reap.

The ultimate destiny of a living organism is dependent on four factors—two immanent and two external to the organism itself: its essential nature and its intrinsic developmental laws; the immediate environment and the deliberate interference of human beings.

II. HUMAN GROWTH

§ 1. *Similarities and Differences*

Man is a composite of body and soul. So human growth is analogous to that of other living beings. It, too, is controlled by developmental laws. Man's ultimate destiny, the goal of his life, lies outside all laws of nature. But his progress to that goal from birth to death is parallel to that of all living organisms.

However, there are differences. Man's organic development rises to a peak around the middle of life and then begins to decline. But one cannot say the same about human development as a whole. As a composite of body and soul man is meant to grow continually through his whole life. Full maturity as a human being is a goal we strive for until the moment of death.

Much depends upon the grace of God and our free cooperation with it. Man is a body-soul complex, a person, a being with intellect and free will. The ultimate goal of his existence lies outside earthly life and its stages: it lies in eternity. But we are not just speaking metaphorically when we compare human development to that of other living things.

§ 2. *Factors Involved*

The factors involved in human growth are more numerous and more complex than those involved in the growth of other organisms.

a) The teleological principles guiding human life: the natural and supernatural goals set for man as a duty and a natural tendency.

b) The peculiar gifts proper to each individual. Each human

person has distinctive gifts and talents. Even grace is conferred in a distinctive way upon each individual.

c) The natural tendencies and traits conferred with human nature itself—the evil ones stemming from original sin and the hereditary ones rooted in family genealogy.

These are the immanent factors inextricably linked with a given human nature. To these we must add:

d) Environmental influences. 1. Sociological influences such as family, marriage, national origin, social status. 2. Psychological influences such as parental training, schooling, religious instruction. All these can influence the decisions of the individual.

e) Individual free will. This is definitely more than just the sum of the above mentioned factors. In spite of everything, man still possesses freedom of choice.

f) Divine grace. It can overturn human life completely and nullify every other factor. But such cases seem to be the exception.

III. THE PSYCHOLOGICAL OPTIMUM

§ 1. *Its Meaning*

We use this term to designate the most opportune moment for providing some particular pastoral or educational direction in a given stage of human development.

Now man is a creature with free will, always open to the grace of God and the promptings of the spirit. So we can only speak of an *optimum*, not of a *necessarium*. In fact, we can also speak of a moment that is *bonum* or *melius*. It would be wrong to regard the opportune moment as a single instant which, if once lost, is gone forever. Nor should one expect absolute success, just because he has stepped in at the most opportune moment. All we can say is that he has the best chances of being successful, if he offers his help at this moment.

§ 2. *Its Importance*

We can appreciate the importance of this concept more fully if we consider cases in which it is disregarded.

1. A child may be compelled to observe some religious tenet or exercise before he is really ready for it. The duty is laid upon him too early.

As a result, the child may develop a know-it-all attitude. Even worse, he may not be prepared to take on the duty properly when the right time comes. There is no deepening or development on his part. The fruit which ripens too quickly, decays faster. This must be kept in mind when we consider the question of first confession and First Holy Communion.

If too much is asked of the child, he may eventually break under the strain. His physical or mental faculties may be overtaxed. Every school curriculum is drawn up with a view to the capabilities of the child at a given age. I knew a precocious child who read Latin at seven and Greek at nine; at eleven he already knew some Chinese. But he died of a brain tumor at the age of twelve.

2. However, the priest or educator may also step in too late. He may introduce him to some basic reality at an age when he should be occupied with deeper questions. The young sapling has already bent in a certain direction, and it is too late to straighten it out. The die has been cast. Other influ-

ences (environment, free will, natural development) have already done their work.

§ 3. *Its Applicability*

Strictly speaking, the concept of a psychological optimum is only valid for the years of growth. And for human beings there are three significant stages: early childhood, puberty, and adulthood. But again we must remember that the concept is not a hard and fast one which can be restricted to a clear-cut moment. Free will and divine grace must always be taken into account, for they can exert influence throughout a person's life.

Moreover, later experiences can rectify faults in previous development. Childhood problems may be cleared up in adolescence, and mature love may solve many earlier difficulties. The threat of death, in old age or in one's early years, can also have a strong effect on one's life. But here we are considering the general course of development.

§ 4. *The Stages of Human Development*

Each stage of human growth has its own peculiar duties and objectives. But some people divide these stages into water-tight compartments. In their view the psychological optimum (for child-care, education, religious upbringing) is a decisive moment which determines everything. If one does not do the proper thing at the right moment, the opportunity is gone forever and usually cannot be recalled. The loss is irrevocable.

There are three significant stages in human growth:

1. Early childhood. From the standpoint of our present study,

this is the stage in which basic moral and religious attitudes are instilled.

2. Puberty (adolescence). In this stage a human being either chooses or refuses to develop into a mature, responsible person.

3. Early adulthood. The young man or woman either develops a mature outlook on life or remains child-like in his attitudes.

4. At some point the person enters full adulthood. This is not a distinct phase of development, but rather the natural outcome of the preceding phases—for good or ill.

Early childhood means a relatively restricted environment. Adolescence brings a broadening environment and opens up wide possibilities. The young person finishes high school, enters college, and decides to major in some field. He begins to make a choice among the countless possibilities open to him.

Adulthood is not reached at any given age. It is determined by other factors. At some point a young man chooses a particular job, marries a particular girl, and sets up residence in a particular neighborhood. In short, he chooses among the many possibilities which were once open to him and thus sets restrictions upon himself.

Now he must face a double-edged challenge and find out,

a) objectively, whether the talents and capabilities he brings from his previous development can stand the test of daily trial and concrete challenges; and

b) subjectively, whether he is mature enough as a person to live in the adult world.

In offering his help, the pastoral minister must keep these two aspects in mind.

5. *Old Age.* Its approach represents a severe crisis for many

people, as is clearly seen in the problem of compulsory retirement. And since it is the last crisis in life, it becomes the most serious of all.

a) Old age involves the accumulated experience of a lifetime and a new form of freedom, as opposed to the restrictions imposed on the younger adult.

b) The old person may display new depths of emotional and mental maturity. Age and wisdom often go hand in hand.

c) Old age brings a certain tranquillity and peace of mind. The old person is no longer troubled by the torments of passion or the ambitious schemes of youth. He once spent sleepless nights worrying whether he would get a certain promotion or position. Now he is honorably retired, and these worries are over for him.

d) Old age brings man to the threshold of death, a reality which every human being must face. Things are now seen in a clearer perspective. Our body decays, but our spirit strains toward its ultimate goal. At this stage of life a man must be clear-sighted so that he can make the final decision, the one which will decide his fate for all eternity. Now he begins to realize that life without God is utter foolishness.

Many old people become truly pious and embrace divine realities with all the enthusiasm of a child. But sometimes there is a touch of melancholy in their situation; they are like the flowers which blossom in late autumn, never to bear fruit of their own.

e) But the body begins to grow feeble in this stage of life. It is much harder for the old person to set out on new pathways, to reform his outlook and his way of life.

PART TWO: PASTORAL DIRECTION IN THE VARIOUS STAGES OF LIFE

I. EARLY CHILDHOOD

A. GENERAL OBSERVATIONS

§ 1. *Its Significance*

Under this heading we are considering the pre-school child, ages two to seven. Even the first year of life has great impact on later development, but we will not discuss it here.

Almost all psychologists divide these five years into two distinct periods; and the division is important for our present study.[1]

Charlotte Buehler divides them thus:

Ages 2–4: the child orientates himself in his surroundings.

Ages 5–7: the child focuses attention on objects around him.

We can proceed to characterize these two periods more concretely:

Ages 2–4: the period of lasting first impressions.

Ages 5–7: the age of questions.

The pastoral significance of early childhood can be summarized in a simple statement. In this period the basic spiritual formation of the child takes place; elementary moral and religious attitudes are instilled. Here we are speaking of the usual situation without discounting the potential influ-

[1] Cf. M. Pfleigler, *Die Psychologie der religiosen Bildung* (Innsbruck, 1934), pp. 74 ff.

ence of grace and free will. Our statement clearly implies that this period of life provides a unique psychological optimum for moral and religious training.

§ 2. *Our Method of Inquiry*

The scholarly inquirer may investigate a particular problem in different ways. He may approach it deductively, working from valid general principles to particular applications of these principles. Such would be the general tendency of a logical inquiry. But a person might also focus his attention on isolated individual phenomena, and treat them as such.

Our present topic is human life itself and its individual manifestations. But instead of restricting oneself to a deductive analysis or an analysis of isolated phenomena, we shall present a typological analysis. In short, we shall examine the various possibilities inherent in phenomena (situations) of the same general type. This would seem to be the only practicable approach to our present subject.

B. EARLY FORMATION

§ 1. *Basic Moral Formation*

Moral attitudes—which ordinarily last a lifetime—are adopted by the child subconsciously. He comes to experience the reality of a moral order or else he does not experience it. We cite three possible situations and their effect on the child's formation.

1. The child does not experience the existence of a moral order.

a) The Situation.

For some reason or other the young child at this impressionable age never discovers that some desires are good and others are bad, that some actions are permissible and others are not, that there are legitimate limits to his freedom of action.

This situation may arise when the youngster is an only child, the baby of the family, or a sickly child to whom parents are reluctant to say no. It is especially serious when someone's refusal to satisfy the child's wish gets him or her in trouble, if, for example, a nurse is fired for her refusal to satisfy the child's wish.

b) The Consequences.

In this early stage of character formation the child becomes a person whose every wish must be fulfilled. Unwittingly he becomes demanding, unruly, unrestrained, and obstinate. In later years he can brook no opposition to his own ideas and wishes. He is deaf, dumb, and blind to the legitimate rights and wishes of his fellows. Thus without realizing it, he becomes a hard-hearted, selfish egotist. He falls into this mold quite naturally, and therefore it is very hard to reform him.

This type of person sees all limits and restrictions as stupid norms imposed arbitrarily by others. Concentrating exclusively on his own wishes, he becomes anti-social and has no regard for other people. Often enough he literally pursues his objections "over their dead bodies."

Such people will grow up to rule their own families with an iron hand. The father proves to be a man of the world, a man without a conscience. And the wife sees motherhood only as an encroachment on her freedom.

Now we can clearly see what is meant by moral formation in early childhood. It refers to the inculcation of certain basic attitudes and behavior patterns which will probably last a lifetime, and unconsciously influence all future moral (or immoral) development.

2. The child meets up with the "moral order," but it seems to be nothing more than a harsh restraint.

a) *The Situation.*

In the impressionable days of early childhood moral injunctions seem to be nothing more than harsh restraints opposing seemingly legitimate desires. In short, the child comes to regard his environment as hostile and heartless. So, for example, poor children cannot get things from their parents which other children get without difficulty. Children brought up by strict parents may also find themselves in this situation. Children brought up in institutions may come to feel that "order," not "love," is the dominating principle. Refugee children may compare their own lot with that of the children born in their new homeland. And if a family suffers a severe reversal of fortunes, the young child may be seriously affected.

b) *The Consequences.*

In this situation much depends upon the child's innate temperament. We will, therefore, consider the consequences from this viewpoint, fully realizing that the problem is quite complex—especially at this stage of life.

The situation makes a deep impression on children with a melancholic temperament. It is imprinted on their mind, never to be forgotten. And their reaction to it is a feeling of weakness and helplessness. They turn into cheerless persons who are chronically depressed, children who never laugh or can only manage a sardonic smile. Eventually they grow up to be bitter pessimists. However, they must get along with other people who seem to enjoy life. So they become pharisaical and deceitful, inwardly resenting the success of others or gloating over their misfortunes.

However, they manage to find other means of compensation. They may turn into thieves or into malicious, spiteful people. They take sadistic pleasure in duping others at every turn.

This type of situation also makes a deep impression on children with a choleric temperament. However, they react strongly against it, and this violent reaction may last a lifetime. These are the "born" misanthropes, the hate-mongers who are just waiting to take their revenge. In early childhood they found order to be a hostile force; now they are prepared to revolt against all order in society. In the revolutions which have broken out throughout human history we find countless atrocities perpetrated by seemingly harmless men. Their suppressed thirst for vengeance suddenly comes to the surface and expresses its full force.

A child harboring these suppressed feelings cannot be a carefree happy tot like other children of the same age. He can turn into a malicious, deceitful little monster. Cruelty to animals and many malicious pranks committed by children can be traced back to this source. The school teacher and the religious instructor often find their hands tied by school policies. They cannot take forthright steps against these baitings; and their helplessness only encourages the child.

In the child of sanguine temperament this situation does not make a deep or lasting impression. He reacts to it quickly, but soon forgets about it. He tends to become a spineless character, shirking all responsibility. Moral restrictions seem to be a senseless burden, nothing more. If he is a talented person, he becomes a carping, sarcastic critic, ridiculing everyone and everything.

The child of phlegmatic temperament is not very much impressed by the situation and has no deep-seated urge to strike back. He becomes a weak, dependent character without self-confidence, inwardly resenting the surrounding environment. He is knocked from pillar to post and develops a fatalistic attitude toward it all.

In its extreme form the attitude is exemplified by those who seem to be "born slaves," even though slavery as such no longer exists in their society. They go through life with their tails between their legs, accepting as a matter of course the arrogant disdain and ill treatment of their fellow men.

If a phlegmatic person is also talented, he is the "nine-to-five man" who idles away time on the job and knows how to avoid the unpleasant realities of life.

3. The child sees the moral order as a source of freedom to which certain legitimate boundaries are attached.

a) *The Situation.*

In the first impressionable years of life the child makes a discovery of great moral import: certain desires and actions can be carried out because they are good; others are bad and cannot be carried out. His kind mother sometimes says yes; but sometimes she says no. Yet it is love which prompts both of these responses. The child comes to realize that his own wishes are limited to some extent by the legitimate wishes of others. Needless to say, this discovery is easier to make in a family with several children.

b) *The Consequences.*

In the first vital years of growth the child learns to get along with others, and his whole existence is well integrated. Order becomes the principle structuring his life from then on. Even when human frailty and temptations overcome him temporarily, he almost instinctively sets out to bring order into his life once again.

* * *

To sum up, the moral order is not an extrinsic system grafted on to human existence. It is the guiding force behind an orderly life, helping us to live as God wants us to live. It is planted in the human heart as a seed, to grow and develop through man's contact with the real world. When the young child experiences order in his first contacts with the world, his own character and personality are integrated into a well-ordered whole; and his moral development is orientated in the right direction. But if he does not experience order in these early years, it is very difficult for him to lead an integrated existence. The basic foundation is laid at this stage of life.

§ 2. *Basic Religious Formation*

1. The seed planted at baptism begins to stir at this age of life. Usually it encounters one of the three fates which we shall discuss below. We must remember that the religious predisposition is not to be equated with the moral predisposition or any other natural tendency. However, it does develop and mature as they do. It is the seed of supernatural life; and its future development is determined by the type of soil in which it is sown (Lk. 8: 5). Childhood environment plays an important role in determining whether this predisposition will mature properly.

a) The seed of supernatural life may take root amid a religious environment which allows it to mature properly. This environment is usually provided by a good Catholic family whose thoughts and actions are motivated by Christian principles. They pray together as a family and bring the child to Mass with them. The whole family atmosphere inculcates an awareness and an appreciation of sacred realities. The child is not pressured into it.

As a result, the child's spiritual life develops easily and naturally into full maturity. It is an integral part of his development.

b) The seed of supernatural life finds itself in an environment which is not religious. It is choked by its surroundings because it cannot develop properly. This great opportunity for laying the foundations of a deeply religious life is neglected. The child remains spiritually undeveloped. Later on in life he will reject religious realities because his notions about religion have remained on a childhood level. He goes through life with questions about religion which were not answered when he asked them in childhood.

c) The religious instinct awakens in an anti-religious environment. The seed is stamped under foot, and divine realities are spurned. This child is imbued with a hatred for God and religion from his earliest years. It is, for all practical purposes, a family trait. However, if the child develops a hostility for his family or his environment, he may ally himself with his former enemy and develop religious interests.

We must remember that grace and free will are always at work. Human development is not bound to an irreversible course determined by iron-clad laws. Anti-religious prejudices may or may not be passed down to succeeding generations, but the basic religious predisposition cannot be rendered extinct.

* * *

The spiritual life, like any other kind of life, can only flourish in a favorable temperature. Extremes of heat or cold will kill it. A child's spiritual life may be stultified by an anti-religious environment. But it can also be squelched by undue pressure and coercion. If he is forced to do too much, he may develop a distinct aversion for religious realities. This was true for the poet Rilke, whose over-pious mother forced him to do more than he was ready for. The old adage is well worth remembering: "*Omne nimium vertitur in vitium.*"

2. *The Two Stages of Early Childhood*

The pastoral minister and the educator can contribute to the development of the child only if they have some appreciation of the psychological factors at work. It is important for them to distinguish between the two stages of early childhood, as psychologists do. The border-line between the stages is not clear-cut, of course, but the following division is widely accepted.

a) Ages 2–4: the awakening of religious dispositions.

In these years the child becomes aware of his relationship to God, and the seeds of supernatural life stir in his heart. All this takes place on a transcendental level which cannot be clearly delineated or described in psychological terms. "In the child, the whole metaphysical order lies sleeping in an indistinct form. How else could they possess an interior awareness of God, infinity, eternity, holiness! For we cannot penetrate to these realities through external means; all we have are empty words" (Jean Paul, *Levana*, 36). And we can add the words of a modern psychologist which are in the same vein. "Since the days of Rousseau men have debated whether young children have a real appreciation of religious realities, or whether this stage of psychic development is reached only at adolescence. Now it may be stated with certainty that the child does possess a religious life, and that this life seems to develop spontaneously from certain basic instincts."[2]

This innate awareness of the God-Man relationship is developed through the child's encounter with religious attitudes and practices in the world around him. The child's idea of God is shaped by what he hears and sees. And this early impression may remain with him for life. If adults constantly threaten the child with the reality of God ("God will punish you"), then God becomes an object of fear for him; and this can have serious after-effects.

This interaction between the child's inner instincts and external conditioning is summed up in concrete terms by E. Nobiling: "The child encounters God in dreams, in communal prayer, in time of need or sickness, in the pricks of conscience or fear, on the occasion of a death in the family, in the rumbling of thunder and lightning."[3]

[2] Eduard Spranger, *Psychologie des Jugendalters* (Leipzig, 1926) p. 289. Additional testimony in Pfliegler, *op. cit.*, p. 74.

[3] *Archiv für Religionspsychologie*, 4 Bd. (Leipzig, 1929), p. 188. Additional considerations in the works of Comenius, Herbart, Maria Montessori, and my book cited in footnote 1.

Thus the child's idea of God is the product of inner feelings and external experiences. God may become the supreme reality for him, embodied in a multiplicity of notions and ideas. And he may adopt many different religious attitudes as a result: love, trust, reverence, fear, anxiety.

On the other hand, the child may not encounter any real religious environment in these early years. As a result, he does not develop a clear idea of God. At best there is a lingering question in the back of his mind. Yet it is quite possible that he may go through the motions of religious worship in his school days without his teachers ever discovering his real state of mind. He can adapt quite easily to his environment.[4]

The child's religious practice—his approach to God—is direct and ingenuous. He can speak to God in familiar terms, and he does not find it difficult at this age. A sense of awe and wonder dominates his thinking. As yet there are no problems or questions on his mind. Later on problems will arise. And if they are not explained, trouble will ensue.

Pastoral Guidelines

1. The child's religious instinct develops quite naturally in an environment favorable to it, e.g., in a devout family.

2. The child should be given an opportunity to participate in religious exercises. Coercion, however, does little good. He should be motivated by a spirit of joy.

3. Children depend on their parents. It is they who should direct the child to God. But if the child's religious practice is motivated only by love for his parents, it will encounter a crisis later on.

b) Ages 4–7: the Inquisitive Stage

Everyone knows that children at this stage never tire of

[4] Cf. Rudolf Binding, *Erlebtes Leben* (1928), pp. 32, 57.

asking questions, sometimes baffling their parents and teachers.

aa) Though it may be hard to believe, it is a fact that through these questions the child develops a quasi-logical concept of God, or at least a clear notion about Him. There is ample proof of this in the technical literature. We cite one comment. "For the first time the child uses logic to arrive at a knowledge of the ultimate cause behind concrete realities. He develops a concept (!) of God or at least a fundamental notion about Him."[5]

bb) Pastoral Guidelines:

1. The child's questions must be taken seriously.
2. They should always be answered.
3. They should be answered in a way which the child will understand.
4. The answers should not be too complex, involving more than is asked.

C. SUMMARY

§ *1. Principles of Childhood Development*

Principle 1. Early childhood is the period of lasting first impressions. Proper or improper development at this stage of life has the most lasting effect. "As the twig is bent . . ."

Principle 2. Early childhood is the period when man unconsciously adapts himself to an ordered or disordered way of life. The wailing infant soon learns to stop crying when he discovers that his screams go unheeded. This is the first primitive type of adaptation. And it is important for the educator to realize that deep-rooted tendencies which have developed

[5] Charlotte Buehler, *Kindheit und Jugend* (Leipzig, 1933[1]) p. 342.

unconsciously can be altered by conscious effort only with great difficulty.

Principle 3. Early childhood is the period when religious and moral dispositions awaken in the child—spontaneously or under the stimulus of environment. They mature through the child's contact with religious attitudes and practices in the world around him. If the environment is hostile or apathetic to these dispositions, they will not develop. Like any other talent they must have support from their environment. And the environment will determine the intensity of these dispositions and the concrete form they take.

Principle 4. All this indicates that parents and educators bear full responsibility for the young child's development. A child may do something wrong, e.g., kick his mother. His parents laugh it off, saying that "he doesn't understand." Now it is true that the child may not be guilty insofar as he does not yet appreciate the wrongness of the act. But this does not mean that the child can do whatever he wants. He must be taught a sense of moral responsibility which is suited to his present stage of development.

In order to bring out the degree of parental responsibility more clearly, we shall contrast it with their responsibility in subsequent stages of the child's development.

In early childhood parents (and teachers) must explain the obligations of the moral order and see to it that they are fulfilled. The child of school age is also taught these responsibilities, but it is up to him to carry them out. The teen-ager should be mature enough to recognize these responsibilities himself, and then carry them out.

§ 2. *Pastoral Direction in These Years*

1. The greatest problem lies in the fact that, although these

years are so important for the future development of the child, they may be neglected.

2. Furthermore, the priest can only act indirectly to change this unfortunate situation.

3. He can exert indirect influence in the following ways:

a) By pointing out the decisive role played by the family and the Christian atmosphere in the home: the value of praying and worshiping as a family.

b) By pointing out the harmful effects produced by a home where the atmosphere is a-religious or anti-religious.

c) By pointing out the dangers threatening the family today: and also the harmful after-effects of a broken home.

4. The priest often has an opportunity to exercise direct influence on the child in orphanages, day-nurseries, and kindergarten classes. This opportunity is not fully appreciated by many priests. Nurseries can do more than keep the child busy while his parents are at work.

5. Many children enter grammar school with undeveloped religious instincts and no moral formation. The first psychological optimum has been completely or almost completely overlooked. The possibility of correcting this situation cannot be excluded; but at the same time the child is faced with new responsibilities which presuppose previous moral and religious development.

The school years are far less important than early childhood for basic moral and religious training. The new lessons may fall on stony ground, like the seed of the Gospel parable (Lk. 8: 6). Our Lord even indicated that the seed would be welcomed at first so that later catechists would not be deceived by first appearances.

PASTORAL DIRECTION

II. THE SCHOOL CHILD

Ages 7–10

Starting school is a significant experience for the child and his parents. The child moves beyond the immediate environment in which he has lived up to this time—his home. These years are also of great importance for the child's education in the narrow sense of the term. However, in the over-all scheme of human development these years ar not as important as the years of early childhood.

A. CHARACTERISTIC TRAITS

§ 1. *Receptiveness*

In these years the child displays a high degree of receptiveness. His memory—as a mechanical ability to store up information—is never so adept as it is at this age. However, the child is not yet able to grasp the logical connections between various data. When he is given reasons for something, he remembers them only by association, but does not see the causal connection.

§ 2. *Enthusiasm*

The school child displays great enthusiasm for everything, but it is a superficial kind of enthusiasm. It may be transferred from one thing to the next at a moment's notice. A real human experience is a situation which makes a deep impression on a person and has lasting after-effects. These years are quite devoid of such experiences. Even important events like the reception of First Holy Communion may leave no imprint on the child's mind.

§ 3. *Group Membership*

At this age the child is very strongly influenced by his "peer-group." His actions are determined, not by personal desires, but by the feelings of the group at a given moment. Class distinctions and differences in family atmosphere mean little to children sitting in the same classroom. The child's religious attitude is also determined by the group, not by his personal feelings. "Religious attitudes are not yet a deep conviction of the person as an individual because this individuality does not yet exist" (Hildegarde Hetzer).

§ 4. *Unquestioning Belief*

As yet the child is not capable of thinking out a position or adopting a critical attitude toward some proposition. His attitudes are motivated by the group and conditioned by his environment. Whether he comes from a devout family or not, he accepts what he hears in school and does what everyone else does. The contrast or complementarity of the two environments makes no impression on him.

§ 5. *Code Morality*

It is quite clear that the moral behavior of the school child is nothing more than obedience to a code imposed on him by others. Those things which are approved by teachers, parents, and older children are good; the things forbidden by them are bad. As yet the child has no internal basis for forming a moral judgment.

B. PASTORAL CONSIDERATIONS

At this age children are likely to have a spiritual life even when no religious atmosphere is evident in the home. But this piety is not to be taken at face value. They will readily take part in all sorts of special exercises, such as school retreats. But it would be better to reserve such exercises for an age when they can make a deeper impression on the child. One must constantly remember the dangers inherent in premature training. No real "change of heart" can take place at this age.

§ 1. *The Main Pastoral Objectives*

1. A thorough grounding in religious doctrine. Only after the child has had years of proper instruction can he make an intelligent, mature decision.

2. A regimen of sound religious practices adapted to the child's present stage of development. They should not be too adult or too babyish, otherwise they will be set aside disdainfully later on and the individual will give up religion altogether. The priest should ask himself whether these practices will stand the test of criticism in the years of adolescence. And it is presumed that the child received some religious formation in early childhood. Previous formation and a proper religious atmosphere in the home are the best guarantee of success. Participation in religious worship should be presented as a privilege, not as an annoying duty.

3. Above all, an introduction to the liturgical life of the Church and to sound forms of communal worship—Mass, the sacraments. Participation in the liturgy is the "pedagogical method of the Church," as Maria Montessori said. At this stage of life it should become a permanent part of the child's religious practice.

§ 2. *First Confession and First Holy Communion*

1. Before Pius X these sacraments were usually received after the age of ten. First Holy Communion to some extent played the same role as baptism did in the primitive Church. It was the first impressive religious event in the child's life. Many autobiographies of people who later came to have doubts about the faith indicate that this memory was their last support.

In the French public school system the situation is still much the same. Children may attend release-time classes on Thursday once they reach the age of nine. This course of instruction closes with the reception of First Holy Communion at the age of twelve.[6]

2. The decree of Pope Pius X, *Singulari Quadam*, was promulgated on August 8, 1910, and it inaugurated a children's "Eucharistic Crusade." Henceforth children were permitted to receive Holy Communion once they appreciated the difference between the sacred species and common bread. There have been cases of pious children receiving Holy Communion at a very tender age.[7]

3. Viewed in historical perspective, the appeal of Pope Pius X was not so novel as it seemed at first. A noted historian reports that Geiler von Kaisersberg, a famous preacher in the fifteenth century, also advocated the early reception of Holy Communion. He set down the following conditions: 1. the child should be able to distinguish the Eucharist from ordinary bread; 2. the final decision should be left to the parents, who would go to Communion with the child in accordance with the custom of the day.[8]

[6] Cf. Leopold Lentner, *Religionsunterricht zwischen Methode und freier Gestaltung* (Innsbruck, 1953), pp. 41, 157.

[7] For example, Little Nelly of Holy God.

[8] A. Veit, *Volksfrommes Brauchtum der Kirche im deutschen Mittelalter* (Freiburg, 1912), p. 175.

The Church always required that the recipient be able to distinguish between good and evil. This moral ability is judged to be present at the age of seven (can. 88, 3). But under the influence of theologians, especially St. Thomas Aquinas, the average age for the reception of First Holy Communion was set at ten.

4. Today the pertinent Church laws are set forth in the Code of Canon Law, which was also initiated by Pope Pius X. Canon 854 sets forth the following stipulations:

§ 1. Holy Communion should not be administered to children who cannot recognize it (*cognitio*) or appreciate it (*gustum habent*).

§ 2. It can be administered to children in danger of death if they can distinguish it from ordinary bread and show proper respect for it.

§ 3. Otherwise, the usual pre-requisites for the reception of the sacraments must be fulfilled: knowledge of the basic dogmas, proper preparation, and due reverence.

§ 4. It is up to confessors, parents, and their representatives to see that these pre-requisites are fulfilled.

§ 5. The pastor must see to it that children do not approach the altar before they reach the use of reason or before they have been properly prepared.

§ 3. *Confirmation*

Confirmation is usually received soon after First Holy Communion. In the Eastern rites it is administered immediately after baptism, symbolizing full membership in the Mystical Body. In the biography of Pope Pius XII (b. 1876), we read that he received First Holy Communion and confirmation at the age of five. The Church desires that children be prepared for confirmation soon after the reception of First Holy Communion.

Confirmation implies that the recipient has reached maturity as a Christian. So it seems only right that it should be postponed until the youth has some appreciation of the obligations he is assuming, perhaps until his graduation from grammar school. At this age the youth is often confronted with inner turmoil, and some may regard it as an inopportune moment. But one might also say that it is precisely the right moment for administering the strengthening grace of confirmation.

The rubrics connected with the administration of this sacrament make it a moving experience. It is conferred only once, by a bishop, in a solemn ceremony.

However, other factors may tend to dim the luster of the experience—the long line of candidates, the shortness of the rite itself, the lengthy preparation, the party to follow. But if these things are set in proper perspective, they can help to make it a memorable experience.

§ 4. *Moral Training*

The developmental principles involved in the moral training of the child at this age are very important.[9]

1. Obedience is the guiding moral principle for the child from ages six to ten. Good and bad are determined by his elders. He has no insight into the intrinsic nature of the moral law.

If parents and priests do not recognize that this is a passing phase, they can do great harm. The child may never be led to a more mature moral outlook. He may stay in a state of

[9] Cf. Hans Frankenheim, *Die Entwicklung des sittlichen Bewusstsins beim Kinde* (Freiburg, 1933); Wilhelm Hansen, *Entwicklung des kindlichen Weltbildes* (Munich, 1933).

moral infantilism, judging good and evil solely from the letter of the law. He never comes to realize that morality is based upon the laws of human nature and our relationship to God. He never appreciates the fact that sin is a revolt against right conscience and the order established by God. All his life he follows a code morality, or else he revolts against authority and rejects the moral order completely.

2. All this obliges the priest and the educator to inculcate a maturer moral outlook in the child. They must make him realize that God is the ultimate source of the moral code now embodied in human authorities, and that He speaks to us through the voice of conscience. It is never too early to teach the child to listen to this inner voice. But this ultimate norm of morality is seldom considered by the growing youth.

III. PRE-ADOLESCENCE

Ages 11–14

Traditionally this stage of development is placed between these ages. It is convenient to use round numbers, but one must allow for reservations, especially in this stage of development. National origin, geographical location, cultural factors, and sex differences all exert an influence. Present-day psychologists emphasize the fact that the political upheavals and technological advances of the last half century have greatly accelerated the growth process. It is worth noting that today the eleven-year-old often leaves grammar school and enters a junior high school.

§ *1. Transition and Its Effects*

1. The main characteristic is the state of confusion and uncertainty accompanying this period of transition. It becomes

more and more pronounced as the child nears puberty itself and the radical changes it will usher in.

2. The source of this confusion is rooted in physiological causes, the activity of the endocrine glands. Through their action the male and female sex organs begin to stir and the body grows at an accelerated rate.

3. This inner activity causes increasing uneasiness in the child, frightening him and often confusing his elders as well. But they must remember that the activity of the endocrine glands is the root cause of it all. They should not make erroneous judgments about the child's dour disposition, assuming that it is due to moral perversity.[10] Catechists often complain that they no longer recognize their once fine students. But modern day teachers should appreciate the causes behind this change.

§ 2. *Characteristic Attitudes*

1. The naïveté of childhood comes to an end. Up to this time the child was an undeveloped human being without an individual personality. His responses and attitudes were dictated by the group to which he belonged. He accepted ideas and beliefs unquestioningly. Now he is able to reason out a question, to accept or reject a given position.

All at once the child notices the difference (or even the sharp contrast) between the religious lessons in school and the attitudes of his parents at home. He finds himself living in two different worlds, whereas formerly it was all one world. He used to go to church without giving it a second thought; now he notices that his parents do not go to church. He begins to display an ambivalent attitude toward religious practice

[10] Cf. M. Pfliegler, *Psychologie der religiosen Bildung* (Innsbruck, 1934), pp. 91-96, 107-110; also Erich Eichele, *Die religiöse Entwicklung im Jugendalter* (Gütersloh, 1928).

even when his parents try to prevent this from happening. He is forced to keep his inner conflicts bottled up inside him.

The child withdraws into himself more and more. He becomes sulky at home and makes a nuisance of himself in religion class. Inside he is tormented with a feeling of helplessness. He wants to break loose from this environment which is so confusing to him. And his unrest finds expression in unruly behavior, flippant answers and wisecracks. He says whatever comes into his head on the spur of the moment, without thinking at all.

2. The youth begins to relinquish the pious practices of childhood. Good children are frightened by the realization that they no longer feel as devout as they used to, that sometimes they feel downright irreverent. They often feel like creating a ruckus when this is completely out of place. The religion instructor must adapt his classes to the situation. He should not judge their attitude toward religious doctrines and practices on the basis of their impudence and restlessness.

Pupils will now begin to have doubts about the ideas they once held. Their inner unrest will prompt them to make bold statements: "There is no God" or "Jesus can't be present in the Eucharist." But as yet they are not capable of having deep-rooted doubts. "The individual can only make a mature decision about his religious life when he has worked out such a life for himself" (Eichele).

The moodiness of the pre-adolescent works itself out more easily in an environment where religious ideals prevail. The complicated environment of the big city only heightens the problems of the transition. The process starts earlier for girls, but the pace varies greatly from one individual to the next.

3. The unrest of this period gives rise to a passion for truth and facts. Pious legends and tales are no longer acceptable. It becames clear that the stork has nothing to do with babies. The modern trend toward early sex education may diminish

the shock of the first wet-dream or menstruation. But there is a danger that children will learn the mystery of life before they can fully appreciate its importance. Curiosity may induce them to experiment with the information they have acquired. It is no secret that there have been "affairs" between twelve and thirteen year olds.

Premature sex experience spoils one's outlook on true love and the real grandeur of sex. It becomes a topic for dirty jokes and distorted humor. But we readily admit that there may be exceptions to this general pattern. And, in any case, serious questions deserve a serious, truthful answer. Such questions will be asked by the pre-adolescent because he is full of questions.

4. The last few months of this stage are singled out by many psychologists as a "negative phase." It would be futile to try to pinpoint it exactly on a calendar, as some attempt to do. But it is certain that in the last few weeks or months of pre-adolescence children display extraordinary obstinacy and stubbornness. They lose all interest in work and become uncooperative. Plagued by inner turmoil they find it hard to use their memory: and their reasoning power is not yet well formed. Many become loners. It is an especially dangerous period for girls because they are caught between the pangs of inner anxiety and the temptations of a budding curiosity.

§ 3. *Pastoral Considerations*

1. The religious instructor maintains control over the unruliness of his pupils through patience, understanding, composure, and self-confidence. He does not allow himself to be baited, but continues to teach with perseverance and logic. He does not use coercion, and he gives consideration to his pupils as individuals. The curriculum also should be adapted to the needs of the age. It is a good time to introduce students to

the stirring pageant of salvation-history and to update their liturgical training.

2. The religious instructor should not let himself be annoyed or discouraged by the impudence or irreverence of his pupils. They are very unsure of themselves and driven by a passionate urge to discover truth and reality in their own way. They need love, understanding, and patience.

3. Mutual contact and cooperation between all those responsible for the child's upbringing—parents, teachers, priests—is of the utmost importance in these years.

IV. PUBERTY

A. ITS INCEPTION AND ESSENCE

§ 1. *Its Inception*

It is almost impossible to delimit with any certainty the age-span in which puberty takes place. The clearest sign of its presence is the first "wet-dream" or menstrual period. But these initial experiences vary from one individual to the next. Sex, climate, racial strain, and cultural factors all exert an influence. Girls mature earlier than boys; and historical circumstances, such as war, accelerate the growth process.

If one wishes to hold to the traditional approach, one could place this stage between the ages of 14 (12) and 18 (16–19). In terms of school life it occurs between junior high school and the end of high school. And there are various stages within the period itself.

In general, we can say that puberty is not a linear process. It moves along fitfully, and there are periods of crisis and retrogression. This is to be expected because it takes place on various levels of human activity—the physical, the emotional, the intellectual.

Physiologically it begins with the secretion of the gonads. More significant is the secretion of the sex hormones which are released into the bloodstream and produce certain reactions in the central nervous system. The endocrine glands are active, contributing to the growth of the sex organs and the development of secondary sex characteristics. Physical and psychic development proceed along the same general lines and interact with one another. But the exact nature of this interaction is not yet known.

§ 2. *Its Essence*

Puberty comes from the Latin word *pubertas* meaning *fertility*.

1. Corporeally it signifies that a living organism of a given species has matured enough physically to be able to propagate the life of the species. This corporeal development proceeds inexorably according to certain natural laws, unless it is disrupted by endocrine malfunction. Hyperactivity of some gland may produce premature development; hypoactivity may arrest proper development.

2. Psychically it signifies that the human being has laid the groundwork for the full development of his own personality, the individuality envisioned for him by God. Hence, it varies greatly from one person to the next, depending on his natural talents and abilities. It implies that the human being is now able to assume responsibility in his culture: he is able to contribute to it and to pass it on to others. The ultimate goal of this development may be called adulthood. It implies that the individual possesses the necessary understanding and

ability to make mature decisions and answer for them before God and his own conscience.

Psychic development is a double-edged phenomenon. On the one hand, it is to some extent related to and dependent on corporeal development; on the other hand, it involves the maturation of a spiritual personality possessing free will. The adolescent still needs training, but now he must consciously cooperate in this process and also train himself. But outside influence as well as free will plays a part in deciding what is to be learned and how it will be learned.

3. Pre-adolescence was merely the prelude to puberty itself. Now the distinctive characteristics of the transition make their full weight felt and radically change the life of the individual. The boy or girl is gradually transformed into a man or woman. Herein lies the source of much trial and tribulation. The adolescent is no longer a child, but not yet an adult. He must bear up under the confusion, and so must his elders. Physically and spiritually he is still unsettled and therefore in danger. And if the surrounding environment is also unsettled, as is often the case, then the transition is even more difficult and perilous.

The over-all result is a state of confusion and disorder. The physical changes frighten and confuse the young person, raising many questions in his mind; but he is afraid to ask advice. He wonders to what extent he is personally responsible for these changed feelings. His external conduct now strikes him as being ridiculous, childish, and incongruous. And he is annoyed to find that grown-ups feel the same way about it. His gait and manner become awkward. To compensate for his uneasiness, he puts on a show of bravado and deliberately acts boorishly. Herein lie the roots of his pompous airs and reckless deeds. He becomes one of the boys and associates with other adolescents. In their company no one yells at him or tells him to take his hands out of his pockets.

In religious matters there is also great uncertainty; just

how much depends to a large extent on his previous training or lack of it. He shuns communal activities, feeling that there is no place for him; and he formulates questions of a rebellious nature. But all this is essentially a passing phase. His utterances are not the expression of a definitive position, but of an inner unrest. And the same is true in the moral sphere.

Much of what we have just said about the adolescent boy also applies to teenage girls. But silliness rather than boorishness is their dominant form of expression. They defend themselves against the adult world by giggling constantly.

4. What is the significance of this developmental stage? At this point the human person begins to develop a real personality. Now is the time for him to become a fully developed individual. Since everything is in a state of flux, one cannot overestimate the significance of any particular moment. But this period does represent the psychological optimum for the development of a mature personality. The developmental process itself is erratic and proceeds at various tempos on different levels. The priest must not become too hopeful or too discouraged over the situation at one particular moment. He should stay close to the adolescent throughout this period and watch over his progress.

B. FOUR BASIC CHARACTERISTICS

§ 1. *The Development of Individual Personality*

A child is a person too. But the word *person* refers primarily to an adult human being who is aware of his environment and his own individuality, who can make free decisions and bear the responsibility for them. Individual personality is the terminus of human development—the human being as a more or less fully developed entity. The young child is a member of the human species, but he is not yet a fully developed individual. His dependence on the group is one indication of this fact. He has not yet attained the ultimate goal of the growth process.

This goal is not handed to human beings on a silver platter. It is something they must freely choose and work out for themselves. It is an adventure full of risks, and there is a real danger that they may never reach the ultimate goal. The adolescent is driven by natural impulses to break free from the group and to develop his individuality. But it is more than a natural impulse: it is also a duty requiring much effort on his part. This process involves several distinct discoveries made during adolescence.

1. The discovery of the "ego." The ego is the core of the individual person, the center of self-awareness. From this focal point the individual looks out on the world and investigates the foundations of reality; from here he makes his free decisions and plans his life. The ego is the focal point of our individuality and self-esteem, the embodiment of our fulfillment as human beings.

This is the first great discovery made by the adolescent. He no longer is content to have others make decisions for him, as they did when he was a child. Overjoyed with the discovery of his own individuality, he may place too high a value on it. But at the same time he is pained by the realization that he is not yet a fully developed individual, an adult. He wants recognition, but does not want to admit his evident immaturity. He pouts continually over the fact that he is treated as a child.

Parents and teachers should appreciate the significance of this transition. They should respect this growing sense of self-awareness and emphasize the need for personal responsibility, without embarrassing the teenager. Otherwise their advice will go unheeded, and they will not be able to exert any influence on them.

2. The discovery of personal freedom. The adolescent begins to appreciate the meaning of free will and personal decision. This discovery may express itself in different ways among children in different environments—city, country, school.

In general, it, too, leads to resentment over restrictions imposed from the outside. Adults will frequently misconstrue it as "contempt for authority." But in reality it is a natural transition from the regulated existence of childhood to the freedom of adult life. It should be regarded as a developmental phenomenon, not as a moral attitude.

However, the teenager should be made to realize that it could become a moral danger if carried to excess. This point can be put across only by someone who has won the teenager's confidence. Otherwise this transitional attitude may develop into a permanent dislike for authority and order; and the person will never grow into a mature adult. The teenager must be made to realize two things.

a) He is still bound by the norms of good order. Now, however, he must adapt himself to these norms in a more mature way.

b) Even the adult must live within the moral and social order. But unlike the child his conduct should be motivated by free will and personal conviction. He must appreciate the necessity for self-regulation and its contribution to his own self-fulfillment.

3. The pre-adolescent child is orientated toward the outside world. The adolescent discovers his own inner world and finds it richer, more attractive, and more mysterious.

One indication of this is his day-dreaming. He can spend hours on end dreaming about an imaginary world or his plans for the future. These dreams may become almost an obsession. It is the time for building castles in the air.

Sometimes this concentration on the inner world leads to an extraordinary productivity. Boys become great poets (for the moment) and girls write voluminous diaries. They are caught up in their new discoveries and can express themselves fluently in prose and verse. Or they may find an outlet in painting. One would think that it was the dawn of a golden age for art and literature. But ten years later they are salesmen or businessmen.

§ 2. *Radicalism*

The radicalism of the teenager is a passionate desire to get to the roots of things. Of course, this desire expresses itself in many different forms depending on the individual's talents, inclinations, and educational level.

1. The adolescent is deeply interested in metaphysical questions. At no other stage of life does he show such a passionate concern for ultimate values. He is often disillusioned by the fact that his teachers cannot answer these questions satisfactorily. And he himself cannot think out a question: he merely encounters it on the experimental level. He takes to reading the philosophers who are causing a stir in his day (e.g., Sartre and Camus), even though he may not understand everything they say. "I need hardly say that I did not understand even one-tenth of what I read; but no one who appreciates the situation would deplore the fact that young people are first attracted by the spirit and tone of what they read."[11]

Now someone may ask: "Where is this type of youth today?" Well, young people today are still the same. When they reach adolescence, they begin to ask these metaphysical questions. But the modern world is filled with the din of fast cars and automated devices. In our society the sports hero represents the pinnacle of success. The adolescent is fasci-

[11] Hans Carossa, *Verwandlung einer Jugend*, pp. 187 f. Trans. *Boyhood and Youth* (London: M. Secker, 1931).

nated and attracted by these standards and values; he is sorely tempted to squelch the questions gnawing at his heart. It is up to the priest to appreciate the inner concerns of the adolescent and to keep them alive.

2. The adolescent approaches problems intuitively and finds little satisfaction in the answers given to him. Any priest or catechist who deals with sixteen- and seventeen-year-olds will notice this. But why is it so?

a) Adolescents will not and cannot believe that these ultimate questions cannot be fully answered by human reason. They regard the intellect as the faculty capable of answering every question. They rely totally on it and refuse to accept its limitations, even though they encounter these limitations every day.

b) The adolescent approaches questions intuitively because his mind is overwhelmed by the thoughts obsessing it. He cannot be bothered with a closely reasoned inquiry. So he must be persuaded that such an inquiry is necessary. His own preoccupations and questions seem more vital and exciting than the dry presentation of his teachers. They range over a wide area, while the classroom lectures seem to be narrow and restricted.

c) The problems he experiences are more pressing and real than the vague answers he receives. This is especially true in matters of faith where an element of mystery is involved.

d) However, the main reason for his reluctance to accept answers is his dislike for hasty definitions and premature solutions. It is a characteristic trait of the teenager. Everything is in a state of flux as far as he is concerned. His questions are the expression of an inner unrest, symptoms of the transformation which he is undergoing.

e) In his own eyes the passion for questions is completely genuine and cannot be challenged. The whole purpose of life is open to question. And his doubts may even engender a disgust for life and a longing for death. Student counselors know very well that teenagers may entertain the idea of suicide.

3. Now we can appreciate the purpose and value of this adolescent radicalism. At some point in life every man is compelled to face up to the ultimate questions: the purpose of life, life and death, time and eternity, God, personal responsibility. In the vital years of adolescence, when the human being is forming his individuality and assuming personal responsibility for his actions, he must necessarily be a passionate metaphysician. Otherwise he will grow up to be just another dumb animal and spend his life eating, drinking, and procreating—nothing more. If he wants to end as a man, he must strive for self-fulfillment. And it is during adolescence that he lays the groundwork for this struggle. The adolescent has a critical decision to make, and this fact must be appreciated fully and properly.

4. The critical decision which occupies the teenager's mind can be a source of annoyance to parents, priests, and teachers. They may easily be tempted to disregard its importance.

The adults around him have already made their compromises with life. They have resigned themselves to their previous failings and mistakes, and find life tolerable as it is. They are content with their lot even if they have not achieved everything they once envisioned for themselves. Parents want their children to be content with life as they are. They have no interest in any critical decision facing their youngsters. They want their children to "adapt," to "be realistic."

But the adolescent is compelled to face this burning question about his future. His whole being revolts against the compromising attitudes of the adult world. He is not prepared to make his decision yet, but he has no respect for "practical" considerations. To be sure, he has it easier than his father who is trying to offer advice. For he is not yet forced to make a clear-cut choice. This is the time of life when he stands suspended between various alternatives, and this can be painful for himself and those around him.

But this state of indecision is quite proper at this stage of life. He has plenty of time to make a decision, and he should not be rushed. We would not want him to set his sights too low, to make an easy compromise with the world. At this stage he is keenly aware of his own weaknesses and frailties, but he does not want to base his decision solely on these weaknesses: nor should he. Parents and teachers should be wise enough to understand this.

5. This radicalism should not be held against the teenager. And it is useless to try to discourage it. However, it does contain two potential dangers to which even the best intentioned may fall prey. Those responsible for his training should keep these dangers in mind.

a) In the swirl of confusion surrounding these years the adolescent tends to forget the importance of perseverance, the value of tradition, and the rightful claims of the adults who are responsible for his upbringing.

b) Furthermore, this radicalism is still nothing more than a vague attitude. As yet it does not have purpose or direction. The young man's powers of judgment are still undeveloped, and he may be captivated by those who advocate scepticism and nihilism. Now is the time when he needs a wise counselor by his side, one in whom he has confidence.

§ 3. *Idealism*

The third characteristic attitude of the adolescent is his moral idealism.

1. At this age the young person directs his attention toward some great ideal which he admires. Never in life will he be so ready to sacrifice everything, even his life, for an ideal. Youth movements will flourish only if lofty goals are set for them. They must have some great ideal to strive for.

Young people are lost without ideals. Only by striving for some lofty goal can they surmount their growing pains. And this idealism also serves indirectly to preserve their moral life. However, it does not launch a direct attack on sin or focus their attention on danger zones. Too much preoccupation with potential sources of danger may become a danger in itself. And excessive clarifications are also uncalled for. But the counselor must give appropriate answers to the questions asked.

An age which can no longer propose ideals to its young people forfeits the right to complain about them. Only a society which is motivated by ideals can still do this.

2. During these years (17–18) the young man begins to think about his earthly goal, his calling in life. And he will only find happiness in a calling which has its roots in the noble idealism of his youth. It is usually at this stage of life that a young person decides to follow a religious vocation, or dreams about "the right girl" for him.

3. The danger threatening this youthful idealism is rooted in the teenager's immaturity. His critical powers are not yet fully developed, so he may readily devote himself to a false ideal. He is very much open to a call, no matter what the source may be.

If the priest is to exert an influence on the young adolescent, he must remember one thing: the youth cannot be dissuaded from some ideal by reasoning or ridicule. Logic did not attract him to this ideal, so logic cannot dissuade him. One ideal can be overcome only by another ideal which is more compelling and more attractive. The example of a flourishing Christian community will succeed where reasoned arguments will not. The priest who is a living embodiment of priestly ideals will attract others to the priesthood. This is his first duty toward his young charges—to set an inspiring example of true Christian living.

§ 4. *Activism*

The adolescent is deeply impressed by everything which smacks of vitality and life. The floodgates of life open up for him, and he is swept along in a stream of activity. Every new venture, every "wave of the future" makes a deep impression on him.

1. New historical movements, especially political ones, often begin by making an appeal to young people. And if they are to succeed in this appeal, they must offer a program of concrete action adapted to the problems of the day. It is very important that the religion teacher realize this.

Dry principles and logical arguments, which seem to have no bearing on life itself, have no appeal for teenagers. Apologetics leaves them cold, and they prefer to attack rather than defend a position even when the supporting evidence is quite strong.

They are more deeply touched by ideals and values which involve action: heroism, nationalism, sports, courage. Their heroes are those who display qualities of leadership, men of action. In school their favorite teacher may be the gym instructor or the athletic director. Thus the religion teacher must possess some of these qualities, and his classes must be up-to-date and forward-looking. His students will perk up when he takes a forthright stand against some pernicious error or contemporary evil. Now is the time to rescue them from the mire of contemporary errors and evils, to call them to the pursuit of higher ideals.

2. An age without real ideals can only offer second-rate substitutes, e.g., social status, the two-car garage. It produces young people who fritter away their time in romantic escapades and drinking sprees. It spawns the empty-headed cynic, the thrill-seeking speedster, and the sadistic gang-member who makes a name for himself—in the tabloids at least.

C. ITS AIM AND PURPOSE

Although much has been written about puberty and the years of adolescence, this stage of life is still commonly regarded as the "awkward age," something which the young person must grow out of. In this respect primitive peoples have shown greater wisdom than we. On reaching puberty the young person was accepted as an adult after undergoing certain initiation rites. Their physical and psychic maturity was put to the test, and they were instructed in the significance of their new role. Once upon a time the social order was a well-regulated community guided by definite principles. It could correct many flaws which had cropped up during the earlier phases of development. But such is not the case any longer.

§ *1. The Main Goal: A Mature Person*

The first goal of puberty is the development of a mature human person, in outline form at least. Physically he is now able to procreate new human life and should appreciate the responsibility involved. Psychically he should be able to face life and make decisions on his own. In short, puberty should produce an intelligent human being who has outgrown the trappings of childhood and developed into a mature individual.

1. *From the Religious Viewpoint*

The vitality of the adolescent, his anxiety to get to the roots of things and to devote his life to some great cause, should lead to an awareness of man's eternal destiny. Thus he will be prepared to make his most important decision, to set the ultimate goal which gives life real meaning and value. If the adolescent never gains this awareness, he will not be able to make this important decision. The consequences could be disastrous.

In any case, this stage of development does represent the psychological optimum for a mature religious formation. The priest and the educator must try to convince the adolescent that man's life is meaningless if it is not founded on an awareness of God. This should be the point stressed in high-school religion instruction. The growing child is now mature enough to appreciate this truth. And he can also appreciate the value and the necessity of communal worship. In this area, however, much depends upon the vitality of his parish and its liturgical worship. It is in these crucial years that new members are recruited for the lay apostolate.

2. *From the Moral Viewpoint*

In this stage of life the adolescent should develop into a mature individual, one who is able to bear full responsibility for his own actions. He should also be able to bear his share of social responsibility before God and his fellow men. The herd-morality of childhood should give way to personal responsibility. He should come to appreciate the intrinsic necessity of the moral order and the need for personal commitment. All the groundwork of a mature existence, both as a human being and a Christian, should be laid by the end of adolescence. The docile child must be transformed into a thinking adult who can direct his own life. Unfortunately, it often happens that confessors and spiritual directors hold up the docile child as the model of a true Christian. They unwittingly try to impose monastic ideals on those who live in the world. This is a complete distortion of the meaning of maturity. The monk can depend upon his superiors and allow them to make decisions for him. The Christian living in the world must know how to make his own decisions in critical situations.

§ 2. *Its Metaphysical Significance*

Since puberty is generally regarded as merely a physiological phenomenon, the man of faith—and particularly the priest—must appreciate its deeper metaphysical significance and offer appropriate guidance.

1. Every being in God's visible creation except man acts according to certain inexorable laws. Only man has been granted the power to decide his own destiny. Iron-clad laws govern the activity of lower creatures: free choice rules the activity of spiritual creatures. Man represents one of God's "risks." This is the root of his dignity and also a source of danger. His life is a hazardous venture because it is possible for him to reject right order, to commit sin. Human freedom is supposed to be used in the proper way. Man is supposed to submit to God's will by his own free choice. But even though man continually commits sin, God does not deprive him of his freedom. For He would be destroying man's nature.

2. In adolescence the human being must come to appreciate his dignity as a free creature and assume the responsibilities attached to this dignity. The time is ripe because he is now mature enough to understand all this and to act accordingly.

The priest and the educator must respect the individual and his God-given nature. They must realize that the teenager's growing sense of freedom is the means by which he attains maturity. And they must show the teenager that adaptation to the divine order is a manifestation of personal growth and maturity.

3. The duties of the priest as an adviser to teenagers might be summed up as follows:

Negatively:

a) We should not censure their opposition to constraint or their desires for personal responsibility. This desire should not be construed as insolence or impudence, even though it seems to be such at the moment. Instead, we should make clear the difference between the right and the wrong use of free will.

b) We cannot spare the teenager from the dangers of puberty. It is precisely through these dangers that he comes to experience freedom and to appreciate its value.

c) Neither should we try to shield him from these dangers by "leading" him along. Such a course of action would do violence to his nature and to God's wishes.

Positively:

d) We must stay close to the teenager in order to offer help when it is needed. But we can do this only if we treat him as a free individual. He does not want our pity. We should be able to gain the confidence of teenagers, especially of those who are really trying to develop their individuality and personal freedom. Or, to put it another way, we should not regard these teenagers as stubborn kids and restrict our attention to the more tractable ones. Otherwise we will end up with a group of "nice kids" who can't stand on their own two feet, and find ourselves despised by mature people. This is not an infrequent occurrence; sometimes it is due to previous training and sometimes to other factors. We must do our best to avoid blame on this score.

e) Teenagers must become convinced that true human dignity is based on the proper use of free will. We must convince them that man preserves his dignity by freely adapting himself to the divine order. Our freedom is orientated toward a definite goal.

f) We must show them that the improper use of free will—the rejection of the divine order—is more than the rejection of an externally imposed code. It is also contrary to our own nature. The objective moral order is also the subjective norm guiding our human nature and our life.

4. This whole matter is so serious and vital that we must say something more about pastoral mistakes in this area. If the priest overlooks the vital importance of puberty or tries to treat the teenager in a childish way, he can do great harm. Why?

a) The teenager's insolence and resistance is quite justified morally and metaphysically. And, at the very least, he feels this instinctively. Thus we find ourselves confronted with a ticklish situation. The teenager is in the right, and the priest is in the wrong. In fact, he is doing the teenager a bad turn.

b) This may have four possible results:

α) Teenagers withdraw from us. They are in danger of doing this anyway because of their radicalism and their desire for independence. Now we are driving them away.

β) The best-intentioned teenagers withdraw from us because we do not take their situation seriously. They expect us to treat them as responsible persons.

γ) Frequently the average teenager gives in to us. He slips into a state of shallow immaturity and pious superficiality.

δ) Even more serious is the danger that the teenager may fritter away his time in the many diversions offered to him. Sports, recreation, and entertainment play a vital rôle in healthy development. But too much attention to these activities may provide an excuse for laziness and a means of escaping responsibility. It can arrest proper development.

§ 3. *A Well-Rounded Training*

In every stage of development this type of training offers the best chance of success. Such a program would include: prayer, proper education, participation in community life, self-control, and appreciation of beauty and essential values, a well balanced diet, and proper habits of dress.

D. PASTORAL CONSIDERATIONS

In these critical years, when the individual is supposed to determine his proper relationship to God, he cannot be satisfied with half measures and mere religious exercises. Failure to reach a decision on this important issue produces an adult who is superficial and frivolous. "God and I" is the great question confronting every human being. And now is the time for him to settle this question. The human race would degenerate into brute animals if every succeeding generation were not faced with this grave and awesome question.

Adolescence is the opportune moment, the psychological optimum, for man to say "yes" to God. The doubts and questions of the teenager, his restlessness and anxiety, serve one over-riding function. His spirit is examining the various possibilities open to it before coming to a decision. Indeed, one of the most basic experiences of the adolescent is the awesomeness of the various possibilities open to him. Failure to reach a definite decision will make him a caricature of a true human being.

§ *1. The Teenager's Religious Life*

The teenager himself is often aware of the contradictions in his behavior which are so obvious to others. He is perplexed by it all. Outward appearances often enough seem to belie the principles we have laid down in the previous section (c, 2).

1. From their outward behavior adolescents seem to be quite unreligious and unapproachable. They deliberately keep to themselves and refuse to participate in the communal life of the faithful.

a) This seems to be true whether they live in a rural community or in a big city. Parents have a hard time getting them to church. When they do go, they may leave when they get the chance. Or else they stay hidden in the choir loft, or lounge around the back of the church. In the large cities many adolescents do not go to church at all. Their parents, who may not have strong ties with the church either, no longer exert any religious influence on their children. Or else they encounter fierce stubbornness. High school students have no qualms about missing Sunday Mass. When they still had to go, their behavior clearly indicated that they were there only because they were forced.

But this a-religious behavior is closely connected with the moral uncertainty and the perplexity surrounding the years of adolescence.

b) This behavior pattern is quite normal for one who is at this stage of development.

Inner uncertainty is a natural condition for the adolescent, and it affects his social behavior. He feels out of place among adults for the same reason. Up to now he took part in various activities as a child. Now he has outgrown childhood, but is not yet ready to participate as an adult. He sees the contradiction between his own inner unrest and the social rôles which are taken for granted by adults in his society.

It is well to remember that adolescents prefer to avoid public activities because they have not yet developed their personality. The self-assurance of adults around them contrasts sharply with their own lack of assurance. They are afraid to expose themselves to public scrutiny because they are keenly aware of their immaturity. They reject force and refuse to be treated as children. They cannot be compelled to do something. In this regard they are quite right.

Pastoral Obligations. The priest must appeal to the idealism of the adolescent, and point out the danger of cowardice. No one wants to behave in a cowardly way. They must come to appreciate the manliness of professing sincere religious convictions and the necessity of belonging to a community of believers. Even their stubbornness and pride have good points, and should be put to good use. The average young man goes to church lackadaisically, out of mere habit, or else he does not go at all. They must see the cowardliness and lack of self-respect betrayed by their shyness in church. To all appearances the adolescent has no real religious life, but one should not be fooled by this.

2. The Real Situation.

a) Anyone who comes in close contact with adolescent boys discovers that they have a burning curiosity about ultimate realities and are deeply interested in the answers to these questions. However, they will reveal this inner concern only to someone whom they trust; and it is not easy to win their trust.

A teacher in a technical trade school used to set aside a few minutes now and then at the end of class for questions. The students could ask questions dealing with life and its problems; but they were to avoid the area of religion since many denominations were present. Finally one day he gave in to their entreaties and allowed them to ask questions about religion. He found himself bombarded with questions about God, Christ, eternity.

Religious instructors in high schools where religion is a subject in the curriculum have a serious and difficult task. They must see to it that the class lectures do not end up in mere debates between themselves and the students; rather, they should stimulate the students to pose their questions openly and to approach the subject reverently. Reverence is the prerequisite attitude for a serious discussion about religious questions. If the students do not yet appreciate this fact, the teacher must make it clear to them. Personal moral problems should be handled in private.

Time and again, travelers have observed the intense interest of young people in religious questions in countries where religious instruction is forbidden. At the present time there seems to be a current of mysticism sweeping over the young people of Russia, according to some reports.

b) Psychologists have always noted that this period of life is the psychological optimum for dealing with the ultimate questions regarding human existence. Many go so far as to say that with the discovery of the ego the individual can now establish a personal relationship with God for the first time. They claim that the spiritual and moral problems confronting the adolescent drive him into the arms of God to find meaning and purpose in life. Their radicalism necessarily leads them to the ultimate reality. However, many stubbornly choose to suppress this inner need.

3. At one time there was a strong movement afoot to cut out

religious training during adolescence. But this movement could not base its validity on the findings of adolescent psychology and has been shown up for what it really is: a piece of atheistic propaganda proclaimed by a political machine for its own purposes. Today it is still vigorous only in atheistic dictatorships.

However, the idea is also entertained by some individuals today who are prompted by good motives.

a) What can be said in favor of this idea? To what extent is it correct as far as religious instruction is concerned?

If the religion course is presented as just another subject and does not concern itself with the student's questions, then it does not accomplish its real purpose. At most, it can contribute to their over-all education by providing a religious view of the world. Religion is not a subject, but an approach to life. It must concern itself with life's problems. The religion teacher cannot allow himself to become pedantic. Every human being must determine his proper relationship to God, and religious instruction should help him to do this.

It is best for the teacher to consider his pupil's vital questions in connection with the curriculum itself. But he should always be prepared to help him at critical moments which may be of decisive importance.

As far as religious practice is concerned, all forms of coercion—direct or indirect—must be avoided. To the adolescent, force represents a type of treatment which he no longer regards as suitable. Teenage boys and girls are uncertain about religion, but they have great interest in ultimate questions. They would rather not have to display this interest openly because they have not yet worked out a new form of participation congruent with their new role in society. They must be drawn out. We might set down the following guidelines for the religious instructor or student adviser:

a) Do not be irritated by their radical questions and irreverent behavior. Radicalism, as we have already pointed out, is a characteristic trait of these years. When they behave in this way, it gives us an opportunity to explain calmly that religious questions can only be dealt with seriously and soberly.

β) We must realize that many adolescents do not take part in religious exercises (e.g., receiving the sacraments) out of a sense of moral honesty. It is a praiseworthy attitude. If we show that we understand them, they will understand us when we point out the dangers of letting this become a permanent behavior pattern. There are strong arguments against using any type of coercion.

If the adolescent is compelled to take part in religious exercises, he may commit sins against the virtue of religion or even sacrileges. Morally speaking, the individual is bound to follow his conscience even if it is an erroneous one. Acting against one's conscience is a sin. Pedagogically speaking, it is a mistake to use coercion at an age when the students are bound to offer resistance to it. Their self-awareness and sense of personal responsibility are growing more definite; and they are justified—psychologically, morally, and religiously—in their opposition to external pressure. They realize this instinctively and pay no attention to their instructor. They may conform to his requests in their outward behavior, but inwardly they resent them. And because they are being forced to act against their own inner feelings, they foster an inner aversion, perhaps even hatred. It is a traumatic experience.

b) What is wrong with the proposal to eliminate religious training during adolescence?

To begin with, eliminating religion courses from the high school program would take the backbone out of the educational curriculum. The Christian religion is the heart and core of Western history and culture. If Christian principles and values are overlooked, the other cultural and educational values will have no unifying force.

The pupil's character-formation would also suffer. While his secular education would continue, his religious training would be arrested at a childish level. When he grew into adulthood, he would be perfectly justified in rejecting these childish notions along with the other trappings of childhood. By far the majority of adults who give up the practice of religion are people whose religious training remained on a childish level.

§ 2. *Is an Easy Transition Possible?*

Is an easy transition from childhood to adulthood possible? This is a serious and important question.

There is no doubt that every human being must experience the transition from childhood to mature adulthood. And the transition is clearly fraught with dangers. But some young people do grow into adulthood without any noticeable break in their religious practices or attitudes. Why?

1. *Questionable Cases:*

In a considerable number of cases the developmental process, as it is experienced, seems to be the determining factor. Puberty has no great impact on some young people and does not create any upheaval. The existing foundation is undisturbed by it. At first glance this would seem to be a happy state of affairs.

However, as a general rule, it seems that the more difficult and challenging the transition, the harder the struggle, so much the better is the final product: a mature, responsible human being.

When the growth process itself causes no more discomfort than a little toothache, the result is usually rather disappointing also. Some people misinterpret this situation and regard this easy development as clear indication of a special calling. Such could be the case, but it is not likely.

This unperturbed development may also be due to the educational process. The child is shielded from dangers surrounding him. In itself this is all right, so long as it is not meant to spare the child from the fundamental experiences of the growth process. Without doubt this is a problem which must be given serious consideration in the minor seminary. The doubts and confusions may crop up later on and cause havoc. Like children's diseases, they are a greater problem for adults.

2. *Healthy Cases:*

a) Here, too, many cases are conditioned by the developmental process as it is experienced by the child. These young people have gone through a healthy, normal development so far. In early childhood a solid foundation was laid, and it has been developed as time went on. All the prerequisites for the development of a mature, responsible, well-balanced person are present. Puberty cannot overturn this foundation. Trials and tribulations cannot shake the existing edifice.

b) This is also the situation with some youths—not all—who from early childhood have experienced the advantages of good home life. They have been brought up in a close-knit family, which has provided them with life's essentials and fostered an optimistic outlook toward themselves, other people, and life itself. Early childhood laid the groundwork for a well-balanced development. They continued to develop with confidence and self-assurance, facing life's experiences as they encountered them. The dangers of adolescence are something they do not avoid. They meet them calmly and mature through them. The value and significance of a good religious family are quite apparent in their case.

c) A third group consists of adolescent boys and girls who develop into deeply religious men and women, even though they do not have the support of a pious family behind them. What is the explanation?

During adolescence they enjoyed the company and friendship of other adolescents who practiced a healthy, religious life. With them they faced the difficult transition from adolescence to adulthood. Catholic youth organizations rectified many early mistakes and deficiencies to be found in the home. It was not the pious direction or the religious moderator which was the decisive factor. It was the experience of taking part in a youthful community living the mystery of faith. This community was their true home during these difficult years.

However, the lack of solid training in early childhood often produces insecurity later on. They feel the pangs of this insecurity and sometimes react by acting harshly toward themselves and others. It is necessary to remind them of the balanced religious outlook they once shared with their fellow-teenagers.

d) Some individuals develop strong individual personalities because in these years the full dimensions of the faith are revealed to them through the example of others or the advantages of a solid religious training. The panorama of a full Christian existence opens up to them at the very moment when they are beginning to appreciate life in all its facets. Even though they may not come from an ideal home, they develop into mature Christians. Indeed, they may suddenly find themselves shocked by the shallowness of those who are nearest and dearest to them.

e) A more specialized instance of this phenomenon is typified by cases where adolescents are given new insight into their confused feelings. In the midst of their doubts and inner turmoil, they are shown the potential value and true significance of all this. As L. Tolstoy once said to a youngster: "When you get the feeling that all your childhood notions about God have collapsed, that there really is no God, don't give way to dismay. It happens to all of us. Your doubt does not mean that God does not exist. It merely means that your childhood notions about God were not solid. You must now try to clarify your own concept of God. When someone from a primitive society ceases to believe in a wooden idol, it does not mean that there is no God. It merely means that He is not made of wood."

E. THE RELIGIOUS CRISIS

§ 1. *The Basic Situation*

Toward the end of adolescence a critical point is reached. The torments and inner uncertainties become almost unbearable, and the adolescent longs to establish inner peace and security. The physiological transitions have run their course, but his psychospiritual development is not yet complete. He wants to put an end to the uncertainties which are consuming his energies, to make a decision. Yet, worn out by inner turmoil, he may put off making a decision and grow out of adolescence without settling anything. The problem is put off or stifled completely.

This mood of indecisiveness may prove to be only temporary, but it may also become a permanent disposition. The religious indifference of the modern world and the lack of proper guidance foster such an attitude in young people.

§ 2. *Psychological Data*

1. On the basis of tests, American psychologists (Stanley Hall, Starbuck) have established that "conversions" take place after the age of sixteen. Here, of course, reference is to the child

in a public school system where religion is not part of the curriculum. Even in this type of environment the religious drive makes itself felt. Indeed such an environment can precipitate the whole problem and force an early decision. "Conversion" here refers to the establishment of a personal relationship with God.

2. According to the Buehler school (Charlotte Buehler, Hildegarde Hetzer), the "critical period" falls somewhere between sixteen and eighteen. The background for their study was Vienna between the two World Wars. According to them, at the end of this period some kind of decision, perhaps only temporary, is reached. "The years of stormy growth and heightened feelings" come to a close.

3. According to Burkhard Winzen (Oscar Kuelpe school) young people from a Catholic background frequently reach this crisis between the ages of twenty-two and twenty-four. Oskar Kupky[12] is of the same opinion.

4. To what are these psychologists referring? Toward the end of adolescence the religious question forces itself upon the teenager—unless it is repressed—and produces a crisis (understood in the medical sense). It may be accompanied by deep psychic unrest. It is worth mentioning Kupky's view that boys are more deeply troubled in the early stages, while girls are more troubled in the final stages. But this seems to be an unwarranted generalization. Anyone who has observed teenagers knows that the symptoms vary greatly according to individual makeup, sex, temperament. This is clear when Frisch and Hetzer report that boys are preoccupied with such problems as "faith and reason" and theodicy, while girls are preoccupied with the question of immortality. One may also question the thesis of this school that only young *men* can

[12] Oskar Kupky, *Die religioese Entwicklung*, p. 36.

reject the faith on the basis of principle. It is more a question of intelligence levels than of sex differences.

§ 3. *The Final Outcome*

1. In presenting the final results of an inquiry conducted by the psychologists of the Buehler school, we must remember that it represents only one study based on testing procedures with many loopholes.[13]

Despite this drawback, however, the study of Hetzer and Frisch is still valuable; for it used not only the questionnaire technique, but also the data furnished by personal diaries. Based on the replies of one hundred adolescent boys and girls it presented the following breakdown: 1. church-goers—thirty-nine boys, thirty-seven girls; 2. belief in God—eight boys, eleven girls; 3. nonbelievers—fifteen boys, no girls; 4. members of quasi-religious sects (e.g., political movements)—twenty-three boys, thirty-one girls.

2. A distressingly large number of young people remain in a state of indecision. Either they do not realize the significance of the developmental challenge, or disregard it, or consider it as a purely physical phenomenon. Many let themselves slip down, and no one stops them. The critical decision is repressed or squelched, and no one is astonished.

3. *The Underlying Reasons*

a) From early childhood on, the youngster's religious tendencies were neglected, and this trend was not corrected in adolescence. The neglected opportunities of childhood (the

[13] The "questionnaire" is widely used today in public opinion research. There are many loopholes in this method. Thus, for example, only 10% of those questioned fill out the form; and among the 90% who do not may be those who prize their inner thoughts the most, those whose answers would be the most valuable.

first psychological optimum) inhibited the child's spiritual growth.

b) Today puberty is often explained as a purely physical phenomenon of growth, with no spiritual side. The second great psychological optimum for establishing a real relationship with eternal realities is wasted.

c) The result is a lack of interest in ultimate questions, and the adolescent grows into an adult who turns a deaf ear to eternal realities. He lives for the pleasure of the moment or devotes himself to his job without seeing the meaning of life itself.

§ 4. *Pastoral Objectives*

The main objective of pastoral guidance during these years is to persuade the adolescent to embrace the Faith as a free individual. How can this be accomplished?

1. We must reveal the grandeur and vitality of the Faith to the adolescent.

2. We must convince him that the Faith is the only solid foundation for our earthly life.

3. A well-rounded religious education is highly desirable, but seldom attainable.

4. The importance of eternal realities must be presented clearly and forcefully, e.g., in such terms as God and you, time and eternity, life with meaning or life without meaning, happiness or damnation, authentic existence or superficiality.

5. In a general program of instruction the most critical doctrines should be given special emphasis.

6. The principal aim of our instruction should be to instill

these convictions in our pupils: I cannot really live without being in union with God; I cannot really live without Christ and His Church. Once these convictions are firmly implanted, other problems and beliefs fall into their proper place and are duly answered. If this conviction is lacking, there is no framework for these other pieces of knowledge.

7. The young man must be given some high ideal to enable him to overcome the dangers confronting him (e.g., his awakening sex drive).

V. EARLY ADULTHOOD (18–25)

A. GENERAL OBSERVATIONS

§ 1. *The Age Period*

This is the age period between the closing years of adolescence and full entrance into the adult world. It is an interim period. The inner unrest of adolescence gradually subsides, and the individual prepares to assume his place in the world. He has made his critical decisions and begins to carry them out, to fulfill his calling in life.

Any attempt to pinpoint this period must be made with great reservations. However, it is usually placed between the ages of eighteen and twenty-five. The transition from high school to college sets this period off nicely from early adolescence.

§ 2. *Contrasted with Childhood and Puberty*

1. Early childhood involves the discovery of the outside world. The child acquires a naive awareness of it. For him the im-

mediate environment and the outside world are identical. The things which are closest to him are the most important—home, family, school, games. He has no over-all picture of reality. God, too, is a part of his environment.

2. Adolescence involves the discovery of the inner world. The teenager discovers his own ego, and it becomes the focal point from which he looks out on the world. A metaphysical curiosity drives him beyond the bounds of time and space, and his subjective outlook opposes all restrictions. Self-control is not one of his strong points. Indeed, day-dreams become projections of his own idealistic projects and ambitions. However illusory they may be, they are very real to him. The religious decision which comes at the end of this period calls for an unqualified commitment to a God who now seems quite different from the God of childhood. It is a difficult decision, and often the individual makes it out of necessity, without fully realizing its consequences. If it comes at the end of a long struggle, it brings a feeling of peace and contentment never to be equaled. The desire for a more settled life heralds the approach of the next age-period.

3. In early adulthood the individual must integrate his inner world with the world outside. In short, he must fashion a metaphysical and psycho-physical *Weltanschauung*.

§ 3. *The Young Woman: A Special Case*

The young woman at this stage of life must be given separate consideration, because certain vital facts apply to her alone.

1. From puberty on, her rate of development proceeds faster than that of a boy. And by the time she reaches this age, there is a sharp difference in status between him and her. This

difference is recognized by legal statutes and social customs.

Marriage, more than anything else, curtails the freedom and carefree nature of youth. And a girl is already eligible for marriage at the age of seventeen or eighteen. According to Canon Law, the minimum age for contracting a valid marriage is fourteen for a girl and sixteen for a boy (c. 1067, 1). This canon, which applies to the universal Church, is not just a legal abstraction; it is based upon the physiological realities of human development. But in our culture it does not represent a common practice.

2. The fact that girls traditionally are eligible for marriage much earlier than boys has no physiological basis. It stems from the fact that it is usually up to the man to support his family. And it may be another ten years before a boy can do this. To the difference in rate of development is now added a radically different outlook on life.

This was brought home to me by a personal experience. I spent fourteen years as a high school teacher. In every class there were twenty to thirty boys and about five girls. One day a sixteen-year-old girl, who was a good student, came up to tell me she was leaving school. She thanked me for everything and blushed when I asked her why she was leaving. Then a boy blurted out that she was engaged and was leaving to take some courses in home economics elsewhere. Suddenly I realized the gulf separating boys and girls of this age. A sixteen-year-old boy is a carefree creature who has little immediate concern about the problems of adult life. And this sixteen-year-old girl had to begin thinking about cooking, ironing, washing, and child care. Thus girls of this age are much more concerned about practical realities than are boys. They are more serious, more sophisticated, and more responsible. For the duties of motherhood, the most demanding role of all, lie not too far in the future.

3. This difference between the sexes deserves the serious at-

tention of parents and educators. It is glossed over in co-educational schools where girls often fall in with the more immature behavior of boys. In such a situation the difference may be covered up, leading to trouble on both sides. I myself am basically opposed to co-education for this reason. But I must admit that wherever I have encountered a co-educational system, I have found only good results.

The girl's eligibility for marriage at an early age often prompts her to go husband-hunting. When she sets her sights on boys of her own age, it can lead to moral catastrophe for both.

B. EARLY ADULTHOOD VERSUS ADOLESCENCE

In order to point up the general characteristics of this growth stage, we shall contrast the young adult with the adolescent on several matters.

§ 1. *Personality Traits*

The Adolescent	*The Young Adult*
1. Habitually subjective.	1. Awareness of objective realities and a growing appreciation of objective standards.
2. He is driven to question everything and succumbs to a mood of doubt. He abhors definitive answers.	2. He looks for answers which will settle his mind, at least for the time being. He tackles each question as it comes along, one after another.
3. A predilection for questions about ultimates. He believes that every problem can be solved.	3. Concern for the immediate problems of life. He is prone to resign himself to the "insoluble."

4. An idealist, who has no respect for "realistic" considerations.

4. A realist who is more closely attached to practical realities and hard facts.

5. Bold and impudent in behavior. Still inexperienced. Little sense of responsibility.

5. Growing awareness that complaints and criticisms put an obligation on the critic too. He knows that his word is taken seriously.

6. Life's infinite possibilities still lie open to him. He is a dreamer, free from restrictions. Slogans are taken literally and are meaningful to him. Ten years later these same slogans are little more than catch-phrases.

6. He freely chooses to put limits on himself by settling upon a particular calling in life with all the restrictions it entails. "We reach a point in life where there is no longer any question about what we can be, only about what we are" (Rudolf Henz, *Begegnung im September*, p. 105).

7. Little appreciation of life's hardships and heartbreaks. A cynical attitude toward life's real problems, motivated not by boorishness, but by a silliness quite natural at this age.

7. The end of a carefree existence. Now he meets his first problems connected with choosing and fulfilling a life's work. Part-time work and study. Academic specialization. The carefree days are over, and he is expected to settle down.

§ 2. *Relationship with the Environment*

1. Great concern for one's personal ego and a tendency to withdraw into oneself. The search for personal identity. Passionate devotion to some

1. The search for a mate. The freedom now enjoyed by girls increases the dangers of illicit sexual behavior. In the Middle Ages it was felt that a girl was

great ideal (which one often sees realized in some adult). Boys may, for a time, leave girls alone completely. Later they will begin to approach them shyly.

excused from Sunday Mass if she could not get some escort.[14]

2. Life is seen as a carefree venture, and the individual lives very much for himself. He has not yet developed a settled existence. The adolescent shuns community life, even that of his family in many cases. His behavior is brusque and gauche. He is happy when left to himself, and adults do not crave his company.

2. The individual returns to the social community, and this is expected of him. He restores his ties with adults, though hard feelings may remain. Younger siblings may sneer at all this.

§ 3. *As Psychological Optima*

1. The basic framework of adult life is decided upon.

1. This framework is put to the test in everyday life.

2. The individual personality is formed.

2. An integrated outlook on life is developed.

3. Maturity is set up as a goal to work toward.

3. The person tests his fitness for adult life.

C. PASTORAL CONSIDERATIONS

It is a sad fact that a considerable number of young people break with the priest at this stage of life. They do not remain in contact with him after leaving youth organizations. So

[14] Veit, *op. cit.*, p. 149.

what should the priest concentrate on when dealing with this age group?

§ 1. *Counseling for Life*

1. The priest must have the young person's trust. He must be ready to discuss problems with him on a person-to-person basis, let him speak his mind, and make sure he understands the nature of the question. He must be prepared to handle questions and problems on vital matters. The greatest danger is lack of understanding, failure to appreciate the young person's difficulties. He must help the young person to formulate his personal *Weltanschauung* and lead a settled life.

2. The priest should arrange general talks on certain pertinent subjects, always allowing opportunity for discussions and questions. For specialized questions, experts in the field should be invited to speak. The purpose of such talks is to help the young man integrate his inner world with the world outside.

3. The priest should encourage the formation of groups which would discuss the Bible, important books, and so forth.

4. All these activities can be offered to both sexes in this age-group. It is a very good idea for them to join together in determining their goals in life and their responsibilities before God.

§ 2. *Participation in the Liturgy*

This age-group in particular should be brought to appreciate and participate in liturgical worship. They can serve in many different rôles—as choir members, prayer leaders, ushers. Young people should give shape and vitality to the liturgical worship of the community.

§ 3. *Preparation for Marriage*

1. Purity and self-control should be presented as the virtues which will do most to insure a happy family life.
2. Pre-marital instruction is an important pastoral duty and quite necessary, even though it often fails to achieve its purpose. The virtuous girl who would make an excellent wife often remains a wall-flower, while the more frivolous girl manages to catch her man. This instruction should also be provided to those who are rushing into marriage too quickly (e.g., teenage marriages) in order to ward off the potential dangers involved. In this area the priest has an implied obligation to exert indirect influence on civil legislation regarding marriage.

§ 4. *The College Student*

1. As we have already said, this is the time when the young person works out an integrated view of life. This involves a danger as far as the college student is concerned. Just at the time when he is capable of doing this, he must concentrate on (major in) some specialized field, one little area of life. This concentration can shut out other considerations regarding life in general. Enamored by the data and the methodology of his own field, he may disregard other important aspects of life.

2. It is most important that precautions be taken to forestall this eventuality. The student must not allow specialization to alienate him from the Faith, or restrict his range of interests.

3. To counteract this danger, many universities in various countries provide courses and seminars on vital topics (e.g., Newman Clubs). Where such opportunities are not available, it is up to the local pastor to look out for the needs of college students.

§ 5. *The Sociological Environment*

Young people in rural regions find it easier to reintegrate themselves into the social community and settle down. In big cities this is not so easy. The anonymity of city life forces young people to fall back on their own resources. They slip away from parochial life, and it is hard to reach them. There is a real danger that they will spend the rest of their life away from the Church. There is need for apostolic organizations such as the YCW to reach young people in various walks of life.

VI. SEXUAL DEVELOPMENT

A. BASIC CONSIDERATIONS

Up to now we have not given much attention to sexual development in the growth process. In this section we shall present an over-all view of this particular subject.

§ 1. *The Sex Drive*

The sex drive is part of man's corporeal nature and serves an important function. It insures the preservation and continuance of the human race. Like every human instinct, its proper use depends upon man's free will. Human beings can use or abuse it, and thus preserve or endanger the life of the family, the tribe, the race.

§ 2. *Sexual Morality*

The morality of sex is under the control of the *lex naturalis*, the natural law. It determines the proper function of the sex instinct and regulates its use. Anything contrary to its proper function is considered to be a disorder, hence, a sin.

There is no Catholic or Christian morality of sex. One can use the term only insofar as baptism adds a supernatural aspect to its use. The holiness of those in Christ's Mystical Body is abetted by the elevation of marriage to a sacrament. And Christianity preaches monogamous marriage, its indissolubility (which existed "in the beginning" [Mt. 19: 5] though it was not acknowledged by the Jews), the ideals of perpetual virginity. The precepts of Canon Law regarding sexual morality may be called the Church's doctrine on sex. But they are a codification of natural law precepts which have their own intrinsic validity.

§ 3. *Manner of Treatment*

In the following section (B) we shall discuss sexual development in the various growth stages, considering the following points: 1. the physiological aspect, 2. the accompanying psychological aspect, 3. the pertinent judgments of moral theology, 4. pastoral conclusions.

§ 4. *Terms and Concepts*

In treating the physiological aspects of sex we shall employ the following terms and concepts.

1. *Sex*—the disposition of all human beings marking them as either male or female from birth onward.

2. *Sex drive*—the innate instinct deriving from one's sex membership.

3. *Libido*—a term introduced by Freud to characterize the

spontaneous, uncontrolled expression of the sex instinct, prompted by the pleasure motive.

Sexual desire and the pleasure attached to it were implanted in man by the Creator as a stimulus to insure the preservation of the human race. It involves the mutual attraction of the two sexes. The pleasure is a purely functional one.

4. *Secretion*—the release of a glandular fluid which is either discharged from the organism (excretion) or directed into the blood stream (internal secretion).

5. *Exocrine glands*—have ducts and excrete substances (e.g., the sweat glands, salivary glands, digestive organs, sexual organs).

6. *Endocrine glands*, or *ductless* glands produce internal secretions called *hormones*. The hormones play a vital role in many areas of growth and development. They stimulate or arrest certain processes, heighten or lower the pace of various physiological activities. Some of the endocrine glands which are significant for our present discussion are the pineal gland (epiphysis), the pituitary glands (hypophysis), and the thymus gland.

B. IN THE GROWTH PROCESS

§ 1. *The Small Child*

At first glance one would think that this stage of development need not be considered from the viewpoint of sexuality. But since Freud made this developmental stage a keystone in his psychoanalytic theory, it, too, must be included in our treatment.

1. *Psycho-physical Considerations*

a) The sex instinct is present as a vague, diffuse sensation which is not yet canalized. Even in these years the sex glands are active, secreting hormones internally. But these hormones only serve the internal development of the body.

b) There is no indication that the young child feels any specifically sexual sensations. It is content when its hunger is satisfied, and discontent when it is not. Thumb-sucking is a carry-over from the days of breast-feeding. The thumb and the big toe become substitutes for the breast. A sexual interpretation of all this is an unwarranted assumption rooted in an adult viewpoint.

c) Even more obvious is the fact that the young child has no conscious awareness of sexual notions.

2. *Theological Considerations*

All the prerequisites for a moral act are absent. In the later years of this growth stage (3–6) the child does display a spontaneous "moral" attitude. He blushes when he is caught telling a lie. He "knows" that he is not to eat candy before dinner. Thus he does possess a spontaneous sense of shame. But all this is part of his native moral instinct, and no conscious deliberation is involved. There are no grounds for a theological judgment of moral guilt.

3. As their children's teachers, adults are responsible for instilling a sense of right and wrong and seeing to it that moral norms are obeyed. In this stage of life basic attitudes are instilled and the fundamental character traits are formed, regarding sex as well as everything else. What does this mean in practice?

a) The child unconsciously learns the meaning of good order or else remains undisciplined.

b) The child either remains a slave to his corporal instincts, or learns the value of self-control through proper training.

c) Right now the child will either develop a sense of modesty or grow up without it. There are many actions, morally indifferent in themselves, which have always been subject to the norms of modesty. Human beings possess a natural sense of shame. If parents let children relieve their needs in public, there is no moral issue involved as far as the child is concerned. But the early habit may have serious consequences for their conduct later on. It can dull their natural sense of modesty and become a moral danger for themselves and for those around them.

§ 2. *The School Child (Ages 7–10)*

1. *Physiological Considerations*

a) Internal secretion is taking place, but it is still directed toward the proper development of the bodily organism. No specifically sexual feelings are attached to it.

b) As yet the sex organs are not excreting sperm or ova. So the accompanying venereal pleasure—*delectatio venerea*—is also absent.

2. *Psychological Considerations*

a) The difference between the sexes is recognized in a vague, ingenuous way. Its significance, however, is not yet appreciated. It is camouflaged by the twofold function of the external sex organs. Indeed, this twofold function may insure the carefree ingenuousness so necessary for the child at this stage of life.

b) As a result, school children mingle freely with each other. There is no tension between the opposite sexes. If boys and girls stay mainly with members of their own sex, it is only because they want to imitate grown-ups. Or else it is due to boyhood "codes" and native girlish shyness.

c) To be sure, some children seem to be corrupted at an early age. They instigate shameless games without really knowing what is implied. Group membership, however, plays an important role in shaping moral attitudes at this age. So a few spoiled apples can lead the whole barrel into moral mischief.

d) The child's native sense of shame is the foundation for his moral conduct. The difference between the sexes goes unnoticed, or else it arouses curiosity and bashfulness. The child is being prepared for the future, and the danger of temptation is also present.

e) The child's moral conduct is determined by the standards of others (code morality). He has no real insight into the meaning and purpose of the moral order. Good and bad are determined by the commands and prohibitions of his elders.

f) When does the light begin to dawn? It may well happen in the last years of this developmental stage. But usually it comes at the beginning of pre-adolescence, when the youth is beginning to question things and look for correct answers. At first it is only a partial awareness. The mother's role is appreciated before the father's role. If there is a danger that the explanation may come from bad companions, parents and educators have a moral obligation to explain things themselves. Nowadays there are sound books on this whole subject.

3. *Theological Considerations*

Any moral judgment must be based on three factors. Objectively we must consider the *gravitas materiae*. Subjectively we must consider the *advertentia* (*plena*) and the *consensus* (*plenus*).

a) In the child's case there can be no *materia gravis*, i.e., no sin of *luxuria* (impurity), because as yet he is incapable of venereal pleasure. At most he may have a certain feeling of tenseness, curiosity, and shyness. In short, he may commit a sin against modesty.

b) As far as *advertentia* is concerned, the child is not yet able to appreciate the significance and seriousness of his immodest conduct.

c) As far as *consensus* is concerned, the child's curiosity is aroused by the whispered comments of adults and even more by their snide remarks and smirks. But he is hardly capable of committing a serious sin.

Analogous Situations: Can the child commit a "murder" at this age? Yes, objectively speaking. Can he commit a serious sin of theft or calumny? Yes, objectively speaking. But in all these cases, it is very doubtful whether the subjective prerequisites for a mortal sin are verified.

d) *Conclusions:*

1) The presumption is against the likelihood of a mortal sin being committed.

2) A sin of impurity is impossible.

3) Thus the word *impurity* should not be used in religion class at all. Instead, the word *immodesty* should be used. When the word *impurity* comes up, it should be explained in terms of modesty and immodesty.

4) Some children develop scruples because of faulty religious instruction. Even though they may get over these scruples later on, they are left with a bitter aftertaste which may turn them against confession for a long time to come.

§ 3. *Pre-Adolescence*

1. *Physiological Considerations*

a) Around the age of ten the pineal gland begins to slow up

its activity. Physiologically it is the central organ contributing to childhood development. And it plays an important role in inhibiting the rate of man's sexual development. But now it begins to relax its control over the sexual functions of the organism.

b) As a result, the period of calm development free from sexual tensions is at an end. The sex hormones begin to exert their influence on the organism.

2. *Psychological Considerations*

This growth stage foreshadows the great transition represented by puberty itself. The youth's growing hunger for knowledge and truth is evident in the area of sex too. In the days of childhood, dreams were an integral part of reality. Now dreams are clearly distinguished from reality. Fairy tales are no longer accepted, and "the stork" is relegated to the realm of make-believe. The young person has vague notions about many things, but he does not yet grasp their true nature and significance. As yet, he does not appreciate the seriousness of his newly acquired knowledge. His "negative" attitude (discussed earlier) crops up here also. Prohibitions arouse his curiosity, and he is tempted by the forbidden fruit. There is a real danger of seduction, and many regard it as a serious threat.

3. *Theological Considerations*

Any moral judgment on the child's conduct at this age must give due consideration to the important transition taking place and the uncertainty accompanying it.

a) *Gravitas materiae*

It is possible that the young person may experience venereal pleasure. In many cases, it is possible that the sex act can be performed. But it is questionable whether such an act would be motivated by venereal pleasure. Here we can only base our judgment on the average case. The priest should definitely avoid going into particulars.

b) *Advertentia* and *Consensus*

The young person cannot yet appreciate the gravity of his action. He has some inkling from the attitude of his parents and from his own curiosity. But his first reaction to the sexual impulses stirring within him is one of confusion and panic.
One cannot say for certain that the young person is yet capable of full, deliberate consent. The negative feelings he is experiencing put him under further moral pressure. It is at least questionable whether the young person can commit a mortal sin of impurity.

§ 4. *Sexual Impulses and Sexual Desire*

A brief consideration of these factors may clarify our comments in the previous sections and in the ones to come.

1. The sexual impulse, like other physiological impulses, is provoked and stimulated by nerval excitation.

a) The accumulation and forced retention of gonad secretion builds up physiological pressure in the organism. This pressure leads to the release (excretion) of the gonad secretion.

b) The other source of stimulation, more constant in its activity, is the internal secretion of hormones into the blood stream.

c) The sexual impulse, therefore, is a physiological reality experienced passively by the organism. It cannot be aroused or suppressed at will, not directly at least.

2. Sexual desire is a strong emotional feeling which takes hold of the organism. It cannot be shaken off at will. It is the

natural culmination of the sexual impulse. Again we are dealing with a passive experience endured by the organism. It is a powerful "*voluntarium*" (instinct) rooted in nature itself. We are not yet dealing with a free act, even though, in retrospect, the intensity of these feelings often confuses and disturbs the individual in his examination of conscience.

3. All this creates a general state of excitation which pervades the whole organism and occupies its attention. Since this state is provoked by internal physiological activity, it cannot be suppressed at will. A direct attack against this excitation may produce neurotic behavior. "When the sex hormones enter the blood stream, the young person is seized with a violent urge to sprout up into manhood or womanhood. But as yet the young person does not know how to direct his burgeoning powers into well regulated channels."[15] The question of morality does not yet enter the picture.

4. The question of moral responsibility crops up for the first time when the individual gives consent to these sexual desires (when he cannot squelch them), when he takes enjoyment in the accompanying of pleasure. But even here we are confronted with difficult questions. How much of this mood is determined by purely physiological factors which are outside the conscious control of the individual? At what precise point does free choice enter the picture? At what point is the young person physically unable to say no? In any case, one can hardly speak about "full consent" in situations where the prerequisites for "full knowledge or advertence" are absent.

5. *Conclusions:* We are confronted with a critical and potentially dangerous situation. But one must be very hesitant to judge that a serious sin has been committed. The priest and confessor can only clarify the situation—so he himself

[15] Friedrich von Gagern, *Die Zeit der geschlechtlichen Reife* (Frankfurt/M., 1952), p. 45.

must have a clear idea about it—offer comfort, and propose suitable diversions. He should never insist upon a direct frontal attack against these feelings. Not only is it useless; it can cause a psychic trauma which will do permanent damage to the individual. The young person needs advice, not reprimands. If the priest's advice seems useless, the young person may lose confidence in him.

Today there are good books and pamphlets on this subject for parents, priests, teachers, and the young people themselves. For parents and educators, there is, for example, Henry V. Sattler, C.SS.R., *Parents, Children and the Facts of Life* (Image Books: Doubleday and Co., New York). Its annotated bibliography suggests books which may well be given to young people as they are growing up.

§ 5. *Puberty (Adolescence)*

1. *Physiological Considerations*

a) The start of gonad secretion internally and externally is accompanied by feelings of venereal pleasure (*delectatio venerea*). The endocrine glands contribute to the development of the so-called secondary sex characteristics and to the internal and external transformation of the organism.

b) Sexual stimulation and excitability (erection of the sex organ) is conditioned by endocrine activity for the most part. At this stage there is little close contact with members of the opposite sex. Only later does this factor begin to produce inner unrest. This is the usual case in a morally ordered environment and applies particularly to girls. Indeed, in such an environment boys at this age often separate themselves deliberately from girls. But it is quite obvious that in many areas today the situation has changed greatly.

c) Sexual excitation (erection) can also be caused by external stimuli, e.g., by touching the erogenous zones of the body intentionally or unintentionally.

Sexual excitation produces the possibility of sexual intercourse. In practice legal medicine makes the following assumptions: the minimal age at which intercourse is possible is thirteen; the minimal age at which actual procreation is possible is fifteen; the minimal age at which conception is possible is thus around the age of thirteen.

d) There are only a few sexual disorders rooted in endocrine malfunction. Both represent extremes, and there is a large "grey" zone between.

Frigidity (*anhedonie*)—almost complete inability to feel sexual excitation or to be aroused sexually. In an evironment saturated with religious overtones the disorder is likely to be embodied in the chaste-weakling type—someone who is too meek and docile, too "good."

Hyperdonie is the other extreme. It is an overly strong susceptibility to sexual excitation. In its extreme forms it is a serious pathological condition. It is often accompanied by symptoms of feeble-mindedness and general psychic weakness. Most sex crimes are committed by the small percentage of people in this category. This fact should be kept in mind when one is reading statistics on sex crimes committed by teenagers.

e) To form a proper moral judgment on this whole question, one must take note of the distinction made by Albert Moll.[16] He pinpoints two distinct components within the sex drive.

Detumescence (*detumescere*—to cease swelling): the erection of the sex organ and the accompanying unrest call for relief. The usual and quickest means of relief is through ejaculation which relaxes the pressure on the organ.

Contraction: that part of the sex drive drawing male and female to the actual act of intercourse.

[16] Albert Moll, *Handbuch der Sexualwissenschaft,* 1926.

Experience would indicate that in an ordered environment the second function comes into play much later than the first. Indeed it may appear for the first time in adulthood. The difference between boys and girls in rate of development must be kept in mind. The girl's precociousness is balanced by her greater shyness and modesty.

Siegmund Freud notes two other components of the sex drive which are pathological in nature.

1. The compulsion towards *exhibitionism.*

2. The compulsion to inflict cruelty on others (sadism) or on oneself (masochism).

2. *Psychological Considerations*

In considering the psychological aspect of sexuality, we are concerned with the effect of physiological changes on the teenager's psychic life.

According to Theodor Ziehen[17] the teenager's psychic life is affected by these changes in two major ways. It is influenced by:

a) the new sensations in the genital zone "having no connection with heterosexual contacts at first"; *b*) the phantasies, produced by physiological stimuli, which frequently are concerned with the opposite sex.

a) *The New Sensations*

Question 1: Is the excitation of the sex organ itself accompanied by feelings of venereal pleasure, or is the pleasure attached to the elimination of this excitation? This leads to another important question: at what point do we have the "*appetitus delectationis venereae*" of which the moral theologians speak?

Answer: We are dealing with a type of excitation which arises spontaneously and imposes itself on the organism auto-

[17] Theodor Ziehen, *Das Seelenleben des Jugendlichen*, p. 14.

matically. It is "*voluntarium non liberum*." Indeed, the excitation may throw the adolescent into confusion. For many this excitation itself is well nigh overpowering and holds them in a vise-like grip. Freud speaks of such a state, in which the physical excitation itself focuses all the person's attention on the completion of act.

There is a point at which the whole process becomes a vicious circle. Certain stimuli produce certain responses which in turn serve as stimuli for other responses. Sexual sensations aroused by external stimuli may trigger endocrine reactions which in turn will produce new sensations.

Question 2: The desire to rid oneself of this excitation could hardly be regarded as a sin. But is self-induced relief a sin; and if so, how serious a sin is it? We find ourselves confronting the problem of masturbation.

We shall consider the theological aspects of the question later on. But according to the traditional moral view, masturbation must be regarded *objectively* as a grave sin (*materia gravis*). It is, according to St. Thomas, an offense against the "*modus conveniens*" and the "*ordo conveniens*."

Masturbation is an attempt to bring about self-induced relief from sexual tension. It is the self-stimulation of the sex organs for the purpose of enjoying the pleasure attached to ejaculation. It is "against nature" because human sex life of its very nature is orientated toward a relationship with someone else. In this view it is presumed that sexual excitation itself is something suspect. Moral theologians base their condemnation of masturbation on the following grounds. 1. The dissociation of carnal pleasure from true love. Legitimate sexual union, motivated by love, is reserved to those who are married. 2. The dissociation of carnal pleasure from spiritual values. 3. The dissociation of carnal pleasure from its natural function and purpose. 4. The danger of establishing a permanent behavior pattern.

In this treatment we are using the term commonly employed by psychologists. In recent times some have coined new terms to pinpoint the essential nature of the act. Havelock Ellis introduced the term *autoeroticism,* and E. Bleuler used the term *ipsation.*

We must depend upon medical statistics for information on the frequency of acts of masturbation. If the statistics are accurate, they are alarming. H. Rohleder[18] claims that eighty-five to ninety-six per cent of all teenagers masturbate, at least occasionally. His data agree with the finding of an English school doctor, Duke, who puts the rate of incidence between ninety and ninety-five per cent. A Catholic neurologist, Friedrich von Gagern,[19] draws the following conclusion: "The high rate of incidence leads one to say that the non-masturbator is the exception!" This psychopathologist, who is a Catholic himself and had a book published by a Catholic firm, can only say: "Many psychologists have strong reservations when they discover that an adult man scarcely masturbated at all during adolescence. 'Isn't sexual repression a typical symptom of a neurotic personality?' they ask." In short, the non-masturbator would be the abnormal case.

These statistics and opinions come from doctors who deal with sick people. Now let us quote the opinion of a Catholic doctor (not a moral theologian) who is also a psychiatrist and director of St. Urban's Sanatorium in Switzerland. Dr. F. Decurtius writes: "Adolescent masturbation is a visible expression (!) of the sexual transition taking place. If it is not practiced to excess, it is not abnormal or pathological. Nor will it cause grave physical or psychic disturbances. For certain people with certain psychic make-ups it can produce neurotic symptoms of a physical (heart palpitation, trembling) or psychological (depression, fear, inferiority feelings) nature."[20]

[18] H. Rohleder, *Sexualphysiologie* (Hamburg, 1923).

[19] Von Gagern, *op. cit.,* p. 119.

[20] *Gesundes Geschlechtsleben.* A collection of articles edited by a pastoral theologian (Dr. Franz v. Hornstein) and a doctor (Dr. A. Faller). Both are

Thus theologians and pastoral ministers are confronted with a new body of data compiled by experts. They must produce counter-evidence or else draw the proper conclusions.

Let us take the following tentative position:

a) The objective investigator and the pastoral minister who deals with this phenomenon, must respect the testimony of competent, trustworthy doctors. This testimony should serve as the basis for a re-consideration and re-evaluation of the whole question.

b) One should not overlook the fact that these views are also a reaction against the exaggerations of an earlier day, especially regarding the consequences of masturbation. Doctors are concerned with their own sphere of competence.

c) I would have strong reservations against regarding the masturbator as the normal case (even in a purely statistical sense) and the non-masturbator as abnormal.

d) The wise counselor of youth will not expect too much from his lectures on sex education. The subject must be dealt with; but the adolescent will have proportionally less trouble if there is not too much said about the matter. To repeat once again, the adolescent who cherishes high ideals will not find himself in the same tight spot as someone who is obsessed with his immediate problems.

In any case, it is clear that the pastoral minister is confronted with a problem which deserves close re-consideration. He will be able to form a wiser opinion if he distinguishes between the various types of masturbation.

a) Masturbation may be rooted in the confusion and introversion accompanying adolescent development. The

---

from the Catholic University in Freiburg, Switzerland. The book bears the Imprimatur of Bishop Franz von Streng (November 15, 1949), who also contributed to the anthology.

young person feels lonely and misunderstood. He escapes into the world of daydreams. After experiencing the physical pleasure attached to masturbation, he may have fits of depression in which life itself seems futile. "He finds himself unable to cope with life and his own problems" (F. Decurtius). Masturbation is as much a cause of spiritual unrest (guilty conscience) as a by-product of the same. Sex instruction does not help. Often it merely serves to focus more attention on the source of his distress. The proper remedy is provided by healthy companionship with other teenagers—sports, social activities, high ideals, personal responsibility.

b) Masturbation may become an obsession because the pedagogue puts too much stress on the problem and its ramifications. Some preachers love to dwell on the subject. Thus they foster an unhealthy concentration on sex and reinforce the tendency to masturbate.

c) Masturbation may be stimulated accidentally by some illness or medical treatment. The patient may be seeking relief from urinary malfunction or some other irritation. It is best not to pay too much attention to this type of masturbation.

d) Masturbation may serve as a substitute for visible manifestations of resentment. The child of melancholic temperament, who sees the outside world as his enemy, may work out his frustration vicariously through acts of masturbation. It is his way of getting revenge on a heartless world.

e) Masturbation may be compulsive in certain individual cases. A congested prostate gland may cause acute discomfort and make mental work almost impossible. The impulse to detumescence (see above, p. 242) may also cause acute discomfort without any "*appetitus delectationis venereae*" being attached. This applies principally to adult bachelors and married men who must practice continence for some good reason. In forming a theological judgment on such cases, one must treat the person not only sympathetically, but also fairly.

f) The danger latent in all these types of masturbation is the possibility of forming a permanent behavior pattern, a vicious habit of masturbation. Thus the problem cannot be taken lightly. Habitual masturbation does not lead to the consequences predicted by the moralists of an earlier day. But it does affect the physical and psychic life of the individual, inhibiting normal development.

g) When masturbation is part of a neurosis complex, it belongs entirely within the sphere of the medical man.

b) *Adolescent Phantasies*

a) These phantasies may be stimulated by endocrine activity. Or they may be rooted in elements buried deep in the unconscious—personal memories or traumatic experiences. At this stage of life the adolescent is involved in a quiet but eager search for knowledge. He leafs through encyclopedias and other books to get more precise information. The most troublesome sources of these phantasies are previous seduction, rape, and, worse still, incestuous experience. Licentiousness, such as that which was rampant at the end of World War II, remains clearly embedded in the minds of young people. Even an instructional piece (e.g., a film about syphilis) intended to forewarn the adolescent, is seldom received in that spirit. It becomes a stimulus for new phantasies.

b) The adolescent's shyness and discomfort with members of the opposite sex are a natural means of self-defense. If it breaks down too soon, the consequences can be disastrous. In its noblest form, it is represented by *Eros*, a pure love for everything good and beautiful (even a beautiful girl). This kind of love is not dangerous. The pages of literature and biography are filled with accounts of a young man's platonic love for some nice girl who seemed to correspond to his ideals of goodness and beauty. Such a relationship can be a great help in overcoming moral dangers and temptations.

A person who never experienced this kind of love missed a great treasure and will always be poorer for it. When sexual desires take the place of this Eros, they are at best a poor substitute. And they often cause a psychic trauma which is least appreciated when it is most serious.

3. *Theological Considerations*

Practical experience clearly indicates that countless adolescents fall away from the Church because they feel that her representatives do not understand them. If we pursue this problem further, it becomes evident that this lack of understanding is evident in two areas: 1. the priest makes moral judgments which take into account only the objective criterion (*materia gravis*); 2. the priest uses a theological casuistry which confuses and perplexes the teenager—and many others.

A) Objectively speaking, every sin against purity "in thought, word, and deed" is *materia gravis*, hence, a mortal sin.

Before the time of St. Thomas Aquinas, theologians were inclined to regard sexual feelings themselves as sinful. According to Caesarius of Arles one was not permitted to receive Holy Communion after a "*pollutio nocturna.*" And later on we read that the person in question had to do penance, fast, and give alms before he could receive. This severe outlook is based not only on the influence of Old Testament laws of purification, but also on the example of St. Augustine and St. Jerome. The former was terrified by his own past, while the latter disciplined his rebellious nature with a harsh asceticism. St. Jerome did not dare to enter a church after a wet-dream. Venerable Bede writes: "Someone who experiences a pollution against his will [!] . . . should do penance for seven days, recite fifty psalms, and fast on Wednesday and Friday." Only St. Athanasius, a pupil of Antonius the desert Father and a renowned ascetic, had a sensible outlook on reactions which are completely beyond the control of human will.

St. Thomas introduced an important distinction which opened up the whole question. Taking pleasure in things that are good and permissible is good; taking pleasure in things that are evil and forbidden is bad. In short, pleasure itself is morally indifferent.

B) Now we must examine the subjective moral criteria: 1. full knowledge or advertence; 2. deliberate consent.

a) The ability to make a free decision is challenged by strong obstacles in this area. This fact must be kept in mind if we are to form a correct judgment.

I. We are confronted with a basic psycho-spiritual condition stemming from nature itself and preceding any intellectual act of knowing or willing. In forming a judgment we must distinguish between the "*voluntarium*" of instinct and the "*liberum*" of free choice.

Next to the instinct for self-preservation, the sex instinct is the strongest.

Sexual excitation (erection) flows naturally from the accumulation of gonad secretion. The accompanying sexual impulses also arise naturally. This is true in the case of man too.

The sexual impulse can heighten in intensity and become sexual desire occupying all the attention of consciousness. The same degree of excitation can also be caused by hormone secretion into the bloodstream. "The sex hormones act directly to cause erections by lowering the threshold of response.

The erections which normally take place at the start of puberty indicate that the pace of hormone secretion has stepped up."[21]

The result is a considerable diminution of the power of the individual's intellect and free will. "Medically we know that feelings of sexual tension adversely affect the activity of the cerebral cortex, the control center of the intellectual processes. Detumescence can be a much stronger drive than the instinct for self-preservation . . . The mind can be overwhelmed by the sex drive to the point where it is more or less incapable of thinking calmly and clearly."[22] The power of free choice may become almost completely disabled. Gagern remarks: "Even when a man knows that the woman has a highly communicable disease such as syphilis, he may be unable to restrain himself from intercourse. The sexual tension is too strong . . . It is quite clear to us that in moments of intense sexual excitement the ability to exercise free choice is greatly curtailed."[23]

II. It is very important to appreciate the dynamism of sexual excitation. Erection is a reflex activity. 1. It can take place automatically and spontaneously 2. without any conscious act of the will. Indeed, it is quite possible that even the physiological precondition required for a conscious act of the will may not be present. If the erection of the sex organ is prompted by endocrine activity, it is produced by the action of specific parasympathetic (*nervi erigentes*) nerves located in the spinal cord. The cerebral cortex may not play a role in regulating this excitation. In such cases, the sexual erection is not initiated or produced by a conscious act, because the stimuli do not pass through the cerebral cortex.

The reflex response may be produced by three types of stimuli.

[21] *Ibid.*, 235.

[22] Von Gagern, *op. cit.*, p. 162; Hornstein-Faller, *op. cit.*, p. 235.

[23] Erwin Wexberg, *Einfuehrung in die Psychologie des Geschlechtslebens* (Leipzig, 1930), p. 17. Trans. *The Psychology of Sex: An Introduction* (New York: Farrar & Rinehart, 1931).

1. External stimuli. a) Some stimulus affects one or more of the five senses; b) it is transmitted to the nerve-control center (brain); c) the sensation is felt; d) then it is perceived consciously; e) the sensation is then transmitted to the nerves producing an erection; f) the arteries leading to the sex organ are opened; g) the sensation is transmitted to the sex organ, exciting the glands and muscles.

2. Internal stimuli. a) Endocrine secretion or the accumulation of gonad secretion may act as the stimulus. b) The stimulus is transmitted directly to the parasympathetic nerves (*nervi erigentes*) without passing through the brain. Thus the erection takes place without any conscious act of awareness or will.

3. Psychic stimuli. a) Dreams, lectures, memory images originating in the cerebral cortex, may act as stimuli b) which are transmitted to the sex organ through the parasympathetic nerves.

Only in cases 1 and 3 can the intellect and will play a role.

III. In attempting to form a moral judgment on this question, we must note the following important distinction. We can treat the question in terms of the objective moral order, working on fundamental principles which are universally valid and unquestionable. These principles as such do not take individual cases into account.

But besides this, we can examine the biological mechanisms at work when a person is in a state of sexual excitation. In such a state a person's "*advertentia*" is fully preoccupied. Overpowered with the intensity of the sexual feelings, he feels that masturbation is the only way to get relief. It seems to be quite legitimate. There is a correspondence between the reflex mechanism of sexual excitation and the general biological condition of the excited person.

b) *Summary*

What was said above would indicate that "*advertentia*

plena" is interfered with. In extreme cases it is hardly present at all. Insofar as we are dealing with a purely reflex dynamism, advertence does not enter the picture at all. It is worth noting that many people, after committing acts of masturbation, wonder how they could have done such a thing. Once the state of excitation has been relieved, rational control and moral norms take over once again. It is a case of *conscientia consequens*, post-factum pangs of conscience. These do not concern themselves with the morality of a certain action or behavior pattern. As yet the adolescent does not fully appreciate the seriousness of his actions or the demands of personal responsibility. The uncertainty and confusion of this period must be kept in mind. When sexual impulses bypass the brain and work directly on the *nervi erigentes*, the physiological prerequisites for *advertentia* are really lacking.

The presence or absence of advertentia helps to settle the question of *consensus*. The priest must constantly remember the important distinction between the *voluntarium* of instinctual drives and the *liberum* of free choice. Sexual excitation cannot be suppressed by an act of the will. The advice of many confessors, urging teenagers to fight directly against these impulses, can cause serious neuroses. A psychiatrist once told me: "It is a sad fact that most neurotic teenagers come from Catholic families." A person cannot fight directly against a condition which is impervious to correction by acts of the will. One can only advise the teenager to distract himself with other activities and ideas which will occupy his full attention.

c) *Counseling the Teenager*

The priest should advise the teenager to avoid external sources of sexual excitation insofar as this is possible. In short, the teenager must avoid all deliberate occasions (*occasio voluntaria*) of sin. He should devote his attention to absorbing mental and spiritual pursuits.

During moments of actual excitation, only indirect counteraction is possible. The teenager should focus his attention on something else which interests him. He must nurture some high ideal, which will protect him from sinning. His heroic qualities must be tapped. The Catholic Youth Movement has succeeded in doing this by proposing high ideals to its members: Christian manhood, beauty, truth. And there is much to be said for the old student sodalities with their Knights of Mary. The sad fact is that today the outside world and the educational process itself offers no high ideals to its young people. Profits and standards of living are not ideals.

Teenagers must lead a healthy physical life—good food, proper clothing, recreation, avoidance of drunkenness and dope addiction. And this must be supported by a sound religious life centered around participation in the sacramental life of the Church. A teenager who lives such a life will not be overpowered by sensual allurements.

What advice should be given to the teenager who commits acts of masturbation? Utilizing the distinction between detumescence and contraction (see above, p. 242), many regard the typical case of adolescent masturbation (p. 251, a) as a desperate attempt to relieve an unbearable state of tension. Thus, in their view, there is no "*appetitus delectationis venereae*" objectively or subjectively speaking. But it is a most difficult matter. "The psychotherapist encounters more than a few cases of masturbation in which he would like to advise the confessor to tell the penitent not to confess these acts any more, though he might well repent having committed them." This is the comment of a good Catholic psychiatrist, Friedrich von Gagern. Theologically, it is based on the conviction that one cannot speak of mortal sin in such cases of adolescent masturbation.

This advice must not be followed as a general rule of thumb. Indeed, it is not intended as such. Why? Because it is difficult to determine whether a given "*pollutio voluntaria*" resulted from frantic urge to relieve endocrine pressure (detumescence). And that is what von Gagern is referring to. Furthermore, if this advice were offered indiscriminately, it could convey the impression that masturbation is a *res indifferens.* It might encourage an habitual behavior pattern.*

But dire threats and warnings are not the proper corrective approach either. Pius X recommended frequent Holy Communion as the "*divinum pharmacum.*" Yet it is not to be regarded merely as something contributing to better morals. In the hierarchy of spiritual values the opposite would be more accurate. And, of course, it is no substitute for a thorough-going moral training.

C. St. Thomas' View

a) Traditionally, moral theology makes a distinction between the sin of impurity and the sin of immodesty. According to the texts the former is objectively "*peccatum mortale* ex *genere suo toto.*" In short, there cannot be any *parvitas materiae.* Every sin against purity, in thought, word, or deed, is a mortal sin. However, sins against modesty may be objectively venial. There can be parvity of matter in this area, that is, in certain kinds of embraces, certain kinds of dress.

b) Regarding the subjective criteria (advertence and consent), St. Thomas first lays down a fundamental principle (S. Th. 1, 2, q. 73, a. 6 corr.): "*Diminuitur autem peccatum ex causis, quae vel judicium rationis vel liberum voluntatis motum diminuunt.*" The gravity of the sin is diminished to the ex-

* Censor's note: It is important to state that any lessening of subjective guilt should be judged in each individual case and that the confessor must always recall that Pope Pius XII in an address to Italian Catholic Action on Sunday, March 23, 1952, on the Christian conscience clearly rejected the opinion that would assert that as a general rule masturbation was not a grave sin on the part of the subject. Thus Pope Pius XII asserted: "We reject, therefore, as erroneous the affirmation of those who regard lapses as inevitable in the adolescent years, and therefore as not worthy of being taken into serious consideration—as if they were not grave faults because, they add, as a general rule, passion destroys the liberty requisite if an act is to be morally imputable." AAS, 44 (1952), 275.

tent that rational awareness and free consent are diminished. St. Thomas then goes on to say (*ibid.*, Resp.): 1. "*Unde causae, quae diminuunt judicium rationis sicut ignorantia,* 2. *vel quae diminuunt liberum motum voluntatis sicut infirmitas,* 3. *vel violentia aut metus, aut aliquid hujusmodi, diminuunt peccatum sicut* (insofar as) *diminuunt voluntatem,* 4. *intantum quod si actus sit omnino involuntarius, non habent rationem peccati.*"

c) Conclusion: Applying these principles to our present question, we would reach the following conclusions. Every sin against sexual morality is objectively mortal sin (*materia gravis*). But subjectively such an act may only be a venial sin. 1. if rational awareness (advertence) is diminished (at the moment of acting), 2. if the freedom of the will is restricted (e.g., by the intensity of the instinctual drive). Finally, 3. if advertence and free will are absent for all practical purposes (*actus hominis*), then there is no question of sin at all, not even a venial one. Only an *actus humanus*, one produced by reason and free will, can be morally culpable.

These principles would indicate that a considerable number of sins of this type cannot be regarded as mortal sins. And this conclusion has no connection with any formulation based on situation ethics, a philosophical view which denies the existence of an objective moral order.

§ 6. *First Love and Romance*

1. *The Significance of Eros*

It is questionable whether the following observations correspond to present-day realities. Perhaps they do in many cases. But in any case the pastoral minister has a duty to appreciate the beauty of pure young love and to preserve it from moral dangers.

In the normal course of events there comes a point in early

adulthood when the young person feels the first stirrings of love toward a person of the opposite sex. It is a pure love (Eros) to which sexual feelings are indirectly attached to a greater or lesser degree.

b) This experience is of great importance to personal development and one's later life. It is part of the wonder of youth and has been a favorite topic for poets and minstrels down through the ages. The words in the *Imitation of Christ* about love for God, apply here also: "*Homo fervidus et diligens ad omnia est paratus*" (1, 25, 46). Pure love preserves and protects the lover. In wartime many people stay chaste and pure for the sake of some loved one far away.

c) If the individual misses this experience, there will be a void in his life which can never be filled. This is especially true of girls.

d) This grand experience in all its wonder and purity can only be experienced once. The second time around it does not have the same depth. Young people must be told this. They will understand. Amorous flirtations only spoil the whole thing. H. Timmerding regards this once-in-a-lifetime experience as "the model and the natural basis for monogamous marriage, because under ordinary circumstances this experience only occurs once."[24]

2. *True Love*

The pages of literature are filled with accounts of this type of love. Perhaps the greatest literary testament is Dante's *Vita Nuova* (Chapters 2 and 15).

a) The individual in love is highly sensitive to every stimulus which emanates from the beloved one. He yearns to be in her presence, to look at her and listen to her. He is captivated by the slightest contact.

[24] H. Timmerding, *Sexualethik* (Leipzig, 1913), p. 50

b) The young person finds himself totally preoccupied with thoughts of his beloved. Letters fly back and forth. He may even find himself unable to work properly.

c) In addition, the young person has an urge to become a new man. He feels that life has just begun for the first time. Young men become eloquent poets, and girls write volumes in their diaries.

d) Even the most reserved people now find countless things to talk about.

e) The lover may see only the good qualities and graces of his beloved, even where others see no such thing. He must not become blind to her bad points.

f) The beloved can almost cast a spell over the lover. Anything which comes between them becomes an object of hate. This can lead the lover into a dangerous type of bondage.

g) At this point, precisely when feelings of true love begin to lose their edge, jealousy can set in. One party begins to fear that this happy state of affairs may not last. It is the beginning of the end.

3. *Forming Moral Judgments*

We are dealing with an experience which has no parallel in later life. And it is only appreciated by those who experience it. Onlookers only laugh. Timmerding[25] compares it to seasickness because only the afflicted take it seriously. Hence it is a good idea to go slowly in passing judgments on this whole matter. Here we are not discussing sexual urges divorced from any feelings of true love.

[25] *Ibid.*, p. 49.

PART THREE: MAN, WOMAN, AND THE FAMILY

I. MAN AND WOMAN

§ *1. The Two Sexes*

The two sexes of mankind give the human race a place among the other living organisms who are subject to this law of nature. Indeed, many see an analogy in the cosmos as a whole, or even regard this as a basic cosmic principle. The ancient cosmologies took as their starting point the duality of the sexes and their ultimate union. According to these systems this duality had a mystical, symbolic origin and was rooted in the tension and complementarity between mind (man) and body (woman). This is the view expressed in Hesoid's *Theogony*. The Greek pair, *helios-gaia* (sun-earth), is paralleled by Indian *parush-praktri* and Chinese *yang-yin*. According to these myths man represents the principle of spirit and woman the principle of matter. Many ancient emblems symbolize the relation between them. Thus, for example, the symbol ♂ represents man, while the symbol ♀ represents woman.

1. *Psychological Significance*

a) No single factor exerts such an influence on our personal life as our sex. All other environmental and hereditary influences (race, religion, education) take second place and have less effect upon our mental outlook and our behavior. And it must be noted that the physical differences between the sexes are far less important than the psychic differences.

This must be kept in mind if we are to appreciate the deeper significance of sex differences in human life and activity.

b) Carl Gustav Carus (1789–1869), the well-known friend of Goethe, spoke about a polar tension between man and woman. He expressed it in terms of an opposition between *consciousness* (man) and *unconsciousness* (woman). Thus we find the following contrasts between them.

Man	*Woman*
a) Self-assurance, freedom, subjectivity, action.	*a*) Closer to the mystery of life and affected by it.
b) Tends to have a dogmatic, critical attitude toward religion.	*b*) More "natural" in outlook and hence has a healthier relationship to God, the source of everything.
c) Reason is his guide. So he is in danger of being coldly rational, obstinate, eccentric.	*c*) She has a deep-rooted orientation toward vitality, openness, and sympathy.

c) Animus-Anima (C. G. Jung)

Despite his predilection and concern for archetypal symbols, both [*animus-anima*] are *empirical concepts,* "unconscious elements which have been engraved into the living organism since the dawn of time and transmitted from generation to generation." *Anima* is the psychic nature of woman as it has seeped into the collective unconscious of man. *Animus*, the psychic nature of man, is the sum of experiences which woman has exerted on man since the dawn of time.

In all these theories man and woman are directed toward each other and complement one another.

2. *Man*

He represents the solar principle. He is the embodiment of the spirit, the creative being, the master of history.

a) In man the sexual drive coexists alongside his work in life. And yet he seems to be more excitable than the female in sexual matters. He is more excitable because otherwise he might lose interest in the purpose of the sexual function, the preservation of the species. His general outlook is more individualistic and aggressive.

b) The man tends to minimize the significance of the sex drive for his personal development.

1. As a philosopher, scientist, or ascetic, his intellectual interests may take up his full attention. He devotes his life to his work, deliberately abstaining from sexual indulgence. The vital forces of instinct are channeled into his work. His work is his whole life. Herein lies the motive behind celibacy. "He who is unmarried is concerned about the things of the Lord, how he may please God. Whereas he who is married is concerned about the things of the world, how he may please his wife; and he is divided" (1 Cor. 7: 32–33).

2. More usually he regards sex as something which could not inflict a mortal blow. So he gives in to his instincts and leads a double life. But it soon becomes apparent that these forces are interfering with his intellectual keenness as well. Some philosophers succumbed to sexual drives and completely reversed their philosophical position.

3. Sex cannot be an essential part of his life's work (as motherhood can be for the woman), and yet he finds himself more prone to the stimulation of instinctual drives. So it is easier for him to end up on the wrong track. He may play the love-game, having one affair after another, or being unfaithful to his wife. And he may offer the flimsy excuse that man is "naturally polygamous."

4. One tragic conflict between husband and wife is rooted in this tension between male and female outlooks. The man devotes his life to his calling, his job, his social re-

sponsibilities. The woman tries to tie him to herself and the family. She suffers from loneliness; he, from lack of understanding. This is the one genuine marital problem. And it is rooted in the tension between the man's natural psychic drives and his obligations as a husband. The spats between Socrates and his wife Xantippe are a classic illustration of the problem.

5. Another tragic situation is the opposite extreme. The man gives in completely to the woman. He becomes the henpecked husband, the scapegoat for every misfortune. He betrays his essential mission in life (Antony and Cleopatra). Thais, a Greek courtesan, incited Alexander to burn the citadel of Persepolis, the residence of the Persian kings. This was against his policies, but in a drunken stupor he acceded to her request.

3. *Woman*

She represents the telluric, chthonic (*tellus, chthōn*= *earth*) principle.

a) She is ordered toward motherhood. Thus the sex instinct is a more integrated part of her life, more natural. But here, too, there seems to be a contradiction. For although instinctively she is more orientated toward sexual mating, she is not as excitable as the male. She is more sensual than he, but in an innocent way. This is often a danger, not for her, but for the man. An amorous overture, which a woman makes quite dispassionately, can be an occasion of sin for him. The ideals proposed to woman are the beauty of motherhood and the divine nobility of virginity.

To counteract the potential danger stemming from woman's sensual disposition, God has gifted her with a stronger sense of modesty and shame.

b) The power of woman's earthy temperament can sometimes make her the master, although nature did not intend her to be. Man, instead of being the master, becomes the slave of a woman, e.g., of a prostitute, a mistress. History presents many examples. In such cases, a woman, who is meant to personify true love in all its grandeur, becomes the devil's instrument.

§ 2. *A Study in Contrast*

Preliminary Remarks

1. In contrasting male and female outlooks, we shall examine the three psychic operations which are distinguished from each other in traditional scholastic philosophy.

2. We can only note typical differences. In a given individual case they may not be verified at all.

3. We shall not consider anomalous cases which seem to contradict the general rule, e.g., the effeminate man or the mannish woman.

4. Still less will we comment on intelligence. Where possible, we shall indicate the effect of the different outlooks on religious attitudes and behavior.

5. The following comments are general observations on human nature which serve as a basis for pastoral guidance. But each case deserves individual attention.

1. *Thinking*

Man	*Woman*
a) A man's thoughts are concerned with general concepts, abstract ideas, universals.	a) A woman is concerned with concrete realities, appearances, individual items.

He tends to be more objective and realistic.

She has a "sixth" sense and is more subjective in judging.

He questions the meaning and purpose of something. Reasons and intellectual considerations are important.

She wonders about the effect of something on her, judges according to the impression something makes on her—good or bad.

Quarrels between a man and woman frequently lead the exasperated man to exclaim: "It's impossible to talk to you." Each is talking on a different plane: there is no real meeting of the minds.

b) A man lives for some idea which he regards as correct.

b) A woman follows the propounder of some idea and relies on him.

He is more stubborn, more fanatic, less guided by instincts.

She is more secure in her instinctive reactions (Carus). Reasons do not concern her as much.

c) In considering some event, a man wonders about its cause and its significance.

c) A woman is interested in the details of what took place.

In discussing a newspaper report men are interested in reactions to it. They discuss its potential good or bad effects.

Women are interested in what the newspaper said about various things—fashions, society news.

d) A man looks beyond the present moment.

d) A woman is quite prone to the influence of the moment.

e) In distinguishing between various things, differences are seen as oppositions.

e) For a woman, oppositions tend to become merely differences. "The opposing items stand, not beside each other but behind each other, on two different levels of consciousness" (Franz Zimmermann).

Either-or

A man tends to exaggerate, to go to an extreme.

Both-and

A woman is more conciliatory, more humane.

A man abstracts and simplifies, puts things into pigeonholes: e.g., The enemy.	A woman feels the injustice of such simplifications because she is more human in outlook.
A man takes a stand. He has a point of view.	A woman sees the relativity involved.
f) Man is the active procreator.	*f*) Woman is the receiver. She is sympathetic.
Man is the creative being. There are many more men in the ranks of the great poets, artists, and scholars.	Woman is understanding, stimulating, exciting. Few women are represented in these fields, and they are not in the ranks of the great.
In areas where feelings and spirit count, men are more productive, e.g., music, poetry.	A woman is richer in personal experience.
Even women's fashions are created by men . . .	And yet women accept them.

2. *Willing*

a) Intensity: a man puts everything into a given project.	a) Perseverance: a woman keeps going at a task.
A man is ready to die for something.	A woman is ready to go on living for something, and this is more difficult.

Talk about the "weaker sex" is nonsense. Each sex is strong in a different area.

A man proves himself by responding to the challenge of the moment.	A woman proves herself by her persistence and endurance.

Females hold on to life more tenaciously than males. More boys are born than girls, but more girls live.

War is a man's business.	Women tend the wounded, the men who have been struck down.
Men have stronger nerves and can master the moment.	Women are subject to the attack of the moment.

In a fireworks display or some such event, the ratio for fainting spells is one man to ten women.

b) Fearful of suffering

b) Able to bear suffering

This shows up even in the area of pathology.

The typical male malady is hypochondria, excessive concern for health.

The typical female malady is hysteria (*hustera=womb*), a passionate mania about pathological symptoms designed to draw attention to herself.

c) Manly heroism is embodied in the warrior, the hero of action, and the great ascetic, the hero of contemplation (Julio Evola). Both have a natural distrust of women.

c) A woman's heroism lies in her fidelity, her love, her helpfulness, as a wife or a virgin dedicated to some high ideal.

Men tend to form clubs, fraternities.

Historically this does not seem true of women.

After his conversion, St. Augustine set out to found a Christian community with his friends.

It collapsed because of the intense opposition of his friends' wives.

Many traditional folksongs tell about deep friendships between men.

No parallel exists in the annals of female relationships.

Women are naturally jealous of one another.

Women do not care to go to female doctors. They regard them as too coarse. The antipathy disappears only if the doctor, too, is a wife and mother.

d) Men like the taste of open confrontation. They rely on their strength and valor.

d) Women try to get what they want in a roundabout way. "Woman's secret mastery over the course of history . . ." (Bernanos).

Danger rouses his courage.

Danger upsets her.

She relies on her own shrewdness and man's foibles. "There is scarce any evil like that in a woman" (Sir. 25: 18).

e) Man's honor rests upon his reputation in public life. He needs this external respect and esteem.

e) A woman's honor rests upon her success as, e.g., a housewife. Her social reputation depends upon her fidelity as a wife or a virgin.

This can be a danger for him and his character development. It may be purely external respect. He may be too worried about being exposed or about even the most unjustified ridicule.

His timidity in matters of religion stems from this need for external respect. In public ceremonies he wants either a place of honor or else the security provided by the presence of other men.

A woman is usually bolder in religious practice. Why? 1. She is not so concerned about public esteem; 2. she is not taken too seriously in the public arena; 3. toward her, even enemies are more courteous, at least more defenseless; 4. she is bolder in this area because she follows the religious leader, the priest.

f) The workings of man's conscience involve perception of the moral order and assent to its demands. His most frequent conflict is between the demands of reason and the demands of instinct.

f) A woman is more naturally incorporated into the moral order. God's will (the Commandments) is her support and her protection.

g) A man tends toward moral "self-determination." He judges

g) The woman leans toward "spiritual guidance." If she falls according to his own lights, and he does not care for spiritual guidance, because subjection to another is difficult to accept.

He is more willing to subject himself to another 1. where the law of community is still at work; 2. if he submits of his own free will (e.g., in a religious Order); if he appreciates the need for discipline and subordination (military life).

outside the order, she still lingers on the perimeter. She lives "more naturally, beyond good and evil." If she freely chooses to make herself subject to some Order, she finds it easier to offer "blind obedience."

h) Where there is a conflict, a man defends his position against the Order by offering pretexts, usually by pointing out the need for prudence and discretion. His way seems wiser, more enlightened, more down-to-earth.

h) A woman's actions are more instinctive than a man's. Frequently she does not feel any guilt and wonders "What have I done that's so terrible?" It's not that she has done anything; rather, she has given free rein to her inner feelings.

i) A man becomes bad or irreligious by making a deliberate decision. In this way he justifies his course of action in his own eyes.

i) A woman simply drops the support she was clinging to. Thus her wicked action seems more malicious. She can perform wicked acts "in good conscience." "Wickedness changes a woman's looks, and makes her sullen as a female bear" (Sir. 25: 16).

j) A man is also able to lead a double life, playing with sex without feeling any moral uneasiness.

j) A woman can live two contradictory types of conduct. Sonya, in *The Brothers Karamazov*, became a prostitute out of compassion for her family. Yet she inveighed against murder as an offense against God, urged Raskolnikov to confess, and accompanied him to Siberia.

However, for a man every action is a deliberate step. So there are always guilt-feelings attached. But he can work off these feelings in time.
(Both men and women are able to work off such feelings. There is no distinctive contrast on this score.)

In Claudel's *Satin Slipper* Proeza offers this prayer: "Virgin Mother, take my slipper. Virgin Mother, protect my wretched foot in your hand. I tell you right now that in a little while I shall see you no more, that I am going to do everything contrary to you."

For a woman the heart is the deciding factor. She may even choose to do evil out of compassion for someone. In *The Brothers Karamazov* Svidrigailov says: "When a girl's heart is pained by something, she is in great danger."

3. *Acting*

a) A man acts according to his conscious deliberation, following reasons as he sees them.

a) A woman acts according to her instincts, following her heart, be it good or bad.

b) A man stands back somewhat from the situation in which he is involved, e.g., the soldier in battle, the surgeon in an operation.

b) A woman tends to be engulfed by the situation. She is not well suited for battle or surgical practice. As a judge, she would tend to have too much sympathy for the pleas of the defendant.

c) His place is the public arena, his occupation. His occupation can become his whole life, a religion in itself.

He is concerned with justice and might. He is tough-skinned.

c) Her place is the family, where she can attain complete self-fulfillment.

She is kind-hearted, compassionate, helpful.

While men dragged our Lord to Golgotha . . .	the women wept and had someone offer him a strong drink so that he would not feel the full shock of the crucifixion.
(Bystanders permitted this act of kindness. Even the executioners respected it.)	(Our Lord took a sip so as not to hurt their feelings, then set the jar aside . . . a perfect example of his tactfulness.
According to "*Casti Connubii*" (Pius XI) man is "the head of the family."	Woman is "the heart of the family."

4. Pastoral Considerations

a) Pastoral ministers must not be tempted to fit every individual case into the schema outlined above.

b) Its sole purpose is to help him in understanding a given situation.

c) Some psychologists reject the validity of a psychic contrast between men and women. They only recognize contrasts between individuals.[26]

d) The first and most important step is to look upon each human being as someone with an immortal soul. "For you are all the children of God through faith in Christ Jesus. For all you who have been baptized into Christ, have put on Christ. There is neither Jew nor Greek; there is neither slave nor freeman; there is neither male nor female" (Gal. 3: 26–28).

§ 3. Men and Religion

1. Summarizing what was said above, we can put down the following traits as characteristic of men:

a) A desire to examine things in the light of his own reason.

[26] For example, Moers, *Das weibliche Seelenleben* (Berlin, 1941).

There is a corresponding danger that he may be excessively critical, obstinate, and quarrelsome.

His objectivity can go so far as to become a professed unconcern for human beings and end up as a complete lack of personal responsibility. He must be brought to realize that this would be a betrayal of his basic nature. For true manhood involves:

b) A share in responsibility. Only where this is offered to him, can he be induced to lend a hand and contribute his own efforts.

c) Respect as the basis of personal honor.

d) A conscience which prefers self-determination and dislikes pastoral guidance which it has not sought. Frequently he is somewhat suspicious of his wife's confessor because the latter knows more about her and may exert greater influence over her.

e) A deep involvement in his life's work. The danger is that his work may become a substitute for religion.

2. *Participation in religious worship.*

a) The number of men at religious services is often far lower than the number of women. This is especially true on weekdays, and understandably so, because he must put in so many hours on his job. The ratio is even more extreme at the communion rail. But in recent years, the situation has been improving.

In Latin countries, particularly Latin America, the number of men participating in religious services is extremely small. Mexico is an exception because there men represent two-thirds of the church-goers (*Orientierung*, 1962, I, 8). Male participation is very good in Ireland, Holland, the United States, and any place where migration is a pertinent factor. Male attendance at Mass is better in rural areas than in cities, but the reverse is often true when it comes to receiving Holy

Communion. In every country there are exceptions—good and bad—to these general observations. Usually the local pastoral ministry is the deciding factor.

b) *A noteworthy comparison*

In Islamism itself and in the countries where it prevails, religious worship is the business of men. This is in accordance with Islamic doctrine and tradition. Women may take part in religious exercises at the mosque only several times a year. Usually the men alone participate. According to Mohammedan doctrine woman does not have a soul.

Islamism is a proselytizing religion, using "fire and sword." This kind of religion can only be practiced by men.

But the interesting fact is that in Islamic countries Christian worship is also more of a man's affair than it is in Western countries. The first time I offered Mass in Bethlehem, on a weekday, two thirds of the congregation were men. The same could become true everywhere.

Men must come to realize that it is really their business to recognize their relationship to God and to manifest it in religious worship. Women will be delighted if they do. Liturgical participation at Mass should never be left to women alone. Anything which repels men must be cut out. Sermons must be geared to attract men. The fine upright men who have leadership qualities are the ones who must be drawn into active participation.

3. Men begin to fall away from religious worship in early adulthood, in short, somewhere between the ages of twenty-five and thirty-five. And this state will continue for years. What are the reasons behind it all?

a) During his college days the problem of religious commitment comes to a head, and he decides to give up religious practices. The result is just as bad if no final decision is made. Indecision produces indifference to religious matters, and this indifference lasts through the years of adulthood. The root cause of this indecision may lie much deeper, perhaps even as far back as the days of early childhood.

b) In adolescence the young man was willing to seek advice from the priest when he was troubled by doubts and uncertainties. Now in adulthood manly pride forbids this course of action. That is why there is not a one hundred per cent transfer from adolescent religious organizations to adult religious organizations.

It is worth calling attention to this interesting fact. The troubled adolescent, as yet unsure of himself, can still regard himself as a Catholic without any feeling of dishonor or disgrace. Everything is still in flux during these years. He is still a Catholic because that is what he has been up to now, because the possibility of remaining a Catholic still lies open to him, because frequently the whole situation is still muddled.

The young adult feels that he must be able to make a forthright profession of religious belief. If he cannot do this, he maintains a state of indecision, perhaps with some feelings of guilt. Eventually he lets the whole matter rest there. His bad conscience produces an unprincipled life which cannot be altered by the surrounding religious environment, even when it is quite strong.

c) The closing years of early adulthood summon the young man to solidify his position in life and to face certain unavoidable realities. Entrance into full manhood is marked by several distinctive events. 1. He places himself within the confines of a particular type of work. 2. He makes certain irrevocable decisions (e.g., marrying a particular girl). 3. He faces certain inevitable demands stemming from the position in which he finds himself. All these events indicate clearly and concretely whether his adolescent ideals and principles are staunch enough to master the demands of life, whether he personally is mature enough to face life's problems. And they show whether his Faith has become the motivating principle of his life.

d) A prime cause of his defection from religious practice is the pressure of moral problems. He is caught up in the conflict between instinct and moral demands, between instinctive impulses and responsible behavior. This is especially true for the unmarried bachelor, but young married men also have such problems. The latter's problems may be intensified by cramped living space and a low salary which does not allow him to support a large family. It is very important for the pastoral minister to stay close to him on an individual basis, and to explain the demands of the moral law, taking into account the physiological and psychological factors noted previously.

e) The difficulty is often intensified by the surrounding environment, by the frivolousness and ridicule of his fellow workers, by the irresponsible outlook fostered in the press. With the help of those who are faithful, the priest must make every effort to keep each individual within the fold. An effective parish ministry is possible only with the assistance of a strong and active body of men.

4. *Pastoral Guidelines*

a) Show respect for men's self-reliance.

Though this self-reliant attitude may be quite unjustified in certain instances, it remains one of the basic characteristics of his behavior. He will not follow advice unquestioningly.

Even the devout man often spends his life wrestling with God. He wants to be able to express his thoughts freely. Many things about the Church bother him. He wants to be able to speak out on these things. And he will participate actively only if he can speak out. Non-practice in many cases may represent a secret protest. The person loves the Church, but this love is not appreciated. He wants to discuss his personal problems with the priest and with his pastor. Frequently this discussion takes the form of a verbal attack. The priest should not be panicked by this. He should meet the other person man-to-man, and present his case. He should let him speak out freely, even if he uses strong language. Then the groundwork for a real dialogue has been established.

The average man wants more than the words of comfort which women are often looking for. And he does not want to hear ex-cathedra pronouncements which rule out any response, even though the priest is an anointed minister appointed to give spiritual guidance. He wants to speak out on a man-to-man basis in order to arrive at the specific answer he is seeking.

b) Do not offer too much spiritual direction, unless a man seeks it out. This will not happen too often. Instead, the priest should appeal to his sense of maturity, even if it seems to be quite undeveloped. This course of action will heap coals of fire on his head. But no pastoral minister should have this aim in mind.

Most moral precepts are rooted in the natural law, which is the bedrock of any moral order. People must be convinced of its intrinsic necessity on the basis of reasoned arguments. This is not realized often enough. Herein lies the way to approach a man's conscience. This objective approach is precisely the thing that appeals to him.

A man must be brought to realize that he has to make the right decision for himself in any given situation. Monastic discipline should not be involved in situations where it does not fit. A monk can ask his superiors when he is confronted with a problem. They can regulate his life in every kind of situation. But the average man stands alone in his public and private life. He cannot run to a priest every time he has to make a decision. His conscience must be well formed so that he can make the right decision in a given situation. We have the duty "to work together to form strong Christian consciences which will be able to find the Christian solution to the many problems confronting them in public and private life" (Pius XI to Cardinal Segura of Toledo, November, 1929).

c) Show respect for men's objective outlook. A man expects the priest to give him a theological judgment which is clear, to the point, and objectively valid. One should never forget that every moral action involves an objective element and two subjective elements: 1. the degree of advertence at the moment of decision; 2. the degree of freedom enjoyed at the moment of acting. An action which may be a mortal sin *in se* (in the textbooks), may be only a venial sin or no sin at all in a given instance. The only sins which really exist are sins committed by people under a particular set of circumstances. So when the priest is dealing with a sinful action, he must let the penitent—man or woman—take part in formulating the final judgment. For only the person who has committed the act can clarify the subjective aspects of the question. That is what a man has in mind when he seeks advice from a priest or confessor. He wants an objective judgment which takes every pertinent factor into account.

It also should be pointed out that a man seldom attaches himself to one particular priest as a confessor. The priest should not try to tie him down to himself, but rather to his duty.

d) Men and Pastoral Work.

Ordinarily the men who might participate in pastoral work are those who have worked through to a solid religious life. Men like and need action.

But a man wants to bear a share of responsibility. He does not want simply to take orders and execute the commands of others. He should not be treated as a messenger boy. He likes to take on certain duties and be responsible for them. The priest should allow plenty of room for his personal initiative in working out a project. He will be delighted.

The priest must also let a man decide how deeply he can involve himself in this work, because he does have other duties. And every effort must be made to enlist the assistance of top-notch men. We must be wary of effeminate types. They will join readily but, in spite of their good intentions, they hinder the apostolate to men. Busy-bodies and the like drive other men away.

e) Men and Confession

Confession is much more difficult for men than women. The latter need to talk up and seek advice. Men tend to give up confession as it loses its matter-of-fact aspect. Freedom in the choice of a confessor is important where men are concerned. It is easier to insure this in large cities.

We should not forget that confession always involves an element of self-abasement, especially where men are concerned. A man is not inclined to reveal his inmost thoughts, his most delicate problems, to another man. In the heart of man there is a small island of solitude. It is noteworthy that scrupulous young men often prefer to unburden themselves to an older woman. Sharing the same sex does not guarantee mutual understanding.

A problem is presented in confessing sins against the Sixth Commandment. Street terminology and the terminology of moral theology differ from one another. The confessor often has to guess at the exact nature of the sin being confessed. It would be dangerous to press for concrete details. Insistent questioning, aimed at insuring *integritas materialis,* has driven countless members away from confession forever.

Ordinarily a man opens his heart not to a "spiritual director," but to God's anointed representative who has the power to give sacramental absolution. This is the aspect which appeals to his manliness and his objectivity. He is looking for a fair, reasonable, objective judgment of his spiritual status, one which takes all the pertinent factors into account. We must never forget that the penitent sees his sin in its concrete historical circumstances whereas the priest, understandably enough, only sees the objective gravity of the sin. He has a one-sided view.

A man is willing to listen to a few brief words of exhortation. But sugary phrases and pious exaggerations disgust him. Deep down he resents this kind of treatment. There is no need to point out that the priest has no right to vent his anger on his penitents as if they had offended him and not God. Though penance is a tribunal, the confessor must remember that his model is not the Christ who will conduct the Last Judgment, but the good shepherd who goes out to seek the lost sheep, or perhaps the happy father rejoicing over the return of his prodigal sons.

It is a good thing that priests have to go to confession too. It makes it easy for them to put themselves in their penitents' place. Human beings are not to be weighed against their deeds. On the contrary, their deeds are to be weighed against their general moral character. The problem facing the confessor is the fact that the penitent is usually unknown to him. He must, therefore, act with reserve and discretion.

f) Manly Piety

Men are often reserved in their public religious activity because, through no fault of their own, they do not play a vital role in parochial worship. In many cases religious services are left to women. Abbot Wöhrmöller asserts that the Christianity "which is offered is, in fact, too woman-orientated. This is what has produced the alienation between men's hearts and religious practice." The situation has improved greatly in recent decades. Franz Zimmermann (*Männliche Frömmigkeit,* 1937) points out how the decline in male religious practice went hand in hand with the decline in communal worship. The beauty of the liturgy, its objective breadth and scope, and its unobtrusiveness made men feel at home with it.

But for a long time our churches have been filled with the trappings of an overly sentimental piety—emotional hymns, statues, holy cards, all sorts of prayers. The celebrant would stand up on the altar, offering the liturgical sacrifice in a foreign tongue, while each individual worshiper prayed as he saw fit.

Now the liturgical revival will surely find support among men and young people. It should make progress slowly and steadily, instilling reverence in everyone. Manly piety can be very child-like and reverential because it tends to be reserved. It can also be very stubborn and filled with protest. Manly trust in God may not take the form of passive resignation. I have seen many men facing death with calm objectivity and a shaky faith.

5. *The Priest and Men*

Rarely does it happen that a priest's ministry is devoted exclusively to men. But here we want to outline the basic qualities required for an effective ministry to men. Pastoral work among men is the most difficult kind. Women are more open and friendly; they come to the priest of their own accord. Men are more inaccessible. So a priest, quite unwittingly, may end up devoting all his attention to women and doing nothing for men.

a) The first positive requirement is that the priest himself be a real man. He should be judicious, objective, selfless, conscientious in carrying out his job and fulfilling his duties, ready to make sacrifices. He should be a person who trusts others and has their trust in return. He, too, insists upon honor and respect, without becoming conceited. He, too, possesses initiative and works out his own plan of action. He is self-reliant, but he is also open to the judicious advice of others. As a pastoral minister he must possess a certain impressiveness, acting naturally, charitably, in priestly fashion. He must treat men as men, showing them the same respect he himself looks for. He must be able to strike up a real dialogue with other men.

b) Negatively speaking, the priest should not be womanish. Feminine qualities are fine in a woman, but laughable in a man. Talking about priests Werner Bergengruen once said: "Many wear their cassock as if it were a bathrobe"; they give the impression of being lazy, shiftless, slovenly slobs. "Others wear it like a dress"; in short, they are always dressed to kill, even on weekdays. A third group "wears the cassock like a toga"; in short, they wear it in a manly way. The toga was a garment for men, not for women. When the priest goes in for too much finery, he compromises his manly dignity. He should not be either a fop or a slob.

There is no room for pious unctiousness—on the pulpit or in social encounters. It turns men's stomachs. And affectation or poses are a poor substitute for real priestliness, which clearly manifests personal closeness to God.

Worst of all is a mixture of unctiousness and pomposity which produces the overbearing cleric.

c) The priest must continue to act as a real man. He shows understanding toward others. He himself is trustworthy, and he regards others as trustworthy too. He is that much better off if he has a sense of humor, if he knows and loves human nature, and is able to forgive people. Every priest has good reason to keep a constant check on his own qualities as a human being, to answer the question once raised by someone: "Take away his cassock, and what's left?"

Beware of sharp-tongued remarks. Irony is a dangerous gift, and there would be no harm in losing it somewhere. Worse still are taunting, sarcastic remarks. A pastor of men's souls must be a model of manly self-control, a living prototype of the four cardinal virtues. Virtue (noble manliness) is a manly quality, as the word itself indicates. Wisdom, prudence, discretion; bravery, fortitude, fearlessness; circumspection, self-mastery, a concern for integrity and justice: all these are typical manly virtues.

d) Then there are those who are not well formed men, those who repel other men: the clerical "martyr," the pious zealot, the stubborn fanatic (who usually cannot help himself). "Eccentricities" should be overlooked and excused for the most part. They are only an object of ridicule when they are consciously cultivated.

Such types as Peppone and Don Camillo are possible only in Italy or in novels. But the relationship between these two men on the human level applies to every priest. Even our opponents, as human beings, deserve their measure of respect and attention.

e) Many priests have stayed away from the company of men and restricted their pastoral work to women. It is very easy for the priest to find himself on pilgrimages surrounded by women—"blessed among women." He can travel from shrine to shrine in their company. He achieves some measure of success, but in the eyes of men he has already played out his hand and has nothing more to offer.

§ 4. *Women and Religion*

1. *More religious than men?*

a) An affirmative answer would seem to be indicated by the fact that there are more women than men at church services, often many more. But this can be attributed to past tradition, as we saw above. The real reason behind their church attendance is the fact that they are more deeply integrated into the moral order which has God as its center. Perhaps we must also note here that the first person in the West to be converted by St. Paul was a woman, Lydia, a dealer in purple.

In any case, we find this recurring formula in the official prayer of the Church—"devotus femineus sexus." There is no parallel formula referring to the male sex. It is erroneous, however, to base one's answer on the fact that woman's emotional life is stronger: "Because woman's emotional life plays a dominant role in her activity, she shows greater warmth and receptivity in her religious practice" (Cornelius Krieg). Religion is not an affair of the emotions. It is true, however, that there is more of an emotional tinge to women's religious practice. This is quite in keeping with her psychic make-up. It may also be due to the fact that she is more defenseless, more helpless.

b) Others answer this question in the negative, pointing out that the overwhelming majority of canonized saints are men. But, say the women, isn't that because men are in charge of the canonization process? No one can prove, however, that anything besides cold facts play a decisive role in these proceedings.

c) For the priest, Genesis 1: 27 provides the point of departure. "God created man in his image . . . male and female he created them." The example of our Lord and the words of St. Paul (Gal. 3: 27) indicate that men and women are equal in the eyes of the Church. The priest must look after the immortal soul of every human being.

It is easiest for him to provide pastoral care to a woman when she is living up to one of the callings and ideals proper to woman—motherhood or consecrated virginity.

2. *Wife and Mother*

Motherhood is woman's first natural vocation. The dignity of this calling, as seen in the light of supernatural realities, represents the ideal for woman. And true female piety as well as the proper pastoral approach to woman finds its best roots in this concept—woman as a loyal, devoted spouse who creates a peaceful home for a man, the heart of the home who takes on the small but vital concerns of everyday life. She exerts the strongest influence on her man, who often returns home from work worn out and irritated. ". . . let wives be subject to their husbands; so that even if any do not believe the word, they may without word be won through the behavior of their wives, observing reverently your chaste behavior" (1 Pet. 3: 1).

A married woman receives the call to motherhood from God in the sacrament of matrimony. Every new birth calls for her full devotion and attention. Her love and concern belong to her children, be they one or many. She is tied down to her small world, and she loves this tie. She can no longer run around in search of a good time, as she did when she was single.

A mother is the first teacher of her children and their first catechetical instructor. She teaches her little ones how to pray. It is primarily she who provides the religious atmosphere of the home, the children's first religious impressions, and the first stages in the development of their religious instincts. It is easy to appreciate the significance of St. Paul's words: "Yet women will be saved by child-bearing if they continue in faith and love and holiness with modesty" (1 Tim. 2: 5).

Women can display great human qualities and great sanctity in fulfilling this role. The priest need only point out its grandeur and beauty to mothers. The married woman has only to be a good wife and mother. The importance which St. Paul attaches to this noble ideal is a forthright answer to those who would minimize it. Speaking of widows with children, he says: "But if anyone does not take care of his own, and especially of this household, he has denied the faith and is worse than an unbeliever" (1 Tim. 5: 8).

3. *The Consecrated Virgin*

Women may consecrate their life to God "to please the Lord" (Cf. 1 Cor. 7: 25–35), becoming cloistered nuns or consecrated virgins working in the world. Secular Institutes combine both possibilities. The unmarried state as such is not to be preferred to the married state (Trent, Sess. XXIV, c. 10), but virginity takes precedence insofar as it is the precondition for devoting one's life to God. The priority of spiritual and eternal realities is clearly manifested in this way of life. The woman's natural, maternal instincts are channeled into loving care of her neighbors—the poor, the sick, the wayward.

In the moral order this ideal stands above the calling to be a wife and mother. In the sacramental order the latter stands higher. The profession of Religious vows is only a sacramental. One of the priest's essential tasks is to keep this noble calling before the eyes of his parishioners.

4. *The Single Woman*

Statistics clearly show that women far outnumber men. So a large percentage of women cannot get married, even though they would like to; and they feel no call to the Religious life. They pose a serious problem to themselves and to society at large, and often to the pastor of souls as well.

a) The reasons behind their plight can be quite varied and quite laudable. One cannot simply peg them as wallflowers. The disproportionate ratio of women to men is one reason. Some stay occupied with the task of caring for aging parents or younger brothers and sisters. Some are poor and find no one who will take them. Some pursue their education and put their natural talents to use. Many are proud girls.

Very often the best girls are bypassed, while more flighty girls find a mate. Young men do not always pick the girls who would make the best wives. So there are always single girls around who remain unmarried, whether they wish to or not. And we must take cognizance of this fact.

b) Many take their lot without any tinge of sadness. But it is safe to assume that the majority never get over a certain feeling of loneliness and solitude. It may lead them to doubt the goodness and wisdom of God, who said: "It is not good for man to be alone."

Their loneliness is a heavy burden. They, like other women, need someone to lean on. As a result, they may go astray, forming illicit relationships and bearing illegitimate children "so that their life may have meaning and purpose." In many instances loneliness leads to a marked sense of ennui, as experience shows.

c) Single women as such do not have any distinctive social or ecclesiastical status. On a parochial Communion Sunday they themselves and other people—including the pastor—wonder to what group they belong. Fortunately, there is no Communion Sunday for "old maids."

d) Some may end up with distorted personalities. Their qualities of goodness and their need for love may turn into the opposite traits. They become heartless, spiteful creatures who spurn other people and withdraw into their own little nook with a pet dog or cat.

One particular type is the "holy Mary," a quarrelsome, obnoxious, sarcastic creature with her own fierce brand of piety. She often gives scandal to outsiders, and frightens priest and parishioners alike.

Even more dangerous is the hysterical woman. Since no one cares to pay attention to her, she calls attention to herself by pestering remarks and erratic behavior.

e) The best way for a woman to forestall the development of such traits is to choose a calling which really suits a woman. There are many such callings—doctor, teacher, nurse, social worker, housekeeper. There is also great merit in giving outlet to one's motherly instincts by helping overworked mothers. Countless single women have found their own way to live up to the ideals of womanhood.

f) The pastor of souls should appreciate their situation and not join in any teasing remarks. He should respect them as women, and not treat them as school girls. They should be persuaded to offer their services to the Church and to the parish. They want to have certain duties of their own, and they will be only too happy to do them when they are asked. They must come to regard their lot, not as a burden, but as their way to salvation.

5. *The Priest and Women*

a) Spiritual Direction

Spiritual direction, in the full sense of the term, should be attempted only by a priest who has the necessary ascetical and theological training, a sound knowledge of human nature, and a good deal of practical experience. In short, he should ordinarily be a devout, older priest.

The term "spiritual director" is often applied to one's regular confessor. But that is not what we are referring to in the following guidelines.

1. Spiritual direction must take due account of the workings of grace in the soul. Charles de Condren says: "In spiritual direction I regarded it as my duty to serve the grace of God and to heed the guidance offered to me by the Holy Spirit."[27]

2. It is not easy to penetrate into the heart of another person. St. Augustine makes this admission: "It would be easier for a man to count the hairs of his head than to assess the feelings and moods of his heart."[28] How much more difficult to penetrate the complex workings of another man's heart when there are so many factors involved! All this indicates that caution and discretion are in order. Cocksureness and a domineering attitude are bad in spiritual direction.

3. Spiritual direction to women living in the world should be aimed at making itself superfluous. It should help them to reach a state of maturity so that they can make their own decisions. This is the basic principle, but it is often difficult to carry it out in practice.

[27] Charles de Condren, *Geistliche Briefe* (Fr. in Br., 1930).
[28] St. Augustine, *Confessions*, IV.

Savonarola once asserted that a person should not take a bite of anything without first seeking the advice of his spiritual director.[29] But this is an application of monastic rule to the conduct of life in the world, where it has no place.

4. The ability to make decisions for oneself does not come easily. St. Augustine, one of the great masters of the human soul who had seen much and knew himself fairly well, found it necessary to ask Simplicianus how he could best give honor to God.[30]

b) Dealing with Women

1. The priest should meet women just as he meets men—openly, freely, and with pastoral concern. He must get over any feelings of extreme bashfulness in the company of women. The strict Oriental code governing social encounters between men and women never took roots in the West. And there is no cause for regret on that score.

2. The priest should not show any favoritism. If he does, it will give rise to jealousy and gossip. He must disregard, and if necessary, repel the preferences shown to him as a man. And he must keep a check on his own likings and preferences. On his death-bed St. Dominic confessed that he enjoyed talking with women more than talking with men, and preferred young women to old women. There was nothing wrong in this, of course, and it did not hurt his cause for canonization. But certain thoughts crop up when a man is at the point of death.

3. Discretion is the watchword when dealing with women who are looking for a shoulder to lean on, especially when they keep coming back again and again. There may be nothing to it. On the other hand, it can become a serious problem. The priest must judge for himself.

[29] J. Schnitzer, *Savonarola*, I, 247.
[30] St. Augustine, *op. cit.*, VIII, 1.

A woman has a right to be heard; she is not to be treated automatically as an hysterical female. In communities where healthy relations exist, it is easier to distinguish between the two types.

"Canonical" old age does not alter the need for discretion on the part of the priest. Karin Michaelis refers to it as "the dangerous age." And psychiatrists note that at this age some women are seized with panic at the thought that the doors of life are closing behind them.

4. Keep visits down to a minimum, to those which are absolutely necessary, and get right down to the point. Priests should not visit women when they are alone, unless this cannot be helped. He must watch out for his own reputation. Each person must do his duty as he sees it, in the light of God's will and his own conscience.

5. A priest should not look to a woman for sympathy and pity. This is unmanly behavior, not in keeping with the gravity and dignity of his state. He should not air his conflicts with "the boss," or his fellow priests, or the lay help. Women will always be ready to show sympathy, even when men will not. The priest living alone, who gets a coughing spell in church, can count on getting a box of cough drops from some anonymous sympathizer.

6. It is fairly safe to say that a priest will not be laid low by the brazen overtures of a saucy woman. There is often more danger in a seemingly innocent friendship struck up for good and pious reasons. The natural tendency of women to show affection and sympathy turns the innocent association into a potential danger.

7. The proper way to treat women is to show them great esteem. An attitude of contempt is rather suspect. Every man regards a single girl or a married woman as a member of the same sex as the Virgin Mary and his own mother. Christ's

disciples can only be concerned about immortal souls and their eternal destiny.

8. A condescending attitude toward women, based on the old notion (which has some currency in clerical and theological tradition)[31] that women are inferior to men, is not a good foundation for a sound relationship between man and woman.

c) In the Confessional

1. According to c. 910, 1, a woman's confession can be heard only in a church, in a spot set aside for confession.

2. The confession itself is to be restricted to material necessary for integrity. The priest should listen with kindness and patience.

3. Where an attempt to obtain material integrity might give rise to misunderstanding, the priest can be satisfied with formal integrity. The difficulty involved in talking about ticklish matters is particularly acute in this situation.

4. In cases of marital conflict the priest should stick to the facts and remain impartial. He should not delve into minute details. If his opinion is sought outside the confessional, he should not proffer an answer until he has talked to both parties.

II. THE FAMILY

The Present Situation

The most painful problem confronting the pastoral ministry today is the breakdown of family life. Its vital leadership role, which used to be taken for granted, is now verified only in individual instances. The functional ministry once exerted by the parochial community, a composite of deeply religious

[31] S.T. Suppl. 9, 52, a 1, ad 2.

families, is no longer in evidence. A tangible symptom of the present crisis is the decreasing number of children per family.

We find ourselves confronted by a strange paradox. Despite the increasing use of birth-control techniques, there is an unprecedented population explosion all around the world. What explanation can be offered?

The population increase is due, first of all, to the high fertility of primitive peoples and a few sound nations, and, secondly, to the progress of medicine. Compared to the early days of this century, today's mortality rate for infants is almost minimal.

§ *1. Dangers Confronting It*

1. *Deteriorating Influences*

A. Artificial birth-control techniques are deliberately used to insure infertility. Why?

a) People refuse to practice the spirit of self-sacrifice which is an integral part of motherhood. Child-bearing involves risks to life and health, curtails personal freedom and social activity. So many married couples choose to have only one child or none at all. In many instances other factors are also at work: an immoral sex life before and after marriage, distrust of one's mate, the rash of divorces, the matter-of-fact attitude toward purely civil or common-law marriages.

b) Child-bearing may involve economic problems. In farm areas the distribution of property among a number of children frequently leads to impoverishment. In urban areas parents may worry about a decline in their living standard and their social status. These modern idols dominate human life even at its inception.

c) Scanty living space, lack of employment, and a low initial income affect a person's outlook and work against the ideals that are preached from the pulpit. Trust in God is not easy to practice.

B. A factor which cannot be controlled is the deteriorating influence of big city life. In large metropolitan areas life is easier, and there are more conveniences at hand. The less challenging life is, the softer people become. Families living in big cities usually die out in the third generation. The polluted city air and the nerve-wracking pace undermine people's health. The isolated individual lives out his days, and that is that.

2. *Undermining Influences*

a) The job system in an industrialized society cannot help but undermine the family. To begin with, it destroys the older system in which work was a common family task. The farmer and his children once worked together in the fields and ate meals in common. The craftsman had a room set aside for work in his home, and his children looked in on him. The family ate and prayed together. Sunday was a holyday and a day of rest for the entire family. Today the automobile drives the family apart on Sundays. Better a drive than sitting around the house, however cozy it may be.

b) Today the worker must spend most of the day at his job, away from his family. Dad eats in the company cafeteria; the children, at some luncheonette. And in the evening various types of entertainment lure them away from the home. The home is nothing more than a place to lay one's head. Children are considered a nuisance, not a blessing.

c) The lack of space plaguing young married couples inhibits the growth of a family. In over-populated nations (Japan, for instance) population experts offer no better course of action than legalized infanticide.

3. *Moral and Spiritual Decline*

a) Freedom of the press, billboards, and sexually orientated advertising foster a cynical, dehumanized spirit and a matter-of-fact attitude toward shameless behavior. Even children breathe in this poisonous atmosphere.

b) The entertainment industry and its advertising campaigns reach every nook and cranny of the country and undermine the foundations of a well regulated life. It upsets traditional standards and the normal routine of life. It offers the poor a counterfeit brand of luxury, mass produced articles, and all the trappings of self-deceit. Personal income is no longer spent on the upkeep of the home. It is used to maintain a shallow show of status and luxury.

c) In rural areas this materialistic spirit destroys the last stronghold of calmness and moderation, the last outpost of self-control and prudent discernment. The exodus to the big cities is frequently nothing more than a deliberate escape from a healthy way of life. City people live in a pluralistic atmosphere, where standards are relative and the community does not exercise a silent restraint on its members. The spread of this atmosphere to rural areas is more serious than most people realize.

d) The declining moral standards in the area of sexual behavior are not only supported by the growing lack of restraining influences; they are given new dignity and prestige. They become the guiding norms, and morality becomes a question of majority vote. When illicit affairs and divorces become a commonplace business, when couples with children become an object of pity, then the moral order is completely out of joint, and immorality is in the driver's seat. People no longer feel it necessary to justify common-law marriages and unsanctioned relationships. They are accepted as a matter of course.

A person who grows up in this atmosphere will not regard

marriage as something "made in heaven," or enter it with a feeling of reverence and responsibility.

e) The ultimate reason behind this disturbing situation is the growing failure of men to appreciate their responsibility before God, the Creator and Law-giver who rules life and all living things. Somehow or other man will find his way back to this ultimate source. And the pastoral minister will have to show him the way.

f) The marriage law reform takes account of the distressing situation. But it is motivated by the same basic spirit and cannot provide any fundamental improvement.

Atheistic Communism started out by advocating the break-up of the family. But it was wise enough to see the economic and social consequences of this policy. Today Russia has the strictest marriage code in the world. This policy has no connection with a moral order established by God. It is merely a prudential decision, but one which is far more sensible than the attitude of Western nations. The Russian policy uses every practicable means to combat the dangers and consequences of family breakup. With every divorce the alimony rate is hiked, until it becomes too much for any husband to pay.

The world-wide dimensions of this problem came to light at the International Congress of Population Experts held in Rome (1950). The only answer offered by one Western expert was "birth control." The retort of the Russian expert was enough to put us to shame. "What, birth control? On the contrary, we need more children."

§ 2. *Protective Measures in France*

This critical situation has aroused the consciences of people in almost every nation and highlighted the need to offer protective counteraction. Here we shall show how France reacted to the crisis and set out to remedy the situation.

Half a century ago the French were regarded as a decadent people. The drop in the birth-rate was greatest in France. It was a call to action, and Christians responded.

In 1906 a league was formed to help large families, the people who had preferred the moral law to the propaganda of a hostile environment. In 1918 a fund was set up to provide these families with financial support. That same year saw the proclamation of the *Rights of the Family,* which was placed on the same par as the proclamation of the *Rights of Man* at the start of the French Revolution. Since 1932 large families have received State support. In 1940 the rights of the family were drawn up in codified form and a Ministry of Family Care was set up. Today it is called the Ministry of Public Health and the Family. In 1945 a Family Ministry was set up to represent its interests before the national government, just as business and labor are represented.

At its congress in Lille (1950), the French Family League set forth the basic rights of the family. The points are scarcely new to Christians, but they underline the need for responsible public action.

1. The family has a right to propagate itself.
2. Parents have the right to educate and train their children.
3. The family has a right to be protected by the State from public sources of danger. Among the dangers mentioned by name were amusement houses, immoral books, lascivious reading material, alcoholism, tuberculosis, improper housing, easy divorces, and prostitution.
4. The family has a right to property and possessions, to a decent home and suitable surroundings.
5. There should not be an excessive inheritance tax which would eat up the patrimony bequeathed to offspring.
6. A suitable family wage is absolutely necessary. Any production system which disrupts the family or weakens family

life by placing excessive demands on the father and mother, must be rejected.

7. Distributive justice requires that taxes, tariffs, salaries, pensions be computed according to the basic needs of the family, not just of the single individual.

8. The family, as a real member cell of the nation, has a right to proper representation in the national legislature. Besides having a voice in his own right, the father is also the spokesman for his children who are not yet of age.

9. All social legislation should be orientated around the concept of the family. It is the seed ground of national greatness and economic growth. Any laws or regulations which are prejudicial to the family must be revised.

It is clear from all this that France is definitely not a decadent country. Similar family organizations, based on the French prototypes, have been established in many countries throughout the world.

§ 3. *On the Theology of the Family*

1. *The Family in the Natural Order*

a) Historically speaking, the family is the oldest and smallest cell of every community which is a by-product of man's social nature. When it is incorporated into larger social units, it brings its ancient, natural rights with it. Such rights as the care and education of children pre-date any other social structurings and are independent of them. The family is older than any other biological grouping—tribe, race, nation—or any sociological grouping such as the community or the State. It is the source and the foundation-stone of all the larger social groupings which developed later on.

b) So it is not true to say that the State comes first historically and is ultimately broken up into the smallest unit, the family.

Quite the opposite is true. But, teleologically speaking, the development of tribes and races was latent in the initial social cell. Man is meant to live in community, as Aristotle pointed out. Only in this sense can we speak of the family as a division of the over-all social setup.

c) The family is also the most perduring community. States come and go; political systems supplant one another. But even in a world of anarchy the family cell remains with its inviolable rights. The most important parental right is the right to educate one's children. This right derives from the fact that they are the procreators and providers.

2. *The Family in the Supernatural Order*

a) One may also say that the family is the smallest cell in the community of the faithful. But this does not mean that all the Christian families taken together make up the whole Church. Still less does it mean that the Church is built up simply through family growth.

b) Sacramentally and historically, the Church came into existence before the sacrament of marriage and the Christian family. This is the most important difference between the family-Church relationship and the family-State relationship. It is certainly true that the natural cell, the family, becomes a cell in the Church through the sacrament of marriage. That is what Matthias Scheeben meant when he referred to the family as a cell and organ of the Church.

The sanctification of family members is furthered in many ways through family life. But in baptism the child immediately becomes a member of the Mystical Body. In short, before they enter a sacramental marriage, the two partners are already members of the Church. And the child born to partners in a sacramental marriage is not yet a member of the Church with sacred rights and obligations.

c) Families in sacramental marriages do not constitute the

whole Church. Unmarried people are also a part of it. The parish is not made up exclusively of families, but of all the faithful.

d) Historically we are confronted with another picture. Christian families existed before parishes and dioceses. And the family is a symbol of the Church insofar as the relationship between husband and wife resembles the relationship between Christ and his Church. ". . . a husband is head of the wife, just as Christ is head of the Church, being himself savior of the body. But just as the Church is subject to Christ, so also let wives be to their husbands in all things. Husbands, love your wives, just as Christ also loved the Church, and delivered himself up for her, that he might sanctify her, cleansing her in the bath of water by means of the word . . . We are members of his body . . . This is a great mystery . . . I mean in reference to Christ and to the Church" (Eph. 5: 23–33).

e) In an earlier section we pointed out the importance of early childhood for establishing basic moral and religious attitudes. So the vital role of the family in developing these attitudes is quite apparent. This fundamental religious development will carry over through the storms of later life.

f) Christian families can survive even when the organizational structure of parish and diocese is overturned. If the hierarchy is scattered, they can carry on the faith, the practice of religion, and even the sacramental life.

The clearest example is the history of Christianity in Japan. In that country the extermination of the Christian faith was carried out with extreme severity. By 1637 it seemed to be complete. No Christian could set foot in Japan. If he did, this very act would symbolize his renunciation of Christianity; for he had to trample on a cross as he left the ship. European merchants apparently were able to do this without feeling too much pain.

In 1865, religious freedom came to Japan. When the first missionaries arrived, they were astonished to find thousands of Catholics who had kept the Faith secretly. For two hundred years Catholic families had represented the Church, taught the Faith to their children, and administered the sacraments of baptism and matrimony.

It is quite conceivable that if there were only a "remnant" left, the family would be the only means of passing on the Faith and the life of grace. Perhaps this is what August Zechmeister[32] means when he suggests the possibility of a father celebrating the Eucharist in the family circle and acting as a pastoral minister. It is a moot question. But Guardini, too, sees the advent of an era when the Faith of many will grow cold, leaving a small band of faithful souls.

3. *Summary*

a) Parents, as the procreators, have a natural and fundamental right where their children are concerned.

b) The Church enjoys primary rights in the religious formation of the children. Canonically speaking, she can exercise this right even against the parents' will. But, practically speaking, she can only perform this function with their cooperation.

c) The State enjoys rights in the area of education only insofar as it represents the family. This is the legal basis and functional purpose of a Family Ministry in the legislature. The State must answer to the family in carrying out its educational program.

d) The State enjoys a preeminent right as far as the educational curriculum is concerned. This is required for the sake of the common good, the foundation-stone on which the State is built.

[32] August Zechmeister, *Das Herz und das Kommende* (Vienna, 1947).

§ 4. *Pastoral Considerations*

As we noted earlier, the functional ministry once exerted by the Christian community is no longer verified on any wide scale. Where it does exist, it inculcates basic values and sound living principles. It plays a critically important role. Any organic community, of its very nature, exerts some power over its members. Other types of organizations are only a poor substitute. In fact, these organizations may infringe upon the rôle of the family and disrupt it.

1. *The Ministry to the Family*

A. Remote Preparation For Marriage

a) Ninety-nine per cent of all young people have the intention of starting a family, at least at some time during their young days. Nevertheless, one of the main projects of a working pastoral ministry is to prepare them for marriage and its responsibilities. This point must be stressed because celibate clerics may not see the urgency of this task or feel suited to give instruction about this vocation in life. Marriage courses, utilizing the services of doctors, psychologists, and educators, are indispensable today. And they are usually well attended.

The purpose of these courses is not to propose some nebulous ideal, but to get across the necessity of a healthy, realistic preparation for a sound marriage. Couples must come to appreciate the beauty and importance of conjugal responsibility.

b) Should the pastoral ministry take on the task of paving the way for marriages between Catholic young people? It is not up to the individual priest, so it is not done. And it is hardly practicable on a local level. But on a diocesan scale this could be done. Such a program, of course, would only offer suitable advice and counsel.

Experience teaches that the best girls often remain unmarried. This should be prevented, if possible. Any such program would have two objectives: to prepare young women to be fine upstanding mothers and to give them the opportunity to find marriage partners.

Werner Schoellgen tells what happened at an educational conference in which the ideals of Catholic manhood and womanhood had been nicely set forth. "One female lecturer, whose competence and prudence were beyond question, torpedoed the whole program with one remark. She noted that up to now all such programs, as far as she could see, had led to one result. The girls well suited for marriage and its responsibilities remained wallflowers, while frivolous girls were grabbed up!"[33]

Thus the pastoral ministry must be concerned with this whole question, at least indirectly. The ministry to young people must look beyond adolescence because this is a transitional period. It must show them how to take their place in the adult world, how to face its wonders and its challenges. There is a broad range of biological factors which can only be explained by competent experts. Many marriages, for example, produce no children because the partners have incompatible blood types.

B. Immediate Preparation For Marriage

According to Canon Law (cc. 1020, 1033) this is a direct pastoral duty.

a) Who should handle this preparation? Ordinarily the pastor himself, preferably an experienced priest rather than a young one. The instructor must possess adequate knowledge, practical experience, confidence, and tact. Ticklish points can be read off. In the borderline area between theology and biology it is best to call in a Catholic doctor. If this is not possible, one can read off the pertinent material from some guide-sheet (e.g., PMI form).

[33] Werner Schoellgen, *Grenzmoral* (Duesseldorf, 1946), p. 27.

b) Points to be covered.

1. According to the Roman Ritual (Tit. 7, c. 1) and canon 1020, 2, those who are to receive this sacrament must be tested on the basic truths of the Faith. This holds true in the reception of any sacrament for the first time. This inquiry should not be conducted along the lines of a school exercise. A conversational approach would seem to be the most practicable method.
2. Canonically speaking (c. 1020, 2) the priest must find out if there are any impediments to the proposed marriage. This should be done even before the banns are announced. The intention of each party must be ascertained, and they must appreciate the fact that marriage is one and indissoluble. Frequently the couple is asked to make a written declaration on these points. When it is a question of a mixed marriage, the couple must indicate in writing that they are prepared to carry out the necessary stipulations.
3. The two partners should be made to realize that they administer the sacrament to each other. In the supernatural order they exercise a noble function. They should also be asked if they have been confirmed (c. 1021, 2). But this is not an obligatory condition.
4. There are two moral duties which should be clearly explained in the pre-marital instruction: 1. what marital chastity involves; 2. the *debitum conjugale* and its limits. This course of instruction should also point out the responsibility of parents to provide a Catholic atmosphere in the home (e.g., through family prayer) and to teach their children the faith.
5. Even if one or both parties refuse to receive marital instruction, the marriage ceremony cannot be denied to them (A.A.S., 1918, p. 345).

C. Confession

Freedom in the choice of a confessor must be preserved.

It is best if an older, more experienced priest hears the confession. The first basic rule of thumb is: *Credendum est poenitenti.* Formal integrity must suffice in some instances. Detailed examination should be conducted only if the person demands it. If both parties go to the same confessor, he must be careful not to break the seal.

A few serious words of paternal exhortation are very much in order, because marriage is a great and important sacrament. In this secret encounter with God's representative, some important point might strike home.

Confession is not obligatory before marriage. The priest cannot refuse to marry them if one party refuses to go to confession and Communion. Better one sacrilege than three.

D. The Marriage Ceremony

The pastor may not overstep the boundaries set for him by Canon Law and the sacramental system. He can advise the couple to have a Nuptial Mass. If it is possible, he can call their attention to religious practices appropriate for engaged couples. Local customs are outside his sphere of competence.

a) In the marriage ceremony itself the rites prevailing in the local diocese are to be observed. The sacramental rite should be performed in a dignified way so that it leaves a lasting impression on the couple. The instruction should be in keeping with the dignity and sacredness of the sacrament.

b) Paraliturgical customs of a religious nature should be preserved. They often date back hundreds of years, to the days when marriage was really a family sacrament. Before Trent the betrothed used to pronounce "I do" in the family circle. Then everyone went in procession to the church to announce the marriage publicly. In those days *in facie ecclesiae* literally meant "in front of the Church doors." Large churches and cathedrals had a special door before which the ceremony took place. A few places still retain the nice custom in which the newly married couple visit the graveyard and invite their deceased relatives to the celebration.

c) The marriage itself takes place during the Nuptial Mass after the Gospel. Frequently the bride or both parties hold a wax candle during the Mass. The candle is lit from the flame of the sanctuary lamp. Another custom practiced in some areas is even more meaningful. At Communion time a single host is divided and given to the couple, signifying their union in Christ.

d) Anything which would cause disorder should be gradually and judiciously eliminated. Relatives and friends kiss the bride in the back of the church after the ceremony. It should be pointed out that this kiss is meant to signify reception into the family circle. Other secular customs connected with the marriage festivities (e.g., throwing the bridal bouquet) should not take place in the church.

2. *The Ministry of the Family*

A. The good religious family is the chief bearer of the functional ministry. Its dedication and uprightness are a living example to the children and the surrounding environment. Every precaution, therefore, should be taken to preserve it intact. The old concept of Christian organizations, which tried to take the place of the family in many areas, often disrupted the family life of Catholics. Excessive demands on society members, aimed at furthering the mission of the organization, must be rejected. For the mission of the family as such is irreplaceable and more important.

The home should provide an atmosphere of peace and protection. It should be a place where the family plays and prays together. Families should attend church and receive the sacraments together. All this requires protective measures and an ordered system. The present-day obsession with information and entertainment is inimical to the family set-up. So the

Church should not add to the problem by setting up too many organizations of her own.

Every family member has an immortal soul and needs a spiritual adviser. The pastoral minister must focus his attention on the individual who is in need. He may thereby exert indirect influence on an entire family, but he should not try to take direct charge of it.

Marital conflicts should be resolved by the husband and wife. If one partner runs to the priest every time a problem comes up, he or she will lose the partner's trust and undermine the stability of the marriage. Advice should be given when it is solicited. But the priest should not pass judgment on some problem until he has heard both sides. In many cases a lesser ideal must be proposed, since the nobler ideal is impracticable.

B. Families living a solid, healthy life of faith are "a city set on a mountain." Through their example they exercise their own kind of ministry.

a) Married people should realize that they enjoy the grace of the sacrament in everything they do as spouses and parents.

b) All fatherhood in heaven and on earth comes from God (Eph. 3: 15). The father is the head of the family and the mother is the heart (*Casti connubii*). They are to live together in love and holiness (Eph. 5: 21 ff.). The father is the religious head of the family, as Christ is the head of the Church (Eph. 5: 23). He is the one who sets an example and directs the prayer life of the family: "a father's blessing gives a family firm roots" (Sir. 3: 9). The custom of imparting a paternal blessing to one's children on certain occasions is no longer practiced to any large degree. Engaged couples come to ask for his blessing, but otherwise the practice has fallen into disuse. It should be revived.

c) Family prayer is a very important practice—Grace before

and after meals, morning and evening prayers. Sundays and Holydays should be celebrated in the home too with Scripture readings. In many homes the Gospel is still read before the family sits down for Sunday dinner. Once upon a time parents would ask their children what the Sunday sermon was about, thus checking their attendance at Sunday Mass and underlining its importance. A crucifix, a small altar, and holy pictures do much to promote a religious atmosphere in the home. It is also a good practice to have a house blessed. The family then lives in a home environment suffused with sacred realities.

d) All these practices enhance the religious life of the family and steel its members against the onslaughts of a secular environment. The home should have a good bookshelf and foster communal prayers, communal readings, and communal undertakings. The priest can also call their attention to special radio and television programs which deserve an audience.

C. Today it is very important that Christian families maintain close ties with one another. This is not easy to do, but it is necessary if they are to exert significant influence on society at large.

The French Y.C.W. movement has helped to further this objective. As its members grew up and got married, they tried to maintain contact with each other. This gave birth to a Christian Family Movement (*Mouvement pour les familles*). They had certain guide-lines and objectives in starting this movement. 1. They wanted to unite their families in a given city into a federation and 2. to exercise an apostolate to all the families of that city. 3. In enlisting members for this federation, they stayed within their own circle at first, wanting only good practicing Catholics. 4. With this federation they hoped to re-Christianize the surrounding environment which was a-religious or anti-religious in spirit and had turned many people into veritable pagans.

They wanted to remain in close contact with each other in the various activities and organizations which occupied their time. They hoped that fraternal love (John 13: 35) would be the distinctive mark of their federation. Such love seemed to be sorely lacking in the conduct of human life. In their words, "Communism is anti-Christian, but present-day Christendom is also anti-Christian in many respects."

INDEX

A NOTE ON THE TYPE

IN WHICH THIS BOOK WAS SET

This book has been set in Electra, a type face created in 1935 by W. A. Dwiggins, the well-known Boston artist. This type falls within the "modern" family of type styles, but was drawn to avoid the extreme contrast between "thick and thin" elements that marks most "modern" type faces. The design is not based upon any traditional model, and is not an attempt to revive or to reconstruct any historic type. Since its birth, Electra has met with success because of its easy-to-read quality. This book was composed and printed by the York Composition Company, Inc., of York, Pa., and bound by Moore and Company of Baltimore, Md. The design and typography of this book are by Howard N. King.